Dream Cars

Text and photographs: Rob de la Rive Box and Mirco de Cet
Cover design: Minkowsky Graphics, Enkhuizen, The Netherlands

Translation: Agentura Abandon, Prague, The Czech Republic
Typesetting: AdAm Studio, Prague, The Czech Republic
Proofreading: Jeffrey Rubinoff

Printed exclusively for MJF Media.

ISBN-13: 978-90-366-2017-8
ISBN-10: 90-366-2017-1

Dream Cars

ROB DE LA RIVE BOX
& MIRCO DE CET

MJF
MEDIA

Contents

Preface

Writing this introduction was not easy since the book describes an extremely diverse selection of cars, "a bit of everything." My personal preferences governed many of the cars I examined and I also tried to focus on less common models, such as Spies (or rather Spiess!) since only one model of this brand exists. Sports cars are spotlighted because they are my favorites, and yours as well, I hope! The models made by Porsche and Ferarri included although they are relatively common and much has been published about them already. Of course, the book does discuss the Fiat Nuova 500 as well as Renault 4CV and the Renault 5 Turbo. You will also find the DKW 3=6 and the BMW dwarf cars. I hope I did not overlook your favorite model of car, but I am convinced that you will find this book interesting as well as informative.

Rob de la Rive Box and Mirco de Cet

AC

In 1902, the London butcher John Portwine retired and devoted himself to his great hobby: automobiles. As Portwine had more money than expertise, he asked John Weller for help. Together, they built a large car which was presented at the automobile show in the Crystal Palace in 1903. They ran out of funds and were forced to concentrate on only one exemplar until a year later, when their joint enterprise marketed a motorized carrier velocipede. The vehicle had two front wheels and one rear wheel placed under the seat of the driver. The "car" was a raging success and in 1907, Autocarriers Ltd., as the enterprise was named, launched a new version for human transport, the so-called Sociable. Autocarriers Ltd., or the AC , began to flourish after the English army commissioned it to equip an entire regiment.

The engine of the Bristol had three Solex carburetors and gave a performance of 105 hp/4750 rpm.

In 1912, AC built a car with four wheels and a four-cylinder engine. Fast, small sports cars followed which soon set the image of the make. During the year 1921, when S.F. Edge was appointed as director, the cars set no less than

The body of the Bristol was a good copy of that of the Ferrari 166 Touring Barchetta.

57 records. In the spring of 1921, an AC rode with a 2.0-liter six-cylinder engine on the circuit of Montlhéry for 24 hours at a speed averaging 82 mph. AC was the first English car to take part in the Monte Carlo Rally in 1925 and it even won the following year. Racing was surely good publicity, but it proved to be very costly and the enterprise eventually went bankrupt. The new owners attempted to present various new models, but were forced to give up shortly after.

The dashboard of the Bristol looked a little disorderly.

Postwar production did not start until October 1947. During the first years, only cars of the model year 1939 were made. Not until 1953 did the company finally present the AC Ace. John Tojeiro, a well-known chassis builder, developed a chassis with fully independent wheel suspension. Apparently the body was a direct copy of the Ferrari 166 MM designed by Carrozzeria Touring, but nobody was deterred by the fact and AC was impressed by the new model. They accepted the design and gave Tojeiro the royalties. The first AC Aces were still equipped with a prewar engine, but an advanced version of the old BMW 328 engine was built by Bristol soon after and AC Bristol became very popular, especially in America. Indeed, the engine gave only 120 hp, but the Bristol had excellent stability on the road, which ensured the car's racing success.

In 1957, AC took part in the 24-hour Le Mans race in France. AC Bristol won second place in its class after a Ferrari. In 1958, a 'special' with a new Tojeiro chassis won first place in its class and eighth in the general classification. The 'ordinary' AC Bristol breathed down its neck and won ninth place.

In 1961, Bristol stopped producing engines. AC switched to the 2.6-liter six-cylinder from the Ford Zephyr and the AC 2.6 was born. In October of the same year, an American Ford V8 engine was mounted in an AC Ace on the advice of the American road-racer Carroll Shelby. In February 1962, the first prototype with a V8 engine and a capacity of 288.4 cu. in. was available. The car was shipped to America where it got the registration number CSX0001 (Carroll Shelby Experimental, Number One). Ford Dearborn saw potential in the project and he gave Shelby the order to build one hundred cars to be sold by the Ford dealers. The famous AC Cobra was born! Even before the first order was dispatched, Fort ordered a second series of one hundred Cobras.

In 1963, Ford produced a new V8 engine with a capacity of 427 cu. in. and an output of 485 hp. This was too strong for the original chassis of the Cobra, so Klaus Arning adapted a new chassis in Detroit which was later built in England. Now two versions of the Cobra were available: the first had a 'small' 289-cubic inch engine for the European market while the second was the Shelby American Cobra with a 427 inch engine. The first model was sold by AC in England, the second by Shelby in America. In 1964, Shelby presented a coupe model of the Cobra. The beautiful aerodynamic body was designed by twenty-seven-year-old Pete Brock. The streamlined sports car could achieve a speed of more than 186.4 mph.

AC later constructed other sports cars, but it never again reached such success as with the Cobra. The car is still very popular and, in fact, is now being offered by various enterprises as a replica. One company claims to possess the original templates for the car while another claims to have purchased the 'exclusive' rights from Ford. Even AC itself took up the battle. In 1997, the Cobra cost no less than £73,136 in England. Even Carroll Shelby's version of the Cobra appeared on the market again in 1997 and was available for $40,000. For a more complete version, $500,000 is a good price estimate and the car will get an original CSX chassis number.

The Bristol was presented at the Earls Court Motorshow in 1957.

The interior of the 427.

Technical specifications

Model:	AC Bristol	Cobra 289	Cobra 427	Cobra Mk4
Years of manufacture:	1957-1963	1963-1965	1965-1968	1985 - present
Production:	463	571	306	not known
Engine:	six-cylinder	V8	V8	V8
Displacement:	12.3 cu. in.	289 cu. in.	427 cu. in.	301.6 cu. in.
Output (hp/rpm):	105/4750	300/5750	480/6000	228/4200
Top speed:	124.3 mph	155 mph	174 mph	135 mph
From 0 to 60 mph :	9.1 sec.	5.5 sec.	4.2 sec	5.3 sec
Wheel base:	7 ft 6 in	7 in 4 in	7 ft 6 in	7 ft 6 in
Length:	12 ft 4.8 in	12 ft 8 in	6 ft	6 ft
Height:	4 ft	4 ft 1 in	4 ft 1 in	3 ft 11 in
Weight:	1,680 lb	2,028 lb	2,150 lb	2,469 lb

Alfa Romeo Montreal

In 1967, Canada celebrated its centenary with a large world exposition in Montreal to demonstrate what Canada could offer to the world and to show how Canadians perceived the future. When Dr. Di Nola, at that time director of Alfa Romeo, found the order on his desk to construct a car of the future for the part of the exhibition, "Town of the Future," he acted immediately. Thanks to this project, the Alfa won much fame. Di Nola contacted the famous designer Nuccio Bertone to take on the design of the body at his expense and the Alfa Romeo Montreal was born.

Both Alfa and Bertone hoped to sell the car as an exclusive model in a small series, which is why the Montreal had to also be a super sports car. Alfa used the basic components of the famous Tipo 33 sports car, which was driven by a 2.0-liter V8 placed in front of the rear axle. The air inlets of the Tipo 33 were located behind the doors. Bertone also planned to use the construction for the Montreal, but the construction was not possible for a production car since the new design had to be a 2+2.

Bertone commissioned the designer Marcello Gandini to draw the body. The design had to suit the existing chassis of the Alfa GTV, which had been used almost without change for years, but the engine itself was not perfected. In Canada, Alfa exhibited two prototypes brought by aircraft from Milan to Montreal. The pearl-shell painted cars got a place of honor at the fair and were celebrated by the press. The exhibition lasted one year and Alfa booked orders for the Montreal the entire time. When there were enough orders, they decided to start the production of the car. The Montreal

The design of the Montreal comes from the drawing board of Marcello Gandini.

was considered a very special project and therefore it was expected to be expensive. Indeed, Alfa charged twice the price of a normal 1750 GTV for a Montreal, the "top-of-the-line-model."

In March 1970, automobile journalists got the opportunity to test the production car.Three years after its introduction, the car resembled the prototype only in its external appearance. Bertone had taken the body thoroughly in hand once again. The air inlets behind the doors remained, but now they had seven instead of six grooves and the nose was changed. The body was self-supporting and the four headlights were partly covered by hydraulically operated grilles. At the Canadians show in Montreal, the whole nose could be opened, but the production version had a long, plain and flat engine hood.

The biggest surprise remained nevertheless hidden under the engine hood. Instead of a four-cylinder, there was a version of the Tipo 33 racing engine. It was a beautiful aluminum V8 with four upper cam shafts and fuel injection from the Spica company from Lavern. The engine had dry-sump lubrication and a forged Wolfram steel crankshaft. In the original version, the engine had a capacity of 2.0 liters. But by adjusting the boss-times-height of valve lift ratio of 3.07 x 2.05 in to 3.14 x 2.53 in, a cylinder volume of 158.2 cu. in. became reality. The compression ratio was reduced from 10 to 9.3:1. Now the engine gave about 200 hp at 6500 rpm, in the Tipo 33 Stradale 230 hp/8800 rpm. Furthermore, the six-gear speed-change box of the racer was replaced by a five-gear speed-change box. The original oil-cooler remained in its place and one more was even mounted under the differential. In the engine, 11 quarts of oil and 12 quarts of water circulated. It is obvious that this liquid needed a certain time to reach the needed temperature. An electronic ignition with two coils and a duplex breaker ensured the right spark. The car had, of course, four ventilated disc brakes and a locking differential.

At first, the journalists were not allowed to drive themselves, but riding alongside the former Grand-Prix rider Consalvo Sanesi, they got a good impression of the car's performance. Some days later, the production version of the Montreal stood on the car exhibition of Geneva. But the press was not unanimously enthusiastic about the futuristic car. *Auto Motor and Sport* claimed that there was a central motor in "these Canadians' cars." This statement was never retracted by the journal. The production model had a frontally placed engine, which created much space, but gave the car absolutely no futuristic appear-

The fuel-injection system comes from the company Spica.

The bucket seats are very comfortable

The dashboard was quite futuristic but not very easy to overview.

ance. On the contrary, many journalists remarked that the Montreal was little, round and looked almost feminine. In the magazine *Autovisie*, Nico de Jong described the car as "pretty as a picture." But when the journalists were allowed to drive the car themselves, they were all of one mind: it was a dream car.
The top speed of the Montreal was about 137 mph. It accelerated as follows:

0-29 mph in 2.1 sec
0-50 mph in 5.4 sec
0-60 mph in 7.4 sec
0-87 mph in 13.6 sec
0-124 mph in 32.4 sec

Such a car, of course, could not economize on gasoline. In a test, the journalists of the Swiss weekly *Automobil Revue* made only 13 miles per gallon. At the speed of 124 mph, this decreased to 10.5 mpg. The Montreal did not become a popular car because it was too expensive. In its seven years of existence, scarcely four thousand were sold.

Technical specifications

Model:	**Alfa Romeo Montreal**
Years of manufacture:	1970-1977
Production:	3,925
Engine:	V8
Displacement:	158 cu. in.
Output:	200/6500 hp/rpm
Top speed:	137 mph
From 0 to 60 mph :	7.4 sec
Wheel base:	92.5 in
Length:	166 in
Height:	47.2 in
Weight:	2,799 lb

Alvis Graber

A Graber Special TC 21/100 from 1954.

The English auto company Alvis was scarcely known in other European countries. Before the Second World War, the enterprise built luxury sporting cars, but after 1945, it launched more conservative models. In 1951, the Swiss coachbuilder Hermann Graber bought the first Alvis chassis in order to furnish it with a cabriolet body. It was the beginning of a long-lasting and fruitful collaboration between the two companies.

Hermann Graber, the only son of a wheelwright, was born in 1904. Graber learned the craft of his father and moved to Paris. When his father died in 1925, he returned to Switzerland to take over the family firm. The 21-year-old Graber was much more interested in the construction of special car bodies and the teams of horses were banished from the workshop. One of the first models was a cabriolet on the chassis of a Fiat 509, which Graber constructed for himself. A short time afterwards, the first order followed. Graber constructed mostly cabriolets on the chassis of Mercedes, Bentley, Talbot and Delahaye.

The enterprise very quickly became famous and the clients rolled in. Each order lasted half a year and there was a waiting list. One surely had to have a special liking for this car to have its expensive chassis equipped with a Graber body. What would you say to a two-person roadster on a Duesenberg chassis? Or would you prefer the same body on the chassis of a Mercedes SSK? Graver presented one or more new models at nearly every motor show in Geneva.

After the war, Graber worked chiefly with English chassis. Thus, he bought his chassis from Rover, Bentley, Armstrong Siddeley and Aston Martin. And in 1950, the coachbuilder bought his first rolling chassis from Alvis. When the annual automobile show in Geneva opened its doors in March 1951, he presented the Alvis Graber. The five-person cabriolet strongly resembled the Graber Bentley, which could be admired in the Bentley stand at the exhibition, but was considerably cheaper. In 1952, Graber bought six rolling chassis from Alvis, all of them of the TA 21 type. Five of them had a cabriolet body and the sixth was built as a 2+2 coupe. In March 1953, this coupe stood beside an Alvis cabriolet in the Graber stand. A client from Zurich bought the car on the spot and drove it until 1957, when he had Graber exchange it for a TC 108G. The car remained in the possession of the family until Mrs. Graber (Hermann died in 1970) sold it to an Englishman in 1976.

In 1954, Graber became an Alvis importer for Switzerland and Liechtenstein. In Switzerland, there was not much demand for an Alvis with a factory body, but on the other hand, an Alvis with a Graber construction was very marketable. In 1954, Graber offered four different models: a cabriolet and three coupes on the

The TE type had four doors. 352 were sold.

A TD 21 from 1961 as five-person coupe. The body was built by Graber.

basis of the Alvis TA 21. In 1954, the cabriolet and the coupe cost 28,500 SFR. Both coupes, with stronger six-cylinder engines, cost 29,700 SFR in comparison to a Chevrolet available in Switzerland for only 14,400 SFR and a Volkswagen Beetle from 5,575 SFR.

In 1955, Graber brought an Alvis to the exhibition in Paris. Aside from the new Citroën DS 19, the Alvis drew the most attention. Due to the fact that their usual coachbuilder, the Mulliner company in Birmingham, was taken over by the Standard Motor Corporation, they could not build any cars for a year. Everybody from Alvis was impressed by the new Graber. Both enterprises agreed that the bodies could also be produced in England, as soon as a skillful coachbuilder could be found. At last, they agreed on the choice of Willowbrook, a firm seated in the small locality of Loughborough. But because of the long tea breaks and many strikes, such an Alvis TC 108 G (the G designating Graber) cost no less than £3,500, an amount for which a modest cottage in England could be built in 1955. Thus, even the coachbuilder Willowbrook was no solution, as the enterprise managed to sell only sixteen cars. One of them stood at the London Motor Show in October 1955. The famous special journal, *The Autocar*, opened the description of the vehicle with the following words: "The most beautiful and best proportioned car exhibited at the Earls Court Show is the 3.0 liter Alvis, the favorite of the true car-spotter." But even this publicity did not help. Over several years, only sixteen cars were sold, whereas Hermann Graber succeeded in marketing fifteen coupes and nine cabriolets.

In 1958, Alvis bought a set of wooden templates, tools and drawings from Graber. In the meantime, the coachbuilder Park Ward took over the production of his competitor, Willowbrook. The cars built by this enterprise between the Bentleys and the Rolls-Royces were now called Alvis TD 21. Graber sold 126 cars in Switzerland alone.

In 1959, Graber offered a "Special" coupe and "Super" Panoramic version of the Alvis TD 21. Two four-door cars of this latter model left the small factory. No car Graber built was identical to another. Much attention was paid to the specific wishes of the clients, with cars appearing with or without fins on the rear mudguards, or with much or little walnut wood in the interior. In 1962, the TD 21 Series II appeared and Graber came out with his "Special" cabriolet, which offered space for five persons. Despite its weight of 3,197 lb, the 15 ft. 3 in. long car achieved a top speed of 106 mph.

In 1957, this spacious coupe was born on the chassis of an Alvis TC 21.

This coupe from 1953 was built on the chassis of a TA 21 G.

The cabriolet cost merely 36,500 SFR, which was nothing when compared with the Bentley cabriolet starting at 87,000 SFR.

The last model built by Graber on an Alvis chassis was presented at exhibitions in 1974 as theTE 21. Now the car was equipped with double headlights mounted not side by side, but above one another.

In 1965, Rover took over the Alvis Company and the production of AlvisTF 21 started.This model remained available until 1966.The GraberTF 21 caught the eye with its headlights which, as on a Mercedes from that time, were placed "behind glass." In December 1966, it was Rover's turn to become a part of the Leyland concern. On August 22, 1967, the last AlvisTF 21 was driven out of the Holyhead Road factory in Coventry. From that time on, the factory devoted itself exclusively to the construction of military vehicles. And what about Graber? He had a small number of chassis in stock which he needed to finish first. But later, he thought: "If you can't beat them, join them," and he switched to the chassis of the Rover 2000.

Technical specifications

Model:	**TC 21**	**TD 21**	**TF 21**
Years of manufacture:	1953-1955	1956-1963	1963-1967
Production:	757	1,086	106
Engine:	six-cylinder	six-cylinder	six-cylinder
Displacement:	182.6 cu. in.	182.6 cu. in.	182.6 cu. in.
Output (hp/rpm):	93/4000	115/4500	150/4750
Top speed:	87 mph	99 mph	112 mph
From 0 to 60 mph:	not known	not known	not known
Wheel base:	9 ft 3 in	9 ft 3 in	9 ft 3 in
Length:	15 ft 2 in	15 ft 9 in	15 ft 9 in
Width:	5 ft 6 in	5 ft 6 in	5 ft 6 in
Height:	4 ft 6 in	4 ft 11 in	4 ft 9 in
Weight:	3,186 lb	3,417 lb	3,483 lb

American Motors Ambassador

Americans were last able buy a new car in 1942. And even though they had not been driving very much during the war, a new car came out again in 1945. For the car factories in Detroit, golden times followed.The manufacturers sold everything they were able to produce. And apparently, the clients did not mind that the models had been designed before the war.

Besides the "Big Three," the "Independents," like Packard, Studebaker, Nash and Kaiser introduced new models too. In 1946, the latter companies had a combined market share of 18.5%. In 1953, this percentage sank to less than 5%. At that time, the supply was much greater than the demand. George Mason, the president of Nash, had seen it coming. In 1946, he had already made an unsuccessful attempt to fuse with Hudson and Packard. In 1952, Mason tried it again and Abraham Edward Barit, the president of Hudson and Packard, accepted his proposal. During the war in Korea, Hudson and Packard was successful, but what would happen when the war was over? A peace was not concluded until

The 1972 Ambassador. The new grill was the most important change that year.

The 1959 Rambler Ambassador as a four-door hardtop sedan. The car was available only with a V8 engine.

1954 and the company had already booked a record loss of $10.4 million. A fusion with Nash in the American Motors Corporation seemed to be the best solution. In 1954, the production of Hudson and Packard was transferred from Detroit to the Nash factory in Kenosha, Wisconsin. The new enterprise, AMC, became a serious competitor for the Big Three. The development department needed to be able to order a larger number of parts from suppliers, and more importantly, to be able to built the Nash and the Hudson on the same chassis. And what's more, Nash gained 1,450 new dealers in the United States.

The cars built by AMC were identical down to the emblem. The Rambler was the small version and the Ambassador the big one. Neither Nash nor Hudson had ever possessed a V8 engine, and therefore they were still being bought from Packard. The engine had a capacity of 352.3 cu. in. and had 223 SAE hp/4600 rpm performance. The Ambassador could also be supplied with a six-cylinder engine with 252.6 cu. in. and 147 SAE hp/4000 rpm. In 1956, AMC had its own V8 engine and the Ambassador was available with the V8 only. The engine was a little bigger than that of a Packard. With a volume of 327 cu. in., its performance was 258 SAE hp/4700 rpm. The strong valve-in-head engine sucked its gasoline-air mixture from a big four-barrel Carter carburetor.

In 1958, Ambassador became an independent brand. To celebrate this event, the Rambler was thoroughly taken in hand. The double headlights were placed horizontally instead of vertically and the car was furnished with rear air shock absorbers. The list of accessories which could be added to the Ambassador was long. Apart from other possibilities, the following extras were available in 1959: the Flash-O-Matic automaton with push buttons ($229.50), overdrive ($114.50), steering booster ($89.50), power windows ($99.50), power brakes ($39.95), or a radio with an antenna ($91.90).

In 1963, the Ambassador was offered in two series, the 880 and 990. The 990 was the luxury design. Here you can see such a car as an eight-person station wagon.

Top of the line: the Ambassador Brougham as two-door hard top coupe. In 1972, the car cost $4,018 in the United States.

In 1961, the Ambassador got a new body as well as a new grill. The performance of the V8 was 253 SAE hp/4700 rpm with a 274 hp duplex carburetor if the four-barrel Holley was mounted on the vehicle. In the meantime, it had become a big car with a length of 17 ft and a weight equal to that of a four-door limousine (3,285 lb) or station wagon (3,505 lb).

In 1963, many other changes were made as well. The car's wheelbase grew from 8 ft 12 in to 9 ft 4 in and the height of the body was 4 ft 7 in instead of 4 ft 10 in. The type indications were changed also. Deluxe and Custom versions were no longer offered, but the Ambassador now came out of the factory as an "880" or a "990."

AMC cars were always known for their low-cost operation, but the 1963 models constituted the top of the line. The models with a gearshift lever on the floor could be delivered with overdrive. For this purpose, a special lever was mounted. If the lever was in the forward position, the driver could use a plain three-gear gearbox. If he pulled the lever, the overdrive kicked in as soon as the car's speed surpassed 26 mph and the foot was taken off from the gas pedal for a short time. The 1963 model cars were technically almost perfect. The American auto specialists' journal, *Auto Trend*, ranked the whole AMC series as the 1963 Car of the Year.

In 1965, the Ambassador was once again given a major facelift. For the first time since 1956, the car could be ordered with a six-cylinder engine which had a capacity of 231.8 cu. in. and an output of 157 SAE hp/4400 rpm. The wheelbase of the Ambassador was extended once again in 1965, this time by 4 in, resulting in an increased length of 5 in. The model could be distinguished easily: the double headlights were again above each other and no longer side by side. However, in the 1969 model, they would again be placed side by side.

In 1967, the most expensive version of the Ambassador was called an SST, which stood for "Super Sport Transport." In 1973, this name was changed again. The same year, the client could choose from four models, the Brougham V8, the Sedan, the Coupe Hardtop and the Station Wagon. All models could be supplied with three different V8 engines.

Technical specifications

Model:	**AMC Ambassador**	
Years of manufacture:	1958	1973
Production:	14.570	49.294
Engine:	V8	V8
Displacement:	327, 304, 360, 401 cu. in.	
Output (hp/rpm):	274/4700, 152/4200, 177/4400 or 259/4600	
Top speed:	99, 106, 112 or 124.3 mph	
From 0 to 60 mph:	not known	not known
Wheel base:	9 ft 9 in	10 ft 2 in
Length:	16 ft 8 in	17 ft 9 in
Width:	6 ft	6 ft 5 in
Height:	4 ft 9.5 in	4 ft 8 in
Weight:	3,561 lb	3,814 lb

American Motors Gremlin

A 1975 Gremlin 'Levi-X.'

On May 5, 1991, Richard A.Teague died at 67 years of age after a life full of cars. During the Second World War, he took evening classes at the Art Center College of Design in Los Angeles and during the day, he drew airplanes for Northrop Aircraft. After the war, Teague started as draftsman at General Motors. In 1951, he crossed over to Packard, where he became "Director of Styling" in 1953. When Packard was closed in 1958, Teague went via Chrysler to American Motors. Here, he designed models such as the Matador, the Pacer, the Javelin, the Hornet and of course, the Gremlin.

The Hornet was the successor of the Rambler American. The first model was the 1970, released in 1969. Teague drew the car as a two or four-door sedan. The Hornet became an immense success, and AMC sold 92,458 in the first year alone.

From the American point of view, the Hornet was a small car, referred by manufacturers in Detroit as a Subcompact, with a wheelbase of 9 ft and a length of 14 ft 12 in. The Hornet was indeed only one centimeter longer than an Opel Rekord. But the Opel Rekord and the AMC Hornet were still large, even in comparison to a Volkswagen Beetle, for instance. The demand for especially small cars increased dramatically during that time. To compete with the Volkswagen Beetle for example, Teague was forced to design, at great cost, an even smaller car. AMC invested more than $40 million in the development of the Hornet and the model consumed a large part of the enterprise's capital.

Fortunately, Teague's new "mini" was considerably cheaper. The development did not cost more than a total of $6 million because Teague had shortened the chassis of the two-door Hornet by 12.2 in so that the wheelbase was only 8 ft. The Hornet was cut across behind the front doors, furnished with a simple rear, and the Gremlin was ready. The car now had a length of 13 ft 5 in, a width of 5 ft 10.5 in and a height of 4 ft 4 in. The Beetle's dimensions were 13 ft 3 in, 5 ft 1 in and 4 ft 11 in respectively. The Gremlin was driven by the same engine as the Hornet. This six cylinder valve-in-head engine was available with 199 cu. in. and 130 SAE hp/4000 rpm or with 231.8 cu. in. and 147 SAE hp/4300

The Gremlin X had, apart from other things, a roll-back canvas roof, a black coated grill and tiltable front seats.

rpm. The car was available in two-door and four-door versions. Teague called the former version a station wagon. The rear window could be opened, of course, but was actually too small to be able to serve as a third door.
In 1972, the Hornet could also be delivered with a V8 engine. To the great pleasure of many clients, this was also the case with the Gremlin. This engine had a capacity of 304 cu.in. But even the client with a SIG engine found something new under the hood. The capacity of the six-cylinder was now 231.8 cu. in. or 258.4 cu. in. and had 112 hp/3500 rpm. With such an engine, the car weighed 2,712 lb and a top speed of 99 mph could be achieved. With the V8, the Gremlin achieved a speed of no less than 118 mph. For the gearing, a three-speed gearbox or an automatic shifting was used. In both cases, the gearshift lever was situated in the floor between the seats or in front of the front seat, which belonged to the standard equipment. In 1978, the last year of manufacture for the Gremlin, the model could not be delivered with a V8, but only with a four-cylinder Audi engine.

Soon the Gremlin could be bought in thirty different colors and "sponsor versions." Here you can see a "Levi's" from 1972 with denim upholstering.

Number of Gremlins built per year:

1970	28,560
1971	76,908
1972	94,808
1973	122,844
1974	171,128
1975	56,011
1976	39,419
1977	27,050
1978	54,747

Beginning with the front bumper and ending with the doors, the Gremlin was actually identical with the Hornet.

Technical specifications

Model:	**AMC Gremlin**		
Years of manufacture:	1970-1978		
Production:	671,475		
Engine:	six-cylinder	V8	V8
Displacement:	198.7 cu. in.	232 cu. in.	304 cu. in.
Output (hp/rpm):	130/4000	147/4310	152/4200
Top speed:	93 mph	99 mph	112 mph
From 0 to 60 mph:	not known	not known	not known
Wheel base:	8 ft	8 ft	8 ft
Length:	13 ft 5 in	13 ft 5 in	13 ft 5 in
Width:	5 ft 11 in	5 ft 11 in	5 ft 11 in
Height:	4 ft 4 in	4 ft 4 in	4 ft 4 in
Weight:	2,579 lb	2,579 lb	2,959 lb

Amphicar

"As a car, it is too much a ship and as a ship too much a car," wrote a journalist in the American auto specialists' magazine, *Car and Driver,* after testing the Amphicar. It was indeed neither a good car nor a good boat. The Amphicar was built by the Deutschen Wagon-und Maschinenfabriken GmbH in Berlin, following the drawings of Hans Trippel. Trippel was an experienced professional. In 1936, when he was 23 years old, he constructed an amphibian vehicle on the

When afloat, the Amphicar reached a speed of 7 mph.

chassis of a DKW. When Adolf Hitler started to extend his car fleet, Trippel was the man who handled "floating cars." These cars had been produced in the Bugatti factory in Molsheim since 1941. The Trippel-Werke GmbH enterprise delivered more than 1,000 of them to the Nazis. All amphibian vehicles had a four-wheel drive.

After the war, Germany was no longer allowed to produce all-terrain or amphibian vehicles. Consequently, Trippel could not offer such a car until 1958. He called the new model "Alligator." For the transmission, he used an Austin-Healey Sprite engine.

The industrialist Harald Quandt was eminently interested in the project and invested in it. Thus, the Amphicar was born in 1961. Trippel would have preferred to have a Volkswagen engine, but the air cooling made this impossible. The Mercedes 190SL engine was too heavy and Trippel tried out the four-cylinder engine from the Triumph Herald. This engine was placed in the rear of the car and drove the rear wheels via a four-speed gearbox. The two propellers could be turned on by the means of an intermediate box. The body was made of 0.06 in thick steel sheets. Weighing 2,315 lb, the vehicle reached a speed of 68 mph on the road. Afloat, the top speed was about 7.5 mph. The driving wheel served at the

The interior of the Amphicar looked nothing like a ship.

Two propellers ensured the propulsion in water.

same time as a helm, as the ship was steered by its front wheels even in the water. Indeed, this demanded some helmsmanship because the rotation circle was no less than 59 ft to the right and 89 ft to the left! Both propellers rotated counter-clockwise for the most part. The ship also had no anchor and easily floated away. The Amphicar could hardly be used when a strong side wind blew. On dry land it went better, but there, the car had to withstand the contemptuous looks of bystanders since it stood so high on its wheels that it looked nearly comical.

Technical specifications

Model:	**Amphicar**
Years of manufacture:	1961-1968
Production:	about 3,000
Engine:	four-cylinder
Displacement:	70 cu. in.
Output:	38/4750 hp/rpm
Top speed:	68-70 mph
From 0 to 60 mph:	not known
Wheel base:	68 ft 11 in
Length:	14 ft 3 in
Width:	5 ft 1 in
Height:	4 ft 12 in
Weight:	2,315 lb

Aston Martin DB2

The power source of the DB2: the six-cylinder engine designed by W.O. Bentley.

Each Aston Martin is something special, as you know. But nobody could ever have guessed that this car would become so famous. Lionel Martin and Robert Bamford pieced the first prototype together in 1914. It became a tiny car for the "Voiturette class." The chassis originated from an Isotta-Fraschini and the engine was from a Coventry Simplex. The model became world-famous and the name Aston Martin appeared very soon in all the newspapers. The name Aston, by the way, comes from a small hill in the vicinity of Aston Clinton in England.

In 1919, shortly after the First World War, a second model appeared. This car was something very special as well. Aston Martins turned out to be perfect for racing. Every time they appeared on the circuit, they booked victories.

In 1947, the company ran deeply into debt. The enterprise was sold to David Brown. This Brown gave the order to W.O. Bentley (indeed, the one and only Bentley) to draw a new engine. The new models were presented in 1949 as DB2. The characters DB referred to the initials of David Brown. The DB2 was baptized on the most ambitious and challenging racing circuit: Le Mans. The first model took part in the murderous 24-hour race. Unfortunately, the Aston Martin could not complete the race. The water pump was designed so badly that the car had to give up, steaming after only six laps, because the cooling had ceased to function.

In the spring of 1950, its teething troubles were eliminated and the first production cars could be delivered. In order to save the nearly lost credit of the make, the enterprise took part in the famous race in Le Mans again in 1951, this time with more success. The Aston Martin not only won in its class, but also reset the class record. In 1952, the same happened again in the Mille Miglia. The Wisdom/Lown duo ended in first place before their colleagues Parnell/Serboli, and far before the first Ferrari.

In total, 411 of the DB2 were built. More than 1,200 hours of work were invested in each car. The body was made, with great care, of aluminum plate and mounted on a tubular chassis. Unfortunately, the car just missed the famous Great Exhibition of London. The model was presented by a dealer in Switzerland on November 24, 1952.

Let us put the curriculum vitae of the 411 DB2's under the magnifying glass. On December 3, 1952, the 195th was sold to the Swiss Walter Lambert. Walter was 33 years old and co-owner of a factory manufacturing machines for the watch-making industry. Besides his Aston Martin, Lambert also possessed a Riley, which he took out of his garage when he was not in a hurry. In April 1953, his Aston Martin had already been driven 6,214 miles and the time came for the first service check. Rolls Royce sends its mechanics all over the world to serve its clients. For the first overhaul of the DB2, an engineer flew specially from England in order to adjust the carburetors. When the odometer showed 10,000 miles, the starter and the coupling were repaired by the same man.

The DB2 had a length of only 13 ft 6 in.

And this is how the DB2 of Walter Herter from Bülach looks now. The stripe over the engine hood was not unanimously approved.

The DB2 possessed a 157.4 cu. in. engine with 108 hp at 5000 revolutions per minute. The top speed was no less than 106 mph. In England, the DB2 was supplied with an even stronger six-cylinder engine. This model was christened Vantage and had an output of 127 genuine hp. When Walter Lambert heard this, he immediately had such a strong engine built in own car. Was he already playing around with the idea of becoming a famous racer? We assume so, because in April 1954, he took part in a special course for future racers in Campione. And during his first race, he showed the Jaguars only his rear lights.

But Campione was not his last opportunity. During a race in the mountains near Reigoldswil in September 1954, Lambert won in his class. The same month, Lambert took part in the Mitholz-Kandersteg race and won fourth place behind the Hans Karl von Tscharner's Ferrari and two Lancias. In 1955, many successes followed and, aside from other victories, he beat his arch-rival Von Tscharner.

But times changed. In 1957 (when Von Tscharner, Scherrer and Seiler stopped racing), the field was dominated by the new Mercedes 300 SL and the Alfa Romeo. From that moment on, Lambert finished in the middle. After the race in Mitholz-Kandersteg, the famous car magazine, Automobile Revue, wrote: "Walter Lambert made a very good impression by steering his heavy, and none too maneuverable, Aston Martin quickly through the bends." The DB2 seemed bit antiquated. Lambert then switched to a Ferrari Berlinetta. For a time, he kept his DB2 for every day use, but eventually sold it for 7,500 SFR to Dr. Guer Reichen. Reichen exchanged the car after a short period for a DB4 GT. The new owner, the garage owner, Patthey, decided to give the car a new paint job. With 45,184 miles on the tachometer, he then sold the car to the collector Pierre Strinati, who exhibited it from November 1963 until May 1984. In 1984, the car was sold to Hugo (Le Beau) Studer. Studer participated in antique automobiles races, but he never used the DB2.

In a racing car like the DB2, the rpm gauge is more important than the speedometer.

On November 14, 1985, he exchanged the car for a Lotus. Garage holder Koni Lutziger became the new owner. He had the car partly repainted and again sold it to Walter Herter from Bülach on April 12, 1986. Hopefully, this last owner will race the Aston Martin, as its makers originally intended.

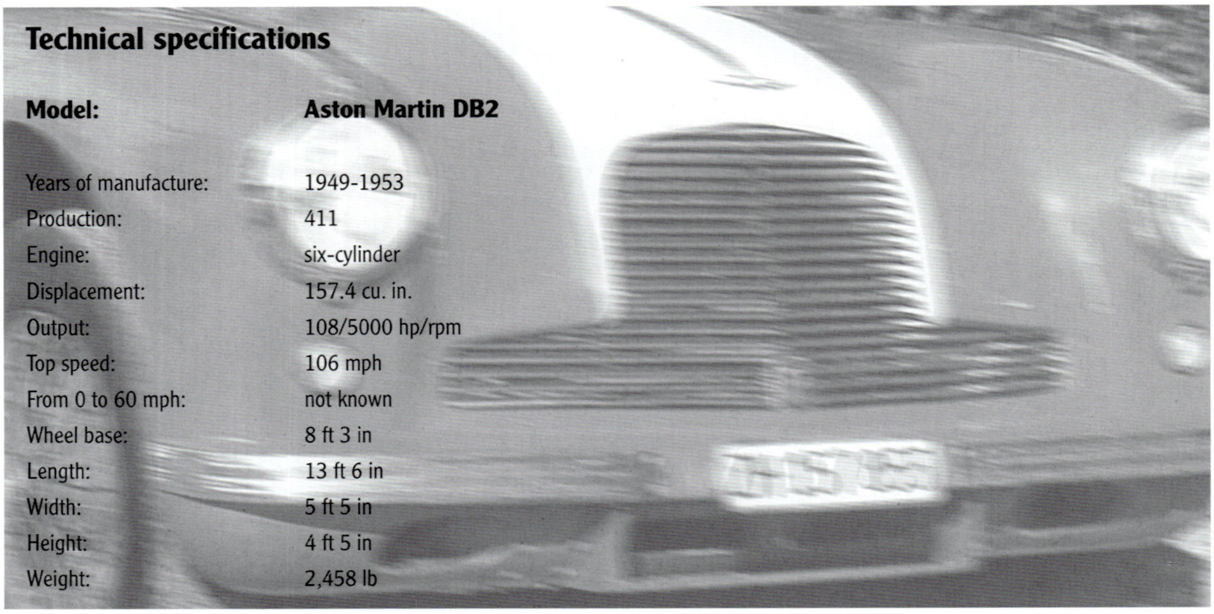

Technical specifications

Model:	**Aston Martin DB2**
Years of manufacture:	1949-1953
Production:	411
Engine:	six-cylinder
Displacement:	157.4 cu. in.
Output:	108/5000 hp/rpm
Top speed:	106 mph
From 0 to 60 mph:	not known
Wheel base:	8 ft 3 in
Length:	13 ft 6 in
Width:	5 ft 5 in
Height:	4 ft 5 in
Weight:	2,458 lb

Aston Martin DB4 GT Zagato

The production numbers of Aston Martins have always been rather modest due to one reason in particular: the enterprise never really flourished. But the cars that left the factory were always top quality. At a press conference during the IAA in Frankfurt in 1995, it was proudly announced that the factory had sold more than 750 cars in twelve months for the first time in its history. In Newport Pagnell, the tradition of excellent craftsmanship still continues. They do not allow themselves to be rushed, they prefer to do their work slowly rather than badly, and they take the time to drink a cup of tea from time to time. And not even Ford, the owner of the factory since 1994, can do anything to change this.

The six-cylinder engine was designed by Tadek Marek and was used in the DB4 for the first time in 1958.

In 1958, Aston came out with a new model, the DB4. Actually, the DB4 was the first new design since the 1930s. The car had English technology with a new aluminum engine under an aluminum body designed and built by Carrozzeria Touring. The factory set a new record: between October 1958 and June 1963, 1,110 DB4s were built.

Eleven of the nineteen DB4 GT Zagatos were delivered with the steering wheel on the right side.

A year after the introduction of the DB4, the DB4 GT was born with a 5 in shorter wheelbase. The car was suitable for the road but was, in fact, designed for the circuit. The DB4 GT remained a comparatively exceptional car. Of this model, only 75 cars with a Touring-body were produced. On the same chassis, 19 cars were taken in hand by Carrozzeria Zagato and the first Aston Zagato was launched by a small Italian factory in 1960. The same year, the model was presented at the London Motor Show in Earls Court. Stirling Moss drove this car during the Easter Race in 1961 on the Goodwood circuit. Because the car had been badly prepared, however, the Englishman ended third behind Mike Parkes' Ferrari and Innes Ireland's Aston Martin DB4 GT. Two Zagatos took part in the 24-hour Le Mans race in 1962, but unfortunately with very little success. After only an hour the car had to be parked on the side of the track with a burnt head gasket. In spite of that, the Zagato was a good racing car and won prizes regularly.

The 36 gallon tank could be filled from both sides.

Woolen Wilton carpets on the floor and Connolly leather on the tilting seats provided luxury.

The Aston Martin DB4 GT contains a six-cylinder engine with two upper cam shafts, a double ignition and three Weber carburetors which were taken from the 302. In the Zagato version, the compression ratio was brought from 9 to 9.7:1, by which the output increased by 11 hp. More interesting is the fact that Zagato succeeded in constructing the car so that it was 240 lb lighter than the DB4 GT of Carrozzeria Touring. And the leather upholstery, the revolving glass windows and thick Wilton carpets on the floor prove that this was not done at the expense of comfort.

The four-speed gearbox originated from the conventional DB4, but the clutch had only two plates and there was a locking differential in the rear axle. The standard version had boosted Dunlop brakes, but in the DB4 GT Zagato there were Girling brakes without boosting. The capacity of the gasoline tank was increased from 23 to 36 gallons, which turned out to be an absolute necessity on the circuit.

Technical specifications

Model:	**Aston Martin DB4 GT Zagato**
Years of manufacture:	1960-1963
Production:	19
Engine:	six-cylinder
Displacement:	224 cu. in.
Output:	313/6000 hp/rpm
Top speed:	43 mph
From 0 to 60 mph:	6.1 sec.
Wheel base:	7 ft 9 in
Length:	14 ft
Width:	5 ft 6 in
Height:	4 ft 4 in
Weight:	2,557 lb

Audi TT

Coupé & Roadster

Well visible: the two gas outlet ends.

Audi comes out with something new each year. Ferdinand Piëch, Audi's big boss, presented his brand new Dream Car at the Frankfurt car exhibition in September of 1995. It was a small 2+2 coupe called the Audi TT (Tourist Trophy). The car had an aluminum body and stood on the chassis of the Audi A3, not yet in production at that time. The engine from the A4 was placed transversally in the front part of the car and drove all 4 wheels. No other solution was possible

The hand-sewn seat upholstery evokes a baseball atmosphere. On the aluminum plate, the passenger can assume a stable position.

The front view of the Audi TT. It could have been designed by the Zagato brothers.

And here is the evidence! The TTS has indeed a canvas roof, but without a rear window.

because Piëch was as strongly convinced of the advantages of four-wheel drive as his famous grandfather Ferdinand Porsche. The car did not have a very modern look; it could have been designed at Zatago's in the fifties. As in the creations of that Italian specialist, there was no trace of luxury in the Audi TT at all. It was a "no nonsense car" with big round gauges in the dashboard, plating visible from inside and a prominent roll bar.

The Audi TT cost as much as the new roadster: 40,000 DM. Roadster? What sort of roadster? The answer was given at the Tokyo Motor Show some weeks later: an open, two-person version of the TT, the TTS. The roadster resembled the coupe, but the small differences made it considerably more interesting. Thus, the turbo engine had much more hp and

Short and to the point. Nothing left to say: the dashboard of the Audi TT.

the maximal rotational moment of the roadster engine was 250 Nm, in comparison with 210 Nm of the coupe version. The roadster had 18 inch wheels with immensely broad 225/40 tires. (The coupe version had 17 inch Wheel.) The big, ugly roll bar was replaced by two smaller ones, located directly behind the seats. Nevertheless, the car was apparently designed for warm countries only. The model had no roof as such, no rear window and only a piece of cloth to protect the passengers from the elements. Even the side windows were missing. The designers of Audi apparently contented themselves with the vent windows as found, for instance, in an MGA of the 1950s.

The TT stood on the chassis of the Audi A3, which would be launched many months later for the first time.

Technical specifications

Model:	**Audi Coupé TT**	**Roadster TTS**
Year of manufacture:	1995	1995
Production:	1	1
Engine:	four-cylinder	four-cylinder
Displacement:	108.6 cu. in.	108.6 cu. in.
Output:	150/5700 hp/rpm	210/6000 hp/rpm
Top speed:	140 mph	155 mph
From 0 to 60 miles:	8.0 sec.	6.0 sec.
Wheel base:	8 ft	8 ft
Length:	13 ft	13 ft
Width:	5 ft 9 in	5 ft 9 in
Height:	4 ft 5 in	4 ft 5 in
Weight:	2,690 lb	2,734 lb

Audi TT Coupe
Roadster Quattro

Seen here in all its glory the new V6 engine 3.2 liter Audi TT.

Both the Coupe and the soft top Roadster Audi TT made their debuts in concept format in 1995. In June 1999, a version of the Coupe Quattro was introduced in the UK, and by 2000, the Roadster had joined its counterpart.

The UK is the largest market for the TT and although it is basically the same car and no doubt sells well in many other countries around the world, it does not necessarily have the same specification as those in the UK.

The car is now available in the UK in three versions, all using the turbocharged 1.8 liter, four cylinder gas engine. The recently added version is capable of pushing out 150 bhp whilst the two older versions remain at 180 bhp and 225 bhp.

The Audi TT Quattro Roadster is one of only two open-top two-seaters to use a four-wheel drive system. The other is the Lamborghini Diablo Roadster. Although the top-of-the-line model is the best equipped, all three share an extensive equipment list featuring alloy wheels, remote control, central locking, leather upholstery and heated front sports seats. A leather-rimmed sports steering wheel, electronic climate control, powered windows and mirror, are rounded off nicely with a Concert radio cassette-player.

The present top-of-the-line 225 bhp model has slightly larger alloy six spoke wheels with wider and lower profile tires, twin exhaust tailpipes and xenon headlights with electronic washers. The two pretty roll-over hoops are not only safety fittings, but are also integral elements of the overall body structure.

Both of the original cars are fitted with a six-speed manual gearbox and the 225 bhp version has a Driver's Information System fitted to transmit any problems directly to the driver. The new 150 bhp version uses a five speed

Two exhaust outlets and six spoke wheels give this TT away. It's the 225 bhp Roadster version.

Front view of the newly presented 150 bhp Audi Roadster. A better price makes it accessible to many more sports car lovers.

manual transmission. All versions are equipped with a powered soft-top and an electrically adjustable glass wind deflector as standard fitments.

Much care has been taken to facilitate use of the soft-top, which can retract at the touch of a button and will take just fifteen seconds to complete its rotation. A tonneau cover is provided after the roof has been lowered to protect the fabric and the working mechanism of the roof.

Safety features are absolutely vital and the TT is fitted with driver and passenger front airbags, side airbags (head and thorax), ABS with EBD (Electronic Brake Force Distribution), EDL (Electronic Differential Lock) traction control governs the front wheels and the latest version of the quattro permanent four-wheel drive system.

In the autumn of 2003, a new and more powerful version was presented to the public: a 3.2 litre quattro version powered by a sophisticated V6 gas engine with the option of the new Audi Direct Shift gearbox and the ability to accelerate to 60 mph in 6.5 seconds and reach a top speed exceeding 150 mph.

Technical specifications

Model:	**Audi TT Coupe/Roadster Quattro**			
Engine:	4 cyl	4 cyl	4 cyl	V6
Cylinder Capacity:	1.8	1.8	1.8	3.2
Bhp:	150	180	225	250
Top Speed:	132 mph	137 mph	146 mph	155 mph(governed)
0-60 mph:	8.9 sec	7.9 sec	6.7 sec	6.4 sec
Wheel base:	7 ft 11 in	7 ft 11 in	7 ft 11 in	7 ft 11 in
Length:	13 ft 3 in	13 ft 3 in	13 ft 3 in	13 ft 3 in
Width:	5 ft 9 in	5 ft 9 in	5 ft 9 in	5 ft 9 in
Height:	4 ft 5 in	4 ft 5 in	4 ft 5 in	4 ft 5 in
Weight:	2,943 lb	2,943 lb	2,943 lb	3,351 lb

Austin-Healey 100S

This small oval grill is characteristic for cars with a four-cylinder engine.

An Austin-Healey 100S is no ordinary Healey, but a real racing car. Donald Healey's 100S was first intended for the American market. The letter "S" referred to the famous Sebring circuit in Florida. Donald Healey would have preferred to christen it the "Sebring," but since this name was already used by another car maker, he had to content himself with the "S."

Between January 1953 and December 1967, a total of 73,728 "big" Austin-Healeys were sold as well as 362 small Healey Sprites. Many different versions of the "big" Healey were constructed. In August 1956, the car was still powered by a four-cylinder engine. Later, the car was available with a six-cylinder engine. Although the Healeys differed from one another, they all had one thing in common: they were designed and constructed for the American market. 89% of all Big Healeys were exported to the U.S. The other 11% were intended for the world market.

In total, 15,826 cars with a four-cylinder engine were sold. Only 55 got the "100S" stamp. When seen from a distance, the car resembles a common 1955 Healey, as its designer, Donald Healey, intended. Healey, a gifted technician, was a competitor with all his heart and soul. He built sporting cars all his life and won numerous races and rallies. He was convinced that an Austin-Healey would evoke a great deal of positive publicity as a racing car. In 1954, he decided to prepare a car for the 12-hour race on the Sebring circuit. The engine was handled by Harry Weslake and after the car was shipped to New York, Healey himself drove it to Sebring, Florida. On March 7, 1954, the Healey was driven by the Englishman Lance Macklin and the American George Huntoon. They would have, undoubtably, won the race if a rocker shaft had not broken, due to the engine running on only three cylinders. The riders were overtaken by an Osca and

The rear of the car was also nearly identical to that of an ordinary Healey.

a Lancia and had to content themselves with the third place in the general classification and champions in their class. But the Healey had demonstrated its potential and Austin in England decided to build more such racing cars.

By the end of 1954, the prototype of the 100S was ready for its first ride. The chassis, originating from a production car, was reinforced in various places by John Thompson. The new body was hammered from aluminum plate by Jensen Motor Ltd. in West Bromwich. The final assemblage was handled by Austin in Longbridge-Birmingham. Nearly all of the 100S-type Healeys were painted white-blue, the American racing colors. None of the cars built by Jensen had a canvas roof or quarter windows. The engine was handled by Morris Motors in Courthouse Green. An aluminum cylinder head designed by Weslake with two horizontal S.U. carburetors was mounted. Both the inflating and deflating valves had larger diameters than the normal Healeys and were operated by a special cam shaft. Even the distributor was new and was placed, not on the right, but on the left side of the engine. The compression ratio was 8.3 instead of 7.5:1 and the output increased from 91 hp/4000 rpm to 134 hp/4700 rpm. Two six-volt accumulators were placed in the rear of the car, as well as a 90-liter tank and two electric S.U. pumps transporting the gasoline to the engine. Close behind the oval grill with the type designation "100S" there was an oil-cooler constructed by the Tecalamit company for trucks. The gear box came from a normal Healey but the gear wheels and the transmissions were different. The gearbox of the 100S had no overdrive and was rather heavy. The short, dual exhaust protruded from beneath the body on the right side in front of the rear wheel. Behind the 5.50-15 Dunlop race tires, there were four hard chrome-plated disc brakes with a diameter of 11.4 in.

In March 1955, the Englishmen had built six cars of the 100S type. The vehicles and the prototype were sent to the 12-hour race at Sebring. One of the cars was driven by Stirling Moss and Lance Macklin. The other cars were lent to American competitors by the American importer. In 1955, a total of eighty cars appeared at the starting line. The race was won by a Jaguar of the D type, a Ferrari won second and fifth and Maserati took third and fourth places. The duet

The engine with an aluminum cylinder head and the ignition on the left instead on the right side of the engine.

The 100S was only available without a canvas roof and quarter windows.

Moss-Macklin came in sixth in the total classification and won in its class.The other Healey 100Ses also passed the finish, but did not get a prize.

All in all, only 55 cars of the 100S type were built and almost all of them were designated for the American market. The 100S is now the most popular Austin-Healey and it should not come as a surprise that various companies specialize in the construction of replicas of this vehicle.

Technical specifications

Model:	**Austin-Healey 100S**
Years of manufacture:	1955-1956
Production:	55
Engine:	four-cylinder
Displacement:	162.3 cu. in.
Output:	134/4700 hp/rpm
Top speed:	140 mph
Time from 0 to 60 mph:	not known
Wheel base:	7 ft 6 in
Length:	12 ft 4 in
Width:	5 ft
Height:	4 ft 5 in
Weight:	1,874 lb

Bentley Continental GT

One of the most important details that Bentley wanted to retain was the famous grill. Here one can see just how well it has been designed at the front end of the car.

At the Geneva motor show on March 3, 2003, Bentley Motors unveiled the production version of their new Continental GT, the fastest road-going Bentley in the 84-year history of the company.The first car will be delivered to the UK home market in October 2004 and to other markets soon after.

The Continental GT was designed and engineered by Bentley at Crewe and will be manufactured there in all-new facilities.The Continental GT is the first Bentley to have been designed entirely in the computer "virtual" world.

The styling story of the Continental GT dates back to August 1999 when Dirk van Braeckel started on a design for an all-new Bentley coupe. It was approved for production by Christmas.

The aim was to create a car with as much room as the most spacious coupes, equip it with the performance and responses of the world's most dynamic supercars and retain the most compact dimensions. The secret of the Continental GT is, in fact, its incredibly compact engine. By using staggered banks of cylinders, the W12 is the shortest 12-cylinder engine on the market. 3K turbochargers were chosen and integrated into the under-hood package. Drive is sent to all four wheels, a first for a Bentley, as is the paddle-operated, six-speed sequential automatic gearbox, a transmission built for Bentley by ZF. Tiptronic allows conventional automatic or a clutchless manual drive.

As can be seen here, all normal adjustments for driving the Bentley can be accessed from the steering wheel. Sumptuous leather abounds and makes for a very comfortable ride.

Once behind the wheel, an ideal driving position is easily achieved. Bentley's ergonomicists have measured New York City professional basketball players to make sure all shapes and sizes are accommodated.

In addition to impressive active safety attributes, the Continental GT has a full raft of passive safety features with two front airbags, four side airbags and two side curtain bags that run along the full length of the cabin. Seat belt pre-tensioners are used for all four seats.

The basis of the chassis strategy is an extremely stiff body, to which the latest suspension technology was applied, featuring an innovative double wishbone arrangement at the front and an exceptionally well-located, multi-link rear

From the side, the Bentley Continental GT looks smooth and well proportioned; the roofline is low and sleek.

axle behind. Air springs are used at each corner in place of conventional coils, each one containing its own infinitely adjustable electronic damper capable of adjusting itself and continuously without the driver ever being aware of it. Braking is being provided by all new–ventilated discs, featuring the latest Bosch anti-lock system with Brake Assist and Emergency Brake Force Distribution.

The role of the company's Volkswagen AG parent has been critical to the process: it was only their £500 million vote of confidence that brought the 20-year-old dream to reality.

Technical specifications

Model:	**Bentley Continental GT**
Engine:	Twin turbo/12 Cylinders
Capacity:	366 cu. in.
Power:	560 PS (552 bhp) (411 kW/6100 rpm)
Transmission:	6-speed automatic
Performance:	
Top Speed	190 mph
0-60 mph:	4.7 seconds
50-75 mph:	3.3 seconds
Overall length:	15 ft 9 in
Width:	6 ft 4 in
Height:	4 ft 7 in
Wheel base:	9 ft

Bentley MkVI and R-Type

The eager purchaser could take this Mk VI Standard Saloon home immediately.

After the Second World War, Rolls Royce transferred the production of its passenger cars from the little village of Derby to Crewe, where only aircraft engines had been built. In 1946, the first cars left the production line. And for the first time, the client could buy either a complete car, or, as before the war, a rolling chassis. The first postwar Bentley left the factory as the Mk VI. Some prototypes of this model had been built already in 1939, but serial production could not be started at that time. In many aspects, the car still resembled its predecessor, the Mk V, but it was equipped with a new chassis with a shorter wheelbase of 10 ft 4 in. And as the engine was mounted in front of the car, the radiator was now located in front of the forward axle instead of behind it.

The Bentley six-cylinder engine had, as did the Rolls Royce, a rather complex cylinder head. The inlet valves were namely overhead valves and the exhaust valves lateral valves. Until 1951, the engine capacity was 260 and afterwards 278.6 cu. in. because the bore for the cylinders was increased from 3.46 to 3.62 in. The gearbox had four driving positions, the first of which was not synchronized. This was no substantial disadvantage, as the car could drive well in the second driving position. In 1952, an automatic gear box could be ordered. The brakes were boosted, but functioned hydraulically on the front wheels and mechanically on the rear wheels. The front wheels were equipped with independent suspension, but in the rear, a rigid axle was mounted.

The first Mk VI left the factory in October 1946 and the last one in June 1952. In total, 5,201 cars were sold, the majority of them Standard Saloons. The four-door version had a steel body made by Park Ward. From the technical point of

The R-Type with a factory body.

The Continental R-Type is one of the most beautiful Bentleys ever built. 207 have been sold in total.

view, the MkVI was nearly identical to the Rolls-Royce Silver Wraith, but the Bentley was a little bit sportier. The Bentley was mostly steered by the owner personally, the Rolls mostly by a driver in livery.

At the London Motor Show of 1952, the R-Type, the successor of the MkVI was presented. The new car scarcely differed from its predecessor. The engine was unchanged and it was also difficult to find any differences in the body. The Standard Saloon was made at Park Ward's and had a larger storage compartment than its predecessor, the MkVI, giving the car extra length, regardless of the fact that the wheel base remained the same.

The special model of the R-Type offered by the factory, the Bentley Continental Sports Saloon, was far more interesting. This fascinating coupe was a creation of the coachbuilder Mulliner. The engine of the Continental Sports Saloon was

The tail end of the Continental was "aerodynamically streamlined."

slightly perfected. The compression ratio was now 7.25 instead of 6.4:1, and the car's top speed was thus about 125 mph. Unlike the other R-Type models, which were geared by an automatic gear box, the Continental was available with a manually hand-operated four-speed gearbox, which gave the car an even sportier character. The R-Type was built from September 1952 to December 1954 and was followed by the S-series.

Although the MkVI and the R-Type were sold mostly with a factory body, some car enthusiasts nevertheless preferred their "own" body. Most frequently, they ordered a rolling chassis. In this version, the car was mechanically complete, but the body ended at the windshield. The construction of the car had to be completed by a selected coachbuilder. Many coachbuilders could give free play to their creativity on the Bentley chassis: VandenPlas, Abbott, Duncan, Harold Radford, Windovers, James Young, Gurney Nutting, Hoopers, Franay, Mulliner, Freestone & Webb, Park Ward, as well as Pininfarina and Graber.

After the war, coachbuilder Harold Radford specialized in the construction of station wagons, which he called the Shooting Brake. Here you can see an Mk VI from 1948.

The body of this R-Type was made by the Abbott enterprise.

Technical specifications

Model:	**MkVI**	**R-Type**
Years of manufacture:	1946-1952	1952-1954
Production:	5,201	2,320
Engine:	six-cylinder	six-cylinder
Displacement:	259.8 and 278.6 cu. in.	278.6 cu. in.
Output (hp/rpm):	not known	not known
Top speed:	90 and 100 mph	170-200 mph
From 0 to 60 mph:	not known	not known
Wheel base:	10 ft	10 ft
Length:	16 ft	16 ft 7 in
Width:	5 ft 7 in	5 ft 7 in
Height:	5 ft 3 in	5 ft 3 in
Weight:	4,078.5 lb	4,145 lb

Bizzarrini GT Europa 1900

Bizzarrini hoped to succeed in selling 30 cars of his new model as the first series, but production stopped at the eleventh car.

At the Torino automobile show, not many novelties were presented. Factories reserved their premieres for Geneva, London or Paris. In 1966, an exception to this rule was made. In the huge Fiat stand, the public could see not only the new Fiat 124 cabriolet, but also the new Dino Spyder (a Dino stood at Ferrari's stand too, but this 206 GT had a coupe body and a transversely placed engine in the rear).

But the new features of the Fiat were not the only surprise. A few minutes before the show opened, another world premiere was pushed onto the Bizzarrini stand, its paint hardly dry. Giotto Bizzarrini had christened his new creation the GT Europa 1900. The two-seater looked like a reduced Bizzarrini GT Strada 5300, but was 23 in shorter, 5.5 in narrower, 3 in lower and no less than 1,323 lb lighter than its big brother. And in addition to that, the model was also cheap. The GT Europa 1900 cost less than half of a Strada and only a little more than a Porsche 912.

The Bizzarrini Europa bore an unmistakable resemblance to its big brother, the GT Strada 5300.

The beautiful body was placed on a steel chassis, and a perfected Opel 1900 engine could be found under the trunk. This four-cylinder engine was placed so far back that it was placed almost directly in front of the rear wheels. The cylinder was taken in hand by the Italian expert Virgilio Conreroirgilio Conrero and equipped with

The large rear window served also as luggage hold cover.

two carburetors. The carter was adapted and could hold no less than 4 gallons of oil. In his handouts, Bizzarrini asserted that the strength of this engine is about 135 hp.

The chassis also showed some technical novelties. The wheels had independent suspension and were provided with disc brakes. The rear disc brakes were situated directly at the ZF locking differential in order to reduce the non-suspended weight as much as possible. The Koni shock absorbers of course were standard equipment and although the car was not intended for the circuit, it could attain a top speed of 124 mph.

Bizzarrini wanted to start with a series of thirty cars, but the car displayed has a chassis number of 11. According to its owner, it was the last one built.

Technical specifications

Model:	**Bizzarrini GT Europa 1900**
Years of manufacture:	1966-1967
Production:	11
Engine:	four-cylinder
Displacement:	115.7 cu. in.
Output:	135/5600 hp/rpm
Top speed:	124 mph
From 0 to 60 mph in sec:	not known
Wheel base:	7 ft 2 in
Length:	12 ft 4 in
Width:	5 ft 3 in
Height:	3 ft 4 in
Weight:	1,433 lb

BMW Dwarf Cars

The 700 could also be purchased as a coupe or as a cabriolet.

The first postwar BMWs were the types 501 and 502. These colossal cars with their heavy six-cylinder and V8 engines were inaccessible for most people. In the 1950s, there was more demand for transport vehicles in Germany than for luxury cars. If BMW really wanted to earn money, other methods had to be found. The solution was found at the Geneva motor show, where the Italian company ISO exhibited its Isette in 1954. BMW and ISO entered into a license contract and one year later, in 1955, the first BMW Isettas left the conveyor-belt. The Germans did not need to change the Italian version very much. They used their own 15.25 cu. in. four-stroke motorcycle engine, mounted the headlamps above the front mudguards and affixed the BMW emblem under the windshield. The Isetta had only one door occupying the whole front part of the car. The steering column was attached to the inner side of the front door. Thus, the front door could revolve on a hinge opening forward and facilitating getting in and out. The motor bicycle engine was placed in front of the rear axle and geared two rear wheels placed alongside each other by a chain. The BMW Isetta had no differential.

In 1956, the factory marketed a strong version, the Isetta 300, with a 18.18 cu. in. single, and instead of 12 hp, it now had 13 hp. But the "gap" between the small Isetta and the large 500 models proved to be too big. Isetta was a low profit business and the sale numbers of the large models were not sufficient, so BMW lost money. Thus a mid-model was presented in 1957, the BMW 600. Although the 600 had to be considered a dwarf model, it afforded enough space for a small family. The

The dashboard of the Isetta.

The BMW Isetta was also available as a three-wheeler. This model was, according to law, a motor bicycle, so a driver's license was not needed.

The dashboard and steering column were attached to the door and revolved with it outwards.

front door concept was preserved, but the 600 also had a rear door on the right side for getting in and out. The rear wheels of the 600 were not placed alongside each other, which made a differential necessary. A 35.5 cu. in. twin-motorcycle engine was built in. As this engine provided nearly 20 hp, this tiny car could develop a speed of almost 62 mph. But in spite of this larger, and above all, less noisy engine, the 600 remained a mini-car which could not offer the same quality as, for instance, the equally inexpensive Renault 4CV or Volkswagen Beetle and production ceased in 1959. The enterprise then presented the BMW 700, which would form the basis for all later models.

The air-cooled engine of the Isetta was placed in front of the rear axle.

Technical specifications

Model:	BMW Isetta	BMW 600	BMW 700
Years of manufacture:	1955-1962	1957-1959	1959-1964
Production:	16,172	83,481	379,699
Engine:	one-cylinder	two-cylinder	two-cylinder
Displacement:	15 and 18.2 cu. in.	35.5 cu. in.	42.5 cu. in.
Output (hp/rpm):	12 and 13/5800	20/4500	30/5000
Top speed:	53 mph	64 mph	74.5 mph
From 0 to 60 mph in sec:	not known	not known	not known
Wheel base:	5 ft	5 ft 7 in	7 ft
Length:	7 ft 6 in	9 ft 6 in	11 ft 7 in
Width:	4 ft 6 in	4 ft 7 in	5 ft
Height:	4 ft 4 in	4 ft 6 in	4 ft 5 in
Weight:	794 lb	1,212 lb	1,411 lb

BMW Roadster

BMW has long been noted for its sporty cars. Many lovers of German cars who are still too young for a Mercedes (but nonetheless have the money for it) prefer a car from the BMW factory in Munich. Until 1985, models were still being drawn in the factory art rooms, but in 1985, BMW laid the cornerstone for its new design studio,Technik GmbH. More than 100 car fans were able to enjoy themselves under the guidance of Ulrich Benz with pencil, paper, plaster and plastic.

One of the numerous designs was a new sporting car. It made its first test drive in less than two years.The model was christened the Z1. It was a two-person roadster which would be sold starting in October 1988.The car was certainly not cheap, but for 80,000 DM the buyer could be sure of an extremely pleasant driving, or riding, experience.The body was a semi-monocoque with a very low sill line.The upper border of the windshield served at the same time as a roll bar.The body was made of steel, but the non-supporting parts like the engine hood, the luggage compartment lid and the side panels were made of plastic.The doors of the Z1 were interesting. A system patented by BMW was used which made it possible for the doors to be sunken into the sills.The door-window glasses than went down automatically by electric control.The wheel suspension came from the BMW 3 series and the six-cylinder engine from the 325i powered the rear wheels. As the space in the car was limited, the spare wheel was absent, but was available for at an extra cost. In the autumn of 1991, the last Z1 left the factory. Exactly 8,000 were built.

In comparison with the Z1, the Z3 looked, again, a bit "ordinary." The body was made of zinc-coated steel instead of plastic.

The frame above the front window was solid to serve as a roll bar as well.

Ulrich Benz, the spiritual father of the Z1, became renowned for his car and so he could not say "no" when Porsche offered him a leading position with a princely salary. The successor of the Z1 was the Z3. This car was designed especially for the American market and was produced in the United States. The Z3 had little resemblance to its predecessor. The model had more of the 507 from the fifties. The Z1 was built in a limited series, but BMW had big plans for the new car. The producer's hope was to dominate a good part of the roadster market with it after the price had been adjusted. The car's price, in the cheapest version with a 1.8-liter four-cylinder engine, was less than the purchase price of the Z1. The more expensive version was equipped with a 1.9-liter engine with two camshafts and four instead of two valves per cylinder. This engine had 140 hp performance, 25 hp more than its smaller brother. But even in this adaptation, the roadster cost only 10% more than the 1.8-liter model. With these two models, BMW dominated a large part of the market and could meet the competition with equanimity. But the competitors of course did not cease to be active. BMW was forced to provide the car with a more powerful engine; there was enough space under the engine hood. In the winter of 1996-1997, the Z3 appeared with a six-cylinder 2.8-liter 24 valve engine and a 3.2-liter from the M series. The last model was no longer called the Z3, but the M Roadster. The program was complete now and there was a Z3 Roadster for each show. They were super fast cars which could rank with the Mercedes SLK or the Porsche Boxster. Obviously, the prices grew with the growing amount of hp. And why not? BMW cars were selling well and in October 1996 more than 35,000 Z3s were produced in

The engine of the Z1, an aluminum six-cylinder with a top camshaft, was placed longitudinally.

A car in which you feel at home.

America. Little more than half of these were exported, mostly to Germany. The rest remained in the United States. Between 250 and 300 cars have been produced per day in the United States since 1997. When necessary, the capacity could be increased to 400.

The Z3 and the BMW Roadster were still selling sporting cars when BMW launched its new model, the Z07. This happened in November 1997 at the Tokyo Motor Show. Even though the car was praised as a prototype, it seemed to be

In Japan, BMW is a hot-selling, prestigious make. Therefore it is not too astonishing that the Z07 was first presented there.

Small but clearly organized: the dashboard of the Z1.

Back into the past: a steering wheel with four spokes

a clear successor to other sporting cars. The Z07 was also available as coupe and was built of an aluminum space frame. The body was made largely of alloys. Some parts were of carbon fiber, a material normally used exclusively for prototypes. As for the motor, the makers were rather secretive, but it is almost sure that the car is powered by the new 5.0 liter V8 engines with 400 hp installed in the M5 during the autumn of 1998. At the time of this book's publication, it is still uncertain how long the car will remain a prototype, but we are quite sure that the model will be introduced onto the market in the 1990s.

The luggage compartment of the Z1 had a capacity of 200 liters.

Technical specifications

Model:	**BMW Z1**	**Z3**	**BMW Roadster**
Years of manufacture:	1988-1991	1995-present	1997-present
Production:	8,000	not known	not known
Engine:	six-cylinder	four-cylinder	six-cylinder
Displacement:	152.2 cu. in.	109.6 and 115.6 cu. in.	195.3 cu. in.
Output (hp/rpm):	170/5800	115/5500 and 140/6000	321/7400
Top speed:	140 mph	121 and 128 mph	155 mph
From 0 to 60 mph:	8.3 sec	11.2 and 7.9 sec	5.4 sec
Wheel base:	8 ft	8 ft	8 ft
Length:	12 ft 9 in	13 ft 3 in	13 ft 3 in
Width:	5 ft 6 in	5 ft 6 in	5 ft 6 in
Height:	4 ft	4 ft 3 in	4 ft 3 in
Weight:	2,755 lb	2,535 lb	3,042 lb

BMW V8

The interior of a 502. Note the two seats and the floor gearchange.

During the Second World War, BMW built not only motorcycles for the Wehrmacht, but also aircraft engines. The Allies, therefore, bombed BMW factories regularly. By the end of the war, the factories in both Eisenach and Munich were largely destroyed. Eisenach ended up in the Russian zone, where production started again very quickly, although most engineers flew to the West. The East Germans built the prewar models under the name BMW. But after 1951, when the BMW factory in Munich produced cars again, they were forced to rename the make EMW. The rotating propeller in the emblem was taken over, but was red-white now instead of blue-white.

The West Germans had to face many more difficulties when trying to launch production again. The factory in Munich was – as much as it was possible – repaired, but as a major part of the preserved equipment and machines was confiscated by the Americans, the factory was forced to start from scratch. At first, the factory produced pots, pans and bicycles and repaired motorcycles. The production of motorcycles got off the ground again slowly as late as 1950 and the first cars stood at the IAA in Frankfurt in 1951. The German competitors were able to build cars for some years already. In Wolfsburg, the Beetles left the production line in great numbers, Opel built its Olympia and a single Kapitän, Ford did good business with the small Taunus and after Carl Borgward was released from a camp for war criminals in 1948, his Hansa stood at nearly each street corner. Mercedes had only the 170 on the program. This relatively small car was driven by a 1.7 liter four-cylinder engine with laterally placed valves.

Before the war, BMW would not have been able to beat its big rival Mercedes, but the situation was different during the post-war period. And so was the car that the factory sent to the Frankfurt Motor Show – it was a real hot

In the 502 V8 Super, the 193.3 cu. in. engine gave an output of 140 hp/5400 rpm. The compression ratio was 9 instead of 7.2:1.

The 3200 CS was, (for the present) the last big BMW. The body was designed by Bertone.

rod! There was a six-cylinder overhead valve engine in the spacious BMW 501, a cylinder volume of 2.0 liters and an output of 65 Hp. The four-speed gearbox was not placed immediately behind the engine, but under the front seat, which improved the weight distribution. The gears were changed by a fashionable gear shift on the steering column. The advantage of this solution was that three persons could sit on the long front seat. The front wheels had independent suspension and the steering mechanism was equipped with a mitre gear and a crown wheel sector, a seldom used but elegant solution. The exhibition in Frankfurt was held in April 1951, but the first BMWs were delivered as late as December 1952. The machines for pressing and the body parts were not ready yet and the first bodies were produced in Stuttgart.

But Mercedes did not wait passively in the meantime and offered, beside the small 170-series, also a 200 and even a 300. Both models were driven by a six cylinder valve-in-head engine with an output of no less than 150 hp in the 300S version. The BMW 501 – available only in black – was, at 2,866 lb, too heavy for its 2.0-liter engine. Thus, it was a big improvement when the car could be ordered with a completely new aluminum V8 engine. A prototype of this model emerged at the Geneva automobile show in March 1954. The new model was called BMW 502. The six-cylinder 501 was still available, but only in the perfected version and for a reduced price. The 501 A had now 72 instead of 65 Hp and cost 14,180 DM in Germany, one thousand marks less than its predecessor. For 12,680 DM, one could get a 501 B. This model differed only by the simpler interior and had fewer accessories than its more expensive brother. Disregarding the 157.4 cu. in. engine, the 502 was nearly identical with the 501, differing only in its built-in fog lamps. In 1955, the six-cylinder engine of the 501 was bored to 126.7 cu. in. and the V8 from the 502 to a 3.2-liter. The latter was able to attain a speed of 106 mph and matched the more expensive Mercedes 300 in every aspect.

During the 37th IAA in Frankfurt, BMW was in the spotlight again. In October 1955, two completely new cars were presented, the 507, a two-person sport car rival to the Mercedes 300 SL, and the 503, a coupe and cabriolet, based on the 502. Both cars were designed by Albrecht Graf Goertz, a German designer who had lived in America since 1936. The

The engine of the 3200 CS gave 160 Hp/5600 rpm, more than enough to bring the heavy car weighing 3,306 lb to a top speed of 124 mph.

The rear door of the 501 opened "vice versa." This facilitated getting in and out.

503 was an excellent vehicle for long rides on the freeway because it could attain a top speed of 118 mph. However, with its consumption of 1 per 5, it was not very economical with the fuel. As for the price, one BMW 503 coupe or cabriolet cost as much as eight standard Volkswagens in Europe, which explains why the big cars of BMW did not sell better. The demand for cars was heavy, but there were not many people who could afford such an expensive BMW. Those who could afford it preferred to buy a Mercedes. After 1958, the BMW six-cylinder engine was no longer available. By the end of 1959, even the 503 and 507 had disappeared. The 502 was produced until 1961, but was renamed BMW 2600, 2600 L, 3200 or 3200 S. The 3200 S was a very fast car, capable of accelerating from 0 to 60 mph in 14 seconds and reaching a speed of 118 mph. Moreover, the model was cheaper than the Mercedes 300 S. But even this car was difficult to market. In October 1961, a third model was added, the 3200 CS. The body of this car was drawn and built by Bertone. The car was placed on the chassis of the former limousines with a wheel base of

Bertone built this 3200 CS cabriolet specially for Herbert Quandt, one of the owners of BMW. It remained a prototype.

93 ft, but looked, notwithstanding its substantial length, very sporty. Even after the production of the big BMWs had been stopped, this brilliant creation of the famous Italian master could be still ordered--surely evidence of the good quality of the car.

Technical specifications

Model:	BMW 501	502	503	3.2	2600	3200 CS
Years of manufacture:	1952-'58	1954-'61	1955-'59	1955-'61	1961-'64	1961-'65
Production:	9,973	5,955	407	3,740	2,365	603
Engine:	six-cylinder	V8	V8	V8	V8	V8
Displacement:	120.3 cu. in.	157.4 cu. in.	193.3 cu. in.	193.3 cu. in.	157.4 cu. in	193 cu. in.
Performance (hp):	65	100	140	120	100	160
Top speed:	84 mph	99.5 mph	118 mph	105.5 mph	99.5 mph	124 mph
From 0 to 60 mph in sec:	not known	not known	not known	not known	not known	not known
Wheel base:	9 ft 4 in	9 ft 4 in	9 ft 4 in	9 ft 4 in	9 ft 4 in	9 ft 4 in
Length:	15 ft 6 in	15 ft 6 in	15 ft 6 in	15 ft 6 in	15 ft 6 in	16 ft
Width:	5 ft 10 in	5 ft 10 in	5 ft 4 in	5 ft 10 in	5 ft 10 in	5 ft 5 in
Height:	5 ft	5 ft	4 ft 8 in	5 ft	5 ft	4 ft 9 in
Weight:	2,954 lb	3,174 lb	3,306 lb	3,240 lb	3,174 lb	3,306 lb

BMW Z4

The BMW Z4 represents the latest in a long line of highly regarded roadsters and could possibly be the prettiest of the Z series. It entered the American market prior to coming to Europe in 2003.There are two versions: Z4 3.0i and the Z4 2.5i.

Both engines are available as an option with six-speed SMG, featuring shift-by-wire technology. SMG allows the driver to shift gears either with the conventional shift lever or by means of two paddles on the steering wheel, enabling him to concentrate fully on the actual process of driving.

Available at the touch of a button as an optional extra, DDC (Dynamic Drive Control) calls up max-

Viewed from the passenger side, the interior of the Z4 looks comfortable and functional.

The deep indentations below the doors make the car look lower than ever. Everything about it is well proportioned.

imum engine power even earlier than usual in the Sports mode, engine management following an even more dynamic and sporting gas pedal control line. To reflect this enhanced response of the engine, the steering also becomes even more direct with speed-related assistance offered by the EPS (Electric Power Steering). When the car is fitted with SMG or automatic transmission, DDC revs up the gears even higher and makes the gearshift even faster.

A feature that will be especially appreciated by lovers of true roadsters is the new and unique 'Engine Sound System,' which is designed to modulate and transmit the noises from the engine intake system into the passenger compartment, generating a particularly sporting engine noise for the occupants.

This is also the first BMW with electric, rather than hydraulic, power steering. With the steering being controlled by software, EPS offers a much higher standard of flexibility in its steering characteristics.

The Z4 is the first open-air BMW to feature a folding roof with a special folding mechanism. This folding mechanism takes up very little space and allows the front part of the roof to extend like a cover over the soft-top, merging flush with the body of the car. As a result, the Z4 requires neither a tonneau cover nor a roof lid. And as an option

An overhead view of the compact engine bay of the Z4 with its choice of 3.0i or 2.5i liter engines.

The rear of the car is dominated by the circular rear lamps and the neat lines of the trunk lid and head restraints.

BMW's new two-seater is available as the only roadster in the world with fully automatic operation of the roof. Runflat tire technology is featured as standard just as on the Z8.

The Z4 is available with a whole range of optional extras, bi-xenon headlights as well as a choice of two HiFi systems developed and optimized especially for the Z4, to provide individual musical enjoyment of the highest standard.

The radio navigation system integrated in the instrument panel uses DVD data for the first time in a BMW and the very dense memory system allows a longer geographic range. The professional navigation system comes also with a retracting color monitor, excellent for reading, thanks to the latest display technology. Both navigation systems may be combined with a telephone.

Visually the Z4 3.0i is differentiated from its smaller engine partner by anthracite chrome headlight settings (as opposed to black), larger oval exhaust tailpipes, chrome kidney grilles with matt chrome bars (as opposed to black bars) and different wheels.

Technical specifications

Model:	**BMW Z4 3.0i**	**Z4 2.5i**
Engine:	3.0i	2.5i
Cylinders:	6	6
Bhp:	231	192
Top Speed (limited):	155 mph	146 mph
0-60 mph :	5.9 sec	7.0 sec
Gearbox:	6 speed manual	5 speed manual
Wheels:	17 inch double spoke alloys	16 inch star spoke design

Borgward Hansa 1500
Sport coupé

Carl F.W. Borgward surely ranks among the most progressive vehicle design engineers of post-war Germany. On July 13, 1948, he returned from an American camp for war criminals in the vicinity of Ludwigsburg. Less than a year later, he presented his first new passenger car at the Salon of Geneva in March 1949. It was the Hansa 1500 – the outstanding feature of which was its especially sleek, ultra-modern body. It was a new start for 58-year-old Borgward, whose factories in Bremen were destroyed during the war.

The Borgward Hansa 1500, the first German car not derived from a pre-war model, was ahead of its time. Its futuristic shape resembled that of the American Kaiser, studied by Borgward in American journals during his captivity. But from a technical point of view, the car was modern. The four-cylinder overhead valve engine was coupled with a four-speed gearbox, which was controlled by a lever on the steering column. The Hansa 1500, which was presented in Geneva in March 1950, was also available with an automatic Hansa-Matic-gearbox, a technical novelty, which no German competitor could offer. The Hansa 1500 was also the first car with a blinker instead of vulnerable direction indicators. The model remained in production until September 1952, when it was succeeded by the Hansa 1800. Altogether, 22,504 1500s were built.

Although participation in racing can cost a fortune, it also brings much publicity for an auto brand. For this reason, Mercedes plunged into the Grand Prix adventure after the war and left its rivals far behind in the dust with its 300 SR sports cars. Porsche specialized in long-distance races, such as the Le Mans, and Borgward tried to attract attention by breaking records. In 1950, a Hansa 1500 equipped with a special body broke no less than twelve records on the circuit of Monthléry, including a drive over a distance of 1000 miles at an average speed of 107 mph. Other successful tests followed and the factory began to take part in races, particularly long-distance ones.

In March 1953, the IAA, the International Automobile Show in Frankfurt opened its gates. There were many interesting things to see. The Fiat 1100, with its new pontoon body, was presented for the first time, as well as the Peugeot 203 and the Opel Olympia Rekord, all new to Germany. The Volkswagen Beetle had an oval rear window and the Ford Taunus 12 M was now also available as a cabriolet. But Borgward also offered many novelties. The Lloyd had hydraulic brakes, and could now be bought – even as an LP 400 – with a body of steel, not wood. The Goliath GP 700 sports coupe could be ordered with a two-stroke engine with gasoline injection. But these were all less important than the magnificent new coupe

This coupe was exhibited in Geneva in 1954. The car is still in Switzerland.

The dashboard of a coupe from 1954.

which Borgward brought to Frankfurt. The Borgward Hansa 1500 was a two-person coupe with an aluminum body. Since the car was not planned as part of a series, the body was hammered out by hand from an aluminum plate. At 18,000 DM, the car was 4,000 DM more expensive than a Porsche 1500 Super. People lined up to catch a glimpse, but they did not seek to buy it. Many of the parts used, including the rear axle, came from the Hansa 500 stock. The new front-wheel suspension was developed especially for the car. The engine came from the Hansa 1500, but the cylinder head was designed by the specialist Karl Brandt, who succeeded in increasing the output of the engine. Two Solex carburetors provided the right fuel mixture, and the car produced an output of 95 hp at 6000 rpm. This had to be sufficient for a top speed of 118 mph. The vehicle was built on a tube chassis and the big drum brakes were nearly as big as the 16-inch wheels.

In the fifties, Diesel engines were a specialty of Daimler-Benz and a 42-hp four-cylinder was created at the beginning of 1953 which could be installed on 1.5 ton trucks. In order to prove how good such an engine was, one was taken from the conveyor and installed into a coupe. At the beginning of April 1953, the press was invited to witness how the coupe, bad-smelling and fuming, attained the speed of 96.3 mph on a closed section of the Autobahn. At the beginning of May, the same car won international publicity on the Mothléry racetrack in France. The Borgward racing drivers Hans Hugo Hartmann, Adolf Brudes, Nathan and Karl Heinz Schäufele were supported in their effort to break the records by two Frenchmen, Poche and Mouche. This led to fourteen records for cars with a Diesel engine. The first 31 miles were covered with an average speed of 84.4 mph. After 3,107 miles, an average speed of 80.75 mph was measured. After 48 hours of racing and pit stops, it appeared that the average speed was still 76.31 mph. On July 12, 1953, the coupe appeared – three of the cars were built in the meantime – for the debut race on the Avusbaan in Berlin. Unfortunately, the car was not fast enough to be able to beat its future rival, Porsche. Borgward used the coupes not only for publicity purposes, but also in order to test the motors. An engine with two upper camshafts, four valves per cylinder and a double ignition were also tested in this way, and compared with an engine using gasoline injection.

The steel coupes were not intended for racing and an output of 80 hp was sufficient.

The coupes had no luggage compartment lid. Luggage could be deposited behind the seats.

For a car factory, no race is as important as the 24-hour race of Le Mans. Winning, or at least taking a good place, at Le Mans attracts crowds of clients to the showrooms. It is no wonder then that Borgward also participated in the prestigious race, but it proved disappointing to him and his colleagues. On the other hand, the same 24-hour race was a great success for the Jaguar C-types, which finished first, second, fourth and ninth. The three Borgwards got the starting numbers 41, 42 and 43, and were supposed to be steered by Poche/Mouche, Brudes/Hartmann and Nathan/Schäufele. The latter team did not even show up at the starting line because they had already totally destroyed their vehicle during the training sessions. Brudes and Hartmann were slightly more successful, but they were forced to abandon the race after three hours of driving (they were then in 36th place,) because thw ran out of gas. On the straight section at Mulsanne, this car attained a top speed of no less than 114 mph. All hopes were thus laid on the vehicle driven by the French team. Their start was more or less a failure and after an hour of driving they held 43rd place. But gradually they gained terrain. After 10 hours, the car reached 30th, after 19 hours 20th, then on to 19th and then even 18th place. The team succeeded in holding this position for three hours until, after more than 23 of the 24 hours, the engine failed, signalling the end of the dream called Le Mans.

At the 1954 automobile shows in Geneva and Stockholm, a new version of the coupe was presented. This time, the coach was made of steel while the doors and the engine hood were aluminum. The cars were more beautiful than the first three and were intended exclusively for use on the motorway. The air inlet on the engine hood was missing. Nevertheless, the interior of the car was again made of leather and there was a normal valve-in-head engine under the hood.

But what remained of the cars which took part in the Le Mans race? The vehicle which had an accident during training was not repaired and was later sold as scrap. The coupe in which Brudes and Hartmann launched from the starting line was brought to total ruin during another race. The car was sold to an automobile fan, got a new coachwork of plastic, but burned completely during a race on the Nuremberg motor-racing circuit and was never restored. The car with the starting number 41, which endured 23 hours, is now in Sweden. Of the two steel cars built in 1954, the one with chassis number 345,023 is still being driven in Switzerland. The car which was presented at the exhibition in Stockholm was later bought by the Swedish Prince Bertil. Whether or not this vehicle still exists is not known.

Technical specifications

Model:	Borgward Hansa	1500	Sportcoupé
Year of manufacture:	1953	1953	1954
Production:	2	1	1
Engine:	four-cylinder	four-cylinder	four-cylinder
Displacement:	91.4 cu. in.	107.3 cu. in.	91.4 cu. in.
Fuel:	gasoline	diesel	gasoline
Output (hp/rpm):	95/6000	42/3700	80/5200
Top speed:	118 mph	93 mph	112 mph
From 0 to 60 mphin sec:	not known	not known	not known

The 1953 Buick

By 1953, the Buick factory celebrated its fiftieth year with a completely new car. Each year, Buick praised its models as "completely new." Yet the "new" often consisted in a different bumper or a larger ashtray. But in 1953, the client finally got something for his money.The new cars not only had a completely new coach, but also (at last) a newV8 engine. It took no less than 5 years to develop the valve-in-head engine.The factory had invested 60 million dollars since 1948. But it was worth the effort.With a dicplacement of 322 cu.in. and a compression ratio of 8.5:1 (the highest ratio for an American passenger car that year), the output was between 166 and 190 hp, depending on whether a two-barrel or four-barrel carburetor. Yet the old familiar eight/in-line-engine had not fallen into oblivion yet. It could be ordered in the 40 Special, the least expensive series of the Buick family.The side-valve engine was able to gain 129 hp from 263.3 cu. in.

The Dynaflow automatic was also improved (80% of all Buicks were equipped with it), as well as the brake system, which was boosted in the Roadmaster Self. In the vehicles with the inline engine, the engine hood could still be opened

In 1952, the Skylark was presented as one of the dream cars of General Motors. In 1953, the model was marketed as the Roadmaster Skylark. The car had genuine spoke wheels and cost $5,000, which may explain why only 1,690 of the model were sold.

In 1953, the Special four-door sedan was the best-selling Buick. More than 100,000 left the showrooms.

from both sides, but the new V8 engine was covered by a hood which opened in a normal way, and thus could be turned on a hinge at the windshield. The public found the cars magnificent, abandoning the old models and helping Buick to a record turnover. In the calendar year 1953, no less than 485,353 cars were sold. Only the manufacturing year of 1950 was better, thanks to the sale of 535,807 cars. In 1952, sales stalled at 321,048, a result with which one could not really be dissatisfied in those days.

No less than 488,755 cars were sold of the 1953 model. This number is the sum of 217,624 of the Special Series, 191,894 of the Super Series and 79,237 of the Roadmaster Series. Incidentally, the latter Series could easily be rec-

The Roadmaster station wagon was, after the Skylark, the most expensive Buick in 1953. Consequently, only 670 of the model were sold.

The dashboard of the Roadmaster-Wagon. Here also, the chrome was not spared.

ognized by the four (instead of three) oval 'holes' in the front mudguards. Of the cars produced in the model year 1953, 172,000 hardtops, 15,500 cabriolets and something more than 2,500 station wagons were counted. The news of that year was the Buick Skylark, a sports cabriolet providing enough space for six people. In 1952, this model was still being presented at the exhibitions exclusively as a dream car.

But in 1953, there were also other reasons to celebrate. Joseph Stalin died, Bill Haley played rock-n-roll for the first time, the Korean War was over, and the seven-millionth car left the conveyor-belt at the Buick factory on June 13.

The Roadmaster (model year 1953) as a four-door sedan.

Technical specifications

Model:	**Buick Super Series**	**Roadmaster Series**
Year of manufacture:	1953	1953
Production:	191,894	79,237
Engine:	V8	V8
Displacement:	322 cu. in.c	322 cu. in.
Output (hp/rpm):	166/4000	190/4000
Top speed:	96 mph	102.5 mph
From 0 to 60 mph in sec:	not known	not known
Wheel base:	10 ft	10 ft
Length:	17 ft 3 in	17 ft 5 in
Width:	6 ft 5 in	6 ft 5 in
Height:	5 ft	5 ft
Weight:	3,902 lb	4,100 lb

The 1946 and 1947 Cadillac

In 1946, 1,342 six-person cabriolets were sold. All of them were from the 62 Series.

In 1939, World War II had already begun for Cadillac. The American government foresaw that the development of the situation in Europe would not allow America to stay outside the conflict. Cadillac thus got, at an early stage, the order to begin producing aircraft engines. Additionally, a conveyor-belt was provided in 1941 to produce Continental engines for tanks. After the production of passenger cars completely ceased in 1942, Cadillac only needed to take a small step to shift over to the war industry. And only 55 days after the last car left the factory, M5 tanks rolled off the same assembly line. On October 17, 1945, a passenger car left the factory again, but it would be many months before it would be possible to speak about regular vehicle production again. In 1945, Cadillac had approximately 100,000 orders for passen-

The dashboard of the 62 Series convertible. All the way to the left of the steering wheel, you can see the handle by which the spotlight could be turned.

The rear light of the sedan above the blinker and directly below the reverse lamp.

ger cars, but only 1,142 clients could be satisfied that year. The first cars of the model year 1946 resembled those of 1942 very strongly. Except for a new grill and different bumpers, the factory was neither able nor willing to change. From the technical point of view, some things were indeed improved, and the Hydra-Matic gearbox in particular was given careful attention and thousands were mounted onto tanks by General Motors. The first post-war Cadillacs were delivered exclusively as four-door sedans (the 62 Series), but after only a few months, the client could choose from eleven different models in four Series. So there was the 'inexpensive' 61 Series, which could be delivered as a four-door sedan or as a two-door coupe; the 62 Series, which could also be purchased as a cabriolet; and the Fleetwood

The four-door vehicle had a length of more than five and half yards and weighed more than 4,400 pounds empty.

The vehicles of model year 1948 got a completely new pontoon body, and the first small fin appeared on the rear mudguards.

Sixty Special, which could only be ordered as a four-door model. Those who could afford a Fleetwood 75 could even choose from five different body designs.

The cars of the model year 1947 remained nearly unchanged. The grill now had five horizontal beams instead of six. In addition to that, the plates protecting the rear mudguards against small stones were no longer made of black rubber but of chrome-plated steel. Inside the car, the eye was drawn to the horn ring, which was half-round instead of completely round. All in all, no great changes were made that could rouse a customer's enthusiasm. But in spite of that, 1947 was a good year for Cadillac, because Cadillac succeeded in selling more cars than their arch-enemy Packard for the first time since 1934 .

In 1948, all cars of the General Motors make got new bodies. The pontoon design made its entry and the old pre-war lines disappeared once and for all. With the Cadillacs of model year 1948, a new era in car design began. On the rear mudguards, the first (modest) fins appeared. Their dimensions were limited in those days, but this would change by 1959. The idea of the fins originated with Harley Earl, a famous designer at General Motors. He was inspired by the sharp tails of the P-38 Lightning fighter plane.

Technical specifications

Model:	**Cadillac Series 61**	**Series 75**
Years of manufacture:	1946-1947	1946-1947
Production:	3,001	1,927
Engine:	V8	V8
Displacement:	346.3 cu. in.	346.3 in
Output (hp/rpm):	156/3400	156/3400
Top speed:	96 mph	87 mph
From 0 to 60 mph in sec:	not known	not known
Wheel base:	10 ft 9 in	11 ft 4 in
Length:	18 ft 3 in	18 ft 10 in
Width:	6 ft 8 in	6 ft 9 in
Height:	5 ft 3 in	5 ft 8 in
Weight:	4,413 lb	4,823 lb

The 1953 Cadillac Eldorado

With the Eldorado Sport Convertible Coupe, the often-cursed panoramic windshield started its career in the production vehicles.

Cadillac, the parade horse from the stables of General Motors since 1909, is considered by many people to be the paradigm of luxury. The vehicle is loved by the rich of the world. Nevertheless, can a Caddy be compared with a Rolls-Royce or an expensive Mercedes-Benz? The vehicle from Detroit remains more widely accessible than a Rolls-Royce or a Mercedes. In 1953, Rolls-Royce built a small number of cars of the Silver Wraith and Silver Dawn models, and perhaps one or two of the Phantom IV. Only a limited number of the Mercedes 300 was produced in Stuttgart. But Cadillac sold 98,612 cars in 1953, including more than 85,000 of the Eldorado type alone. Can such a car still be called exclusive? But in the end, don't forget the Eldorado Special Sport Convertible Coupe, a cabriolet of which only 532 could be sold, and only with difficulty. Why so few? In this case, the main culprit was the price. The car cost $7,750 in America, which was a lot of money, especially compared with the 'normal' Eldorado cabriolet, available for only $4,144.

The Special Coupe could be recognized by its sporty spoke wheels and 'cut-out' doors. All vehicles had whitewall tires.

The V8 gave 210 hp, enough to bring a vehicle weighing 4,400 pounds to a speed of 112 mph.

General Motors has built many dream cars. The designers entertained themselves with luxurious prototypes, but they also constantly searched for models to attract the broader public. Dream cars always featured a detail which was later built into the production vehicles. For instance, the designer Harley Earl designed the Buick XP-300 dream car in 1951 with its memorable and impressive windshield. "A Cadillac with such a panoramic windshield makes every other car look antiquated," Earl told the top man at Cadillac, Don E. Ahrens. Ahrens trusted Earl and the car which "was built because of the windshield" became an immense success. In 1953, it was the most expensive model the factory offered. And it was clear to everybody that the designers had devoted care to even the smallest details. The chassis of the car was three centimeters lower than that of the normal cabriolet and the top was made of white or black Orlon which could be hidden under the panels. The spoke wheels were not imitation. The interior was equipped very luxuriously. The seats, side panels and dashboard were covered with genuine leather and the chrome was dazzling. The car was equipped with all the accessories the factory was able to provide at that time. All these technical novelties were electrically driven and the vehicle had a twelve-volt instead of the normal six-volt battery. The Eldorado Sport Convertible Coupe was marketed again in 1954. It did not bear comparison with the 1953 version. It cost "only" $5,738 and 2,150 were sold.

Technical specifications

Model:	**Cadillac Eldorado Sport Convertible Coupé**
Year of manufacture:	1953
Production:	532
Engine:	V8
Displacement:	331 cu. in.
Output (hp/rpm):	210/4400
Top speed:	112 mph
From 0 to 60 mphin sec:	not known
Wheel base:	10 ft 6 in
Length:	18 ft 4 in
Width:	6 ft 8 in
Height:	5 ft
Weight:	4,442 lb

Chevrolet Corvette

Louis Chevrolet (1878-1941).

The Chevrolet Corvette was big news in 1953. The Corvette was originally designed as the dream car for the Autorama, the yearly automobile show of General Motors which toured America. Harley Earl wanted to construct a sporty, two-passenger dream car for the show. When his boss saw the drawing, he became so enthusiastic that he immediately showed the new design to GM's top man Harlow Curtice. Curtice also realized that a driving prototype had to be made so that the car could be taken into production without many changes. Usually, such undertakings last two to three years, but Curtice and the others at General Motors had only seven months. But the plan was successful, and on January 1, 1953, the Corvette, as the car was baptized, stood on a swivel plate in the Waldorf Astoria Hotel in New York. The technicians made a special chassis with a short wheel-base for the car and the body was made of plastic, which was very unusual for that time. The mechanical parts were collected from the conveyor-belts: a six-cylinder engine, a fixed rear axle, four drum brakes and an automatic gearbox with two driving positions. Americans found the vehicle fascinating and the orders poured in thick and fast. The introduction of a genuine American sports car meant that people were no longer dependent on European models.

The sudden demand for the Corvette had inevitable drawbacks. The factory did not succeed in equipping the production lines in time and thus all the cars had to be produced manually in the production year of 1953. Only 314 vehicles were delivered, which was not sufficient to provide all American dealers with showroom model. Management then decided to sell the first Series to an exclusive group of clients, as a first promotion of the model.

With its length of 167 in, the Corvette was a small vehicle, only 7 in longer than a VW Beetle.

The side windows of the first Corvette had to be screwed to the doors.

All the cars from 1953 had a white body and a red interior. Some were even delivered with Chevrolet Bel Air wheel hubcaps. But there were also different engines. In some cars, engines from pick-ups were mounted. In other cases, the existing engines were enhanced to as high as 150 hp. Chevrolet expected much from the Corvette. They were even convinced that the demand would be so great that the factories would not be able to manage the orders. To prevent this, a new factory was built in St. Louis in great haste, where it should have been possible to produce 100,000 Corvettes per year – a rather exaggerated number, as there were only 3,640 clients remaining in 1954. Many orders had been cancelled due to difficulties in delivery and the high price of the car. The Corvette cost more than double that of a normal Chevrolet cabriolet.

And was the Corvette really a sports car? Its six-cylinder engine had been developed in 1932 and could not be rebuilt into a racing engine. The average American client could not understand why such an expensive car had side windows which could not roll down and be inserted into the doors, but which were fastened with screws, as was the case in the twenties. At the end of 1954, there were still 1,100 Corvettes unsold in St. Louis, and it seemed that nobody would buy them. Only 647 were sold in 1955 despite the fact that the car could now be delivered with a V8 engine. However, the most important reason why nobody was willing to buy a Corvette anymore was that Ford presented the Thunderbird on October 22, 1954. The public had been waiting for this introduction and Ford succeeded in selling 16,155 in that

The dashboard of the first Corvette with the revolution counter in the middle.

first year. In 1956, the second generation of Corvettes appeared on the market. The selling number increased from 3,467 in 1956 to 6,339 in 1957, 9,168 in 1958 and more than 10,000 in 1960. The fact that Chevrolet never abandoned the model was thanks first of all to Ed Cole, who never lost his confidence in it, but also to a technician of Russian origin, Zora Arkus-Duntov, who made Corvette what it is now: the only American sports car.

Technical specifications

Model:	**Chevrolet Corvette (first series)**	
Years of manufacture:	1953-1955	
Production:	314; 3,640; 647	
Engine:	six-cylinder	V8
Displacement:	353.4 cu. in.	264 cu. in
Output (hp/rpm):	152/4200	228/5200
Top speed:	102.5 mph	112 mph
From 0 to 60 mph in sec:	not known	not known
Wheel base:	8 ft 6 in	8 ft 6 in
Length:	13 ft 11 in	13 ft 11 in
Width:	6 ft	6 ft
Height:	4 ft	4 ft
Weight:	2,711 lb	2,789 lb

Chrysler Woody

Before the war, station wagons in America were always built with a partially wooden body. The big automobile companies delivered the cars ready-made, but the client could also choose a furniture manufacturer or cabinet maker 'around the corner.' In 1941, Chrysler surprised the automobile works with its Town & Country, a genuine Woody with an engine hood, mudguards and roof made of steel. The factory did not refer to the model as a station wagon, although the vehicle possessed all the advantages of such a car. It was very spacious and offered places for seven people, but the rear end was curved like a normal passenger car.

In July 1941, the conveyor belts at Chrysler for the production of passenger vehicles were stopped and not even a thousand Town & Countries had been sold. When the vehicles of model year 1946 left the conveyor belt, they kicked up a lot of dust. Chrysler could not deliver any wooden station wagons yet, but instead other Woodys appeared in the showrooms.

Thanks to the perfection of the Town & Country from 1941, which was more a limousine than a wagon, the Woody cabriolet and a four-door sedan appeared. And again, much was said about the Town & Country at Chrysler. This time, the cars were built on the chassis of the New Yorker, Chrysler's top-of-the-line model. The new models were powered by the eight-cylinder in-line engine from the New Yorker, and were certainly not cheap. The bodies were made nearly completely by hand. A Woody cabriolet cost $2,725, nearly $600 more than the New Yorker with its steel cabriolet body.

Walter Percy Chrysler.

In 1946, Chrysler marketed the Town & Country again. This time, the vehicle had nothing in common with a station wagon: it was a full-blooded cabriolet.

In 1947, the fourth Woody could also be ordered from Chrysler. This model no longer stood on the chassis of a New Yorker, but on that of a Windsor. The four-door Woody was powered by a six-cylinder side-valve engine. Also, the model was expensive, with its sticker price of $2,366, and its high maintenance costs. So it was written in the manual: "Just as any yacht is refurbished every season, so too should the beauty and luster of the wooden body be maintained by periodic varnishing." And indeed, it was necessary for the vehicles to have a new layer of clear lacquer each year. But even this maintenance could not prevent the body from letting wind through and eventually rotting. But nevertheless, the cars were beautiful and not surprisingly, the first clients came from sunny California.

The 1948 Town & Country cabriolet was mounted on the chassis of the New Yorker.

A Chrysler Woody Wagon from 1949. The car had the chassis of the Royal, and was thus powered by a six-cylinder engine.

In 1948, a coupe variant of the Woody was added to the range. It was actually the first hardtop coupe in the world. The orders rolled in, but Chrysler built only seven. The first station wagon from Chrysler since 1942, a Woody, appeared on the chassis of the cheap Royal in 1949. The wheel-base was extended by 4 in specifically for this purpose.

The last genuine Woodys left the factory in 1950. Later models had bodies made completely of steel, on which the wood was screwed as decoration. The maintenance of these cars was, of course, much cheaper. In 1950, the Woody coupe was also introduced. In 1948, Chrysler had already built seven Woody coupes, but 1950 production sped up. The old eight-in-line engine, which had been used since 1931, was replaced by a super-modern V8 engine in 1951. The coupe had a body made completely of steel with wooden parts screwed to it. The period of wooden coachwork had vanished forever.

Technical specifications

Model:	**Chrysler Woody cabriolet**	**four-door**	**station wagon**	**coupe**
Years of manufacture:	1946-1948	1946-1948	1949-1951	1948-1951
Production:	8,368	3,994	698	
Engine:	eight-cylinder in-line engine	six- and eight-cylinder in-line engine	eight-cylinder in-line engine	eight-cylinder in-line engine
Displacement:	323.4 cu. in	205.5 and 323.4 cu. in.	323.4 cu. in	323.4 cu. in
Performance (hp):	137	116 and 137	137	137
Top speed:	87 mph	84 and 87 mph	84 mph	87 mph
From 0 to 60 mph in sec:	not known	not known	not known	not known
Wheel base:	10 ft 7 in	10 ft 7 in	10 ft 7 in	10 ft 7 in

Citroën C3 Pluriel

A view of the Pluriel with its roof down. Sun and fun is what this car is all about.

The funky Citroën C3 Pluriel combines all the practicality of a supermini with all the fun of a convertible, while remaining eye-catching and loveable in each of its many different guises.

Named 'Cabriolet of the year' at the prestigious Geneva Motor Show, this friendly, fun little Citroën is all curves, with a profile that sweeps over the smooth hood into the windscreen before arching dramatically over the roof and straight down to the trunk. From the side, the high waistline gradually rises towards the centre of the pillarless window area before leveling off at the rear of the car. Stylish 15" alloy wheels on 1.6i 16V models serve to nicely round off the car's great looks.

All over the vehicle are neat design touches: uniquely-shaped headlamps, techno-style light clusters at the rear, as well as prominent chrome C I T R O Ë N lettering which runs the full width of the rear window. Large chrome chevrons on the hood leave people in no doubt that this is a true Citroen product.

Pluriel is a versatile car.

The two tone dashboard can clearly be seen in the tidy interior of the Pluriel.

From the side the curvaceous lines of the Pluriel can be seen swooping over the front and through to the rear of this pretty little car.

Once inside the cabin, you will notice that the curvaceous theme continues, exemplified in a two-tone dashboard, featuring aluminum-effect spherical air vents, a semi-circular instrument panel and centrally located digital display. Further styling details include curved door handles, elliptical door bins and round speaker housings.

But its real strength lies in its ability to change body configuration according to the weather or the driver's mood. Even on the move, the full-length, electrically operated, multi-layered fabric roof can be retracted to eight different preset positions, while at the same time all four electric windows can be lowered to create a truly open-air feel.

If you want to have a wind-in-your-hair experience, the strong but light arches can be easily removed and stored tidily away and the two rear seats can each be tipped forward to create a large, flat loading area.

The car is available with the choice of two gas engines, a 75 hp 1.4l unit and a 110 hp 1.6l 16V option.

With the 1.6l 16V version, you get alloy wheels and an anti-theft alarm and the Company's acclaimed rally-style SensoDrive gearbox, bringing drivers the excitement of rally-style paddle shift gear changes.

In addition, all models are equipped with ABS, EBD (Electronic Brakeforce Distribution) and EBA (Emergency Braking Assistance) plus four airbags and four 3-point inertia reel seat belts

Technical specifications

Model:	**Citroën C3 Pluriel**	
Engine:	4-cylinder	4-cylinder 16 valve
Capacity:	83 cu. in.	97 cu. in.
Cylinders:	4	4
Power (hp/rpm):	75 / 5400	110 / 5750
Top Speed:	101 mph	117 mhp
0 – 62 mph:	13.9 sec	12.6 sec
Fuel consumption:	41.5 mpg	42.8 mpg
Transmission:	5 speed manual	5 speeds SensoDrive
Brakes:	Ventilated discs	Ventilated discs
Wheels:	15 inch	15 inch Alloy
Tyres:	185/65 R15	185/65 R15
Length:	12 ft 10 in	12 ft 10 in
Width:	5 ft 7 in	5 ft 7 in
Height:	5 ft 1 in	5 ft 1 in
Wheel base:	8 ft	8 ft
Weight:	2,504 lb	2,579 lb

Citroën Traction Avant

André Citroën was born Roelof Limoenman in the Netherlands. His son, Levis Bernard, earned his living as a diamond dealer in Amsterdam. During a visit to Warsaw, he met Amelia Masza. They married, and when the young couple settled in Paris in 1870, he Frenchified his name by adding two points above the 'e.' Since then, his name was Bernard Citroën.

Levis Bernard had five children. His second son, André Gustav, graduated as an engineer in 1898. In 1908, André Citroën took over the bankrupt auto factory of Mors. During World War I, when there was a great demand for shells, he signed a contract to produce 50,000 shells daily in a factory he had built at the expense of the state at the Quai de Javel in Paris. After the war, he shifted over to the production of automobiles. In 1924, he made the first car body in Europe made completely of steel. André Citroën produced all the taxicabs in Paris, connected a part of Paris to the electrical network, and put his name on the ten thousand lamps used for the illumination of the Eiffel tower. And Citroën financed exploratory journeys through Africa and Asia, of course with a Citroën. In 1933, a Citroën Rosalie covered a distance of 186,411.35 miles nonstop. In the same year, André Citroën presented his new car, the 'Traction Avant.' Such a car demanded a new, modern factory. André decided to tear down the factory at the Quai de Javel and build a new one in its place. At the opening, no fewer than 6,500 guests were testimonial witnesses to the presentation of his latest creation, the Traction Avant.

But after he exceeded the limit of 150 million French francs in 1934, the banks turned the tap off. In order to earn money, Citroën further increased production. But unfortunately, all the cars had to be brought back to the factory because of guarantee work. The costs became insurmountable and André Citroën went bankrupt in December 1934.

By the end of 1952, the Traction was equipped with straight instead of slightly curved bumpers. In France, yellow lamps in the headlights were obligatory.

With a button on the dashboard, the front window could open slightly, guaranteeing good ventilation.

The enterprise was taken over by the tire giant Michelin. Citroën died on July 5, 1935, poor and abandoned by everybody. It is sad that he did not live to see how his Traction Avant would become one of the most popular European cars. He would never know that in 1957 alone no less then 759,111 were sold.

The birth of the Traction Avant, or the 7A as it was officially called, was a difficult delivery. There were countless technical problems, which seemed nearly unsolvable. For instance, Citroën had wanted to equip the car with an automatic gearbox. But its construction was so unreliable that Citroën decided at the last moment to mount a manually geared box. But this gearbox, which was developed in only fourteen days, also caused many problems. The wheels of the Traction Avant had independent suspension, and the propulsion was of course through the front wheels, a relative novelty at the time. Only a few German car makes, for instance the DKW, used such a system. But the car arrived and became a big success. People who drove only a single time in the vehicle remained faithful to the model. It had everything expected of a car in those days: excellent road stability, security, plenty of space and a very special self-supporting body.

In June 1941, the 88,066th and the last pre-war Traction Avant left the conveyer belt. During the war, the factory was bombed twice, but was repaired in June 1945. And of course, the production of the Traction Avant started again. The model was marketed as 11 LégPre (light-weight), as 11 Large (broad) and as 15-6. The numbers 11 and 15 referred to the number of the hp and the '6' to the number of cylinders.

The car was the spitting image of its predecessor, but could be recognized by the grooves in the engine hood (the pre-war model had 'small doors'). During the first year, only 1,525 cars could be produced. And for the most part, these vehicles were produced with components which had survived the war.

The Traction Avant had been technically perfected. The engine output of the four-cylinder increased from 56 hp/3800 rpm to 59 hp/4000 rpm, the output of the six-cylinder from 77 hp/3800 rpm to 80 hp/4000 rpm. The wheel-base of the vehicle remained unchanged: 114.5 in for the LégPre and 121.65 in for the Large and 15 Six. In 1953, the Familiale returned to the market. This model, with a wheel-base of 128.7 in, offered plenty of space. Between the front and the

If you wanted plenty of space in the rear, the Familiale was the best choice. But what is your opinion about the space in the Large? Here, the rear seat of a Large from 1954.

The Familiale was the biggest Traction Avant and offered plenty of interior space. Here, a car from 1953.

rear seats, there were three additional small, tiltable seats. In 1952, the body was substantially changed for the first time. The capacity of the luggage compartment was enlarged by 50 percent. In previous models, the spare wheel was screwed to the outer side of the luggage compartment lid; now, it was placed on its inner side.

In April 1954, Citroën again presented a technical novelty. Namely, the rear wheels of the 15 Six were equipped with hydro-pneumatic suspension. The torsion rods were replaced by metal balls containing a gas mixture, held under pressure by a pump which was powered by the engine. The 3,079 vehicles equipped with such a spectacular suspension actually served as test cars for the sensational Citroën DS.

Despite many rumors about the appearance of this completely new large Citroën, the four-cylinder engine of the Traction Avant was given careful attention again in 1955. The compression ratio was increased from 6.5 to 6.8:1, enhancing the output to 63 hp/4000 rpm. The LégPre 130, the Large 125 and the Familiale now attained a top speed of 75 mph.

On July 18, 1957, the last of the 759,123 Traction Avants left the factory at the Quai de Javel. The 11 Familiale was accepted in Paris by a dealer from Saint-Malo. With a production time of 23 years, 4 months and 15 days, the Traction Avant set a new world record. Never had a model been on the program so long without interruption. In total, 759,111 Traction Avants were built: 700,961 in France, 31,750 in Belgium and 26,400 in England.

Technical specifications

Model:	**LégPre**	**Large**	**Familiale**	**15-6**
Years of manufacture:	1945-1957	1946-1957	1954-1957	1946-1957
Production:	not known	not known	not known	not known
Engine:	four-cylinder	four-cylinder	four-cylinder	six-cylinder
Displacement:	116.6 cu. in.	116.6 cu. in.	116.6 cu. in.	175 cu. in.
Output (hp/rpm):	56/3800	58/3800	59/4000	77/3800
Top speed:	76 mph	73 mph	71.5 mph	82 mph
From 0 to 60 mph in sec:	not known	not known	not known	not known
Wheel base:	9 ft 6 in	10 ft 1 in	10 ft 8 in	10 ft 1 in
Length:	14 ft 7 in	15 ft 3 in	15 ft 9 in	15 ft 7 in
Width:	5 ft 4 in	5 ft 9 in	5 ft 9 in	5 ft 10 in
Height:	5 ft	5 ft	5 ft	5 ft 2 in
Weight:	2,358 lb	2,469 lb	2,623 lb	2,921 lb

Cizeta

Do you recognize the Lamborghini Countach? The Cizeta's design was by the same designer, Marcello Gandini.

There is no other town in Europe where so many auto factories are (or were) situated as Modena. This small Italian town is the port of registry for Ferrari, Maserati, Lamborghini, Scaglietti, Fantuzzi and, until 1994, Cizeta. Those who did not hear about the latest car make need not be ashamed. But those who visited the motor show in Geneva in the early nineties might remember Claudio Zampolli, the small, lively, gesticulating Italian. He was inseparable from his car, the Cizeta. In the beginning, the brand was still called the Cizeta Moroder, after Giorgio Moroder, the man who financed the super car. Moroder wrote, apart from other things, the song "Love to Love You Baby" for Donna Summer and the music for the film "Top Gun". Claudio Zampolli was born in Modena and worked for Lamborghini, among others. This company sent him to America in 1973, with a mission to set up a dealers' network there. But Zampolli decided to start a business in California, with Ferraris and Maseratis. In 1985, he founded the company Cizeta Automobili, with the aim to build a super sports vehicle in Modena. And he was successful with the first attempt. It was a very special automobile, with a V16-engine equipped with 64 valves and eight upper camshafts. By the spring of 1989, the prices for luxury sports cars were incredibly high and the first test drives were executed. The Cizeta was presented at the Los Angeles motor show in 1989. A few orders followed.

The shape of the interior was given the highest care, as might be expected for a vehicle costing as much as $630,000 in 1993.

The V16 was placed askew in front of the rear axle, directly behind the two bathtub-shaped seats.

The body of the new vehicle had been designed by Marcello Gandini, the designer responsible for the design of the Lamborghini Countach at Bertone's.The excellent engine came from the drawing tables of theTecnostyle Company, led by three former colleagues of Lamborghini.

The emblem of the car consists of three wolves, two of them blue and one yellow, the colors of Modena.The three wolves were afraid neither of the springing horse of Ferrari nor the bull of Lamborghini. But the horse and the bull also had no reason to turn tail before the wolf.When the prices of expensive cars fell down like a house of cards, nobody was interested in the Cizeta brand anymore.The factory was forced to close its gates in 1994. It now seems that Zampolli succeeded in selling only seven vehicles in total.When the enterprise was closed, there were still four of the cars in the factory hall.

Technical specifications

Model:	**Cizeta V16T**
Years of manufacture:	1989-1994
Production:	7
Engine:	V16
Displacement:	365.8 cu. in.
Output (hp/rpm):	412/8000
Top speed:	204 mph
From 0 to 60 mph:	4.5 sec
Wheel base:	8 ft 9 in
Length:	14 ft 7 in
Width:	6 ft 9 in
Height:	3 ft 8 in
Weight:	3,747 lb

Daimler SP 250 Dart

The fibreglass body of the SP 250 Dart was a complete change of construction methods for the Daimler Company and did have its problems.

Edward Turner is best known for his designs of motorcycle engines rather than car engines. But it was he who designed a new V8 for the Daimler Company during the late 1950's, and it would be these very engines that would be fitted in the new Daimler sports cars.

During the period, the Daimler Company was struggling financially and not much money was available for investment. Therefore, it was difficult to launch the desperately needed new cars. With the American market in mind, it was decided that Daimler would develop a new sports car and fit this new V8 engine in it. Although there were two engine sizes being developed, 2.5 liter and 4.5 liter, the initial engine installed was the 2.5 liters version. The chassis of the car was inspired by the Triumph TR3A sports car and made from fibreglass, a huge departure in body construction for Daimler.

The car was finally presented at the New York Motor Show in April 1959 and was named the Daimler Dart. Unfortunately the Chrysler Corporation already had a Dodge by the same name and complained shrilly. The name, therefore, was changed to the SP 250.

The American market had been very buoyant up to this point and sales should have been good but a recession hit the United States and suddenly Daimler had a very small market for their new sports car.

The car was far from perfect and there were problems with the early engine and their cooling system. There were also problems with the quality of the fibreglass body, but most of these were rectified when Jaguar bought out Daimler in 1960.

Interior of the SP 250 Dart.

A side view of the SP 250 Dart, showing the large rear wings of the car and the long front wings with their lights.

During its nine year production period, the SP 250 received little change to its bodywork or to its mechanics. In 1961, items that had been extras were fitted as standard and two years later, a heater was made standard along with a trickle charge socket.

The coachbuilder Hooper built a special two-door saloon version and the odd policeman had one as his squad car. Production ceased in 1968.

A well kept car, the interior of the SP 250 was comfortable and luxurious for a sports car.

Technical specifications

Model:	**Daimler SP 250 Dart**
Engine:	V8 water cooled
Bore/Stroke:	76.2/69.85
Capacity:	155.4 cu. in.
Power:	14 bhp / 5800 rpm
Wheel base:	7 ft 8 in
Length:	13 ft 4 in
Width:	5 ft 5 in
Weight:	27 lb
0 – 50 mph:	6.8 sec
Top Speed:	123.7 mph

De Soto

The De Soto brand was founded by Walter P. Chrysler in 1928, to compete with Oldsmobile, Nash and Pontiac, and he succeeded fairly well since the vehicles were good and cheap. The demand for cars immediately after the war was so great that every car producer struggled to meet it. But after the market was saturated, slowly but surely, De Soto began to have problems. In 1953, only 129,963 cars were sold and the number fell to 69,844 in 1954. The managing director of De Soto was declared responsible, fired and replaced by 'Tex' Colbert. Colbert got a budget of $250 million and gave Virgil Exner the order to design a marketable car. Exner came up with a completely new model. The design was

In 1955, the Fireflite was the new top-of-the-line model from De Soto. The car was powered by a V8 engine, which gave 203 hp.

so absolutely new that it was spoken of as the 'Forward Look.' On November 17, 1954, the models were presented to the broader public.

The cars of model year 1955 were called the Firedome and the Fireflite. Both models were powered by a 291 cu. in. V8 engine. Thanks to the mounting of a four-barrel carburetor, Firelite was able to provide 203 hp. Both cars had a wheel-base of 10.5 ft and were painted in gaudy colors, especially the Fireflite.The clients lined up for De Soto again. Exner was a great hero, and rightly so, as De Soto sold 129,767 cars in 1955. After three years, they began to stagnate again. After only 19,411 cars were sold in 1960, it was decided to close the gates forever.

Technical specifications

Model:	**De Soto Fireflite**
Year of manufacture:	1955
Production:	64,362
Engine:	V8
Displacement:	291 cu. in.
Output (hp/rpm):	203/4400
Top speed:	102.5 mph
From 0 to 60 mph in sec:	not known
Wheel base:	10 ft 6 in
Length:	18 ft 2 in
Width:	6 ft 6 in
Height:	5 ft 6 in
Weight:	3,891 lb

De Tomaso Vallelunga

The front wheel suspension: very nice from a technical point of view, but not very reliable.

In 1963, automobile history was made at the Torino automobile show. Lamborghini presented his first car, the 350 GTV, Maserati exhibited his first four-door limousine, and Ferrari tried to enchant the show with the 250 LM. But there was also an Argentinean, Alejandro de Tomaso, who tried to sell his own latest product situated in the corner of the hall. De Tomaso had baptized his car, Vallelunga. And it became the first vehicle de Tomaso succeeded in producing in a (small) series.

De Tomaso was born on July 10, 1928 in Buenos Aires. He left Argentina in 1954 and he tried to earn his living in Italy as a racing-car driver, racing with Osca and Maserati, among others. After two years, he married the wealthy American Elizabeth Haskell. Haskell was also enthusiastic about racing and they traveled from one race circuit to another. In 1957, de Tomaso decided to build cars himself. These were, of course, race and sports vehicles, which unfortunately never went beyond the prototype phase. This changed with the arrival of the Vallelunga. The small corner of the hall the Argentinean had hired was just big enough for the car, a table, and two chairs. On the wall, De Tomaso hung a rolling chassis. The car press did not notice this stand, or did not want to. Only a journalist from *English Autocar* paid attention to the Vallelunga. He wrote, among other things, that the chassis very much resembled that of the Lotus Elan. He found the open body to be a bad copy of a Porsche RS Spyder, but certainly interesting from the technical point of view.

The chassis consisted of a hollow beam, through which the water and brake hoses passed. The Spyder's aluminum body had been created from a drawing by de Tomaso by Carrozzeria Fissore. The engine, an advanced four-cylinder originating from the Ford Corsair, was placed in front of the rear axle. De Tomaso declared that he would build at least one

Vallelunga was a small car, specially intended for (small) Italians or Argentineans.

The interior of the Vallelunga: sporty and professional.

The engine compartment could be accessed through the rear window.

hundred of the model so that the vehicle would be admitted to the GT class. But this statement was a bit premature, as the car remained only a prototype. The real Vallelungas appeared on the road as coupes.

Also, the body of the first two coupes was made of aluminum. It is not clear who designed this last model. DeTomaso claims to have drawn the coupe himself, but some experts think it was designed by Guigiaro. Tom Tjaarda (designer of the deTomaso Pantera) insists that Mario Fissore was responsible for the Valelunga coupe. The result was impressive and the Museum of Modern Art in New York even gave the vehicle a prize for being 'an example of progressive technology.'

The coupe looked like a cross between a Ferrari 275 GTB and a Dino 206 GT, but was much smaller. The plastic body was made at Carrozeria Ghia. It was not a car for daily use since the luggage hold, with a capacity of 52 liters, was too small. The car could not be called truly reliable and somebody who was taller than 5.9 ft could hardly sit upright in it. A driver whose feet were a little too broad regularly pushed two pedals at the same time.

DeTomaso never succeeded in making the one hundred cars he had promised. He still claims to have done this, but his bookkeeping proves that he did not deliver more than fifty. And even if you add in the few prototypes, the car nevertheless remains a rarity.

Technical specifications

Model:	**De Tomaso Vallelunga**
Years of manufacture:	1965-1966
Production:	from 50 to 60
Engine:	four-cylinder
Displacement:	91.4 cu. in.
Output:	104/6200 hp/rpm
Top speed:	137 mph
From 0 to 60 mph in sec:	not known
Wheel base:	7 ft 7 in
Length:	12 ft 8 in
Width:	5 ft 2 in
Height:	3 ft 5 in
Weight:	1,212 lb

Delahaye 135

The body was made by the Saoutschik company.

Before and immediately after World War II, some of the most beautiful, but also often the most bizarre, cars were built. Specialists at Saoutschik, Figoni et Falaschi and Guilloré built many of their amazing creations on the chassis of a Delahaye 135 M or MS.

The Delahaye 135 had already been designed in 1935. It was then called the 135 S. This sports car was equipped with a six-cylinder engine possessing a capacity of 3 liters and an output of 119 hp. In 1936, the valve-in-head engine was

The Swiss coach-builder Hermann Graber combined this body with the chassis of a 135 MS in 1946.

The 2+1 looks excellent even from the rear.

The dashboard of the Delahaye by Saoutschik. The Cotal box was controlled by a small lever to the left side of the steering wheel.

drilled to 3.6 liters. This model was called the 135 MS. The MS was able to attain a top speed of 93.2 mph, a fabulous speed for that time. The front wheels had independent suspension and were switched by an electromagnetic Cotal box while the clutch pedal was used only when moving from a stationary position.

In 1946, Delahaye brought the 135 M onto the market again. In the normal version, the 217 cu. in. engine gave 95 hp/3800 rpm, but this output could increase to 110 hp when, for instance, three carburetors were installed. The 135 MS was normally equipped with three Solex carburetors, a higher compression ratio (8 instead of 7.1:1), and an output of 130 hp. Of course, the MS consumed more fuel than its 'smaller' brothers, so the gasoline tank had to be enlarged (100 instead of 90 liters). The 135 M could be delivered with a four-speed gearbox including an electromagnetic Cotal box. The standard MS was equipped with the Cotal box. Most clients ordered their Delahaye as a rolling chassis.

Technical specifications

Model:	**Delahaye 135 M**	**135 MS**
Years of manufacture:	1946-1954	1946-1954
Production:	not known	not known
Engine:	six-cylinder	six-cylinder
Displacement:	217 cu. in.	217 cu. in.
Output (hp/rpm):	95/3800	130/3800
Top speed:	87 mph	93 mph
From 0 to 60 mph in sec:	not known	not known
Wheel base:	9 ft 8 in	9 ft 8 in
Length:	depended on the body	
Width:	5 ft 9 in	5 ft 9 in
Height:	depended of the body	
Weight:	2,127 lb	2,127 lb

DKW 3=6

The three-cylinder two-cycle engine of the F93. Each cylinder had its own bobbin.

Like the Citroën driver, the driver of a DKW remained faithful to the brand. Because of the front wheel drive, perhaps? It might be so, because when you got used to it, the stability on the road was much better than that of a car with a rear-wheel drive. Or, was it because – in the case of the DKW – of its beautiful design? Surely, the price was not the reason, as the car was relatively expensive. For instance, you could buy a beautiful Ford Taunus 15M for the same amount. And then, you at least had a four-cycle engine which did not stutter or stink and into which you could pour normal gasoline instead of a mixture with two-cycle oil. In addition a Taunus was more spacious, at least as fast and also much more economical.

But the auto fan bought a DKW and tolerated all the disadvantages. This was exactly the case with the proprietor of an F93. This model was built in Düsseldorf as the 'Grosser DKW 3=6' between 1955 and 1959. Under the engine hood, there was a three-cylinder two-cycle engine of the third generation. The first generation of engines had already been tested in prototypes before the war and the second generation was mounted between 1953 and 1955 in the smaller, but primarily narrower DKW Sonderklasse. The 'primeval engine' was tested in the Russian zone of Germany in 1945. In 1950, the 3=6 was mounted in the IFA F9, three years before the West Germans.

With this '3=6', DKW claimed the three-cylinder two-cycle engine was equivalent to a six-cylinder four-cycle engine. This was partly correct, because both engines made the same number of strokes per crankshaft revolution. But the two-cycle engine produced better performance than the four-cycle engine. A DKW engine with 54.7 cu. in. gave no less

The 'Grosser DKW 3=6' was presented in Frankfurt in the autumn of 1955.

The owner (she restored the vehicle herself) of an F93. Note the door, which opened in a 'bad' direction and was thus mortally dangerous.

than 38 genuine horsepower. Such output could not be attained by a four-cycle engine. But the latter did not smell as bad as the two-cycle engine.

From autumn 1954, the DKWs were equipped with the so-called Shell-Mixer, which made it possible to pump normal gasoline, then automatically mixed with oil from an oil tank. Before, the fuel had to be mixed by the driver himself. A certain quantity of two-cycle oil was added to a jerrycan with gasoline. The mixture had to be shaken well, because too little oil caused a jamming of the pistons and too much oil caused blue smoke to emanate from the exhaust. But when everything was mixed properly, it was a delight to ride in a DKW. In those years, the opinion was that the road stability of a vehicle with a front-wheel drive was best tested in the turns, when a lot of gas was given. But when you passed through the turn too fast, the DKW could not be trusted anymore. Additionally, a DKW engine

The dashboard of the DKW. Note the handle of the steering column gearchange.

The F93 was 4 inches broader than its predecessor, and afforded more space for the passengers.

You can bet that not all that luggage went on their trip.

gave you a pleasant feeling only at high revolutions, so drivers actually always drove too fast. In the standard version, the vehicle was able to attain a speed of 75 mph. But the three-cylinder engine demanded enhancement. Different enhancement sets were available, by which the compression ratio could be increased from 7.1 to 8.2:1. Also, the injector could be replaced by three independent Amal motorbike carburetors. Then, a top speed of 87 mph could easily be reached. A normal DKW needed 25 seconds to accelerate from 0 to 60 mph. But an enhanced exemplar managed it in just 19 seconds. It did not matter that the carburetors had to be adjusted regularly – that was part of the hobby.

The DKW did not have a self-supporting body, but a beam chassis with heavy cross braces and, of course, an independent front wheel suspension with a high-positioned transversal spring. The body was thus an example of German solidity. It was beautifully finished and the plates were thick enough not to corrode too quickly. The doors, however, still opened incorrectly, a problem which was modified in some types by 1958.

DKWs were also assembled outside Germany by the company Hart Nibbrig and Greeve NV in Sassenheim, the Netherlands. The first car from there, an F93, left the conveyor belt on January 20, 1956 and the thousandth unit had already left by October 30 of the same year. By 1961, about 13,500 cars had been produced.

Technical specifications

Model:	**DKW F93**
Years of manufacture:	1955-1959
Production:	157,330
Engine:	three-cylinder
Displacement:	54.7 cu. in.
Output:	38/4200 hp/rpm
Top speed:	78 mph
From 0 to 60 mph:	25 sec
Wheel base:	7 ft 8 in
Length:	13 ft 10 in
Width:	5 ft 7 in
Height:	5 ft 9 in
Weight:	1,973 lb

Dodge Challenger

About 500 Challengers with the 7.2-liter Hemi engine were delivered in 1970. With its 425 hp, the vehicle attained a top speed of 143 mph.

On March 9, 1964, the first Ford Mustang left the conveyor belt. The vehicle was a hit. Never were so many cars of one model purchased during the first year of manufacturing. But of course, the competition had not fallen asleep. The Chrysler Corporation presented the Plymouth Barracuda on April 2, 1964, only a month after the introduction of the Mustang. Ford sold 121,538 Mustangs and Chrysler 'only' 23,443 Barracudas.

Dodge, another brand from the Chrysler concern, took up the battle on August 27, 1969. The car of model year 1970 was baptized the Dodge Challenger. The Challenger stood on the chassis of the Dodge Coronet, the wheel-base of which was shortened by 6.9 in for this purpose. The vehicle appeared in two basic versions: the Challenger and the Challenger R/T. Both models could be delivered as cabriolets or as hardtop coupes. A 3.7 liter six-cylinder engine was mounted in the normal Challenger. The R/T was available with one of eight Dodge V8 engines. The smallest V8 had a capacity of 5.2 liters and an output of 230 hp. The stronger engine had a capacity of 5.6 liters and 275 hp, 6.3 liters and 335 hp or 7.2 liters with 375 to 425 hp. The engine with 375 hp had three double carburetors and the 425-hp version had two four-barrel carburetors.

By the summer of 1970, the range was enriched by two models, the cheaper Deputy and the T/A, intended for racing in the TransAm series. This T/A was powered by a 5.6 liter V8 engine with 290 hp. The car could be recognized by the tailpipes, which ended under the doors on both sides of the vehicle. On May 29, 1971, a Challenger won the 500-mile race in Indianapolis.

In the meantime, the environmental control rules and safety regulations became more and more stringent in America and product ranges from the factories markedly decreased. The Challenger was available only as a coupe and was now called either Challenger or Challenger Rally. The cars differed only in small details. Also, the number of engines became limited. There was a six-cylinder with 3.7 liters and 110 hp, a V8 with 5.2 liters and 150 hp, and a V8 with 5.6 liters

Of the 88,000 Challengers sold in 1970, 83,838 were hardtop coupes.

The Challenger of Frua more resembled a Maserati than a Dodge.

and 240 hp. In 1974, Dodge celebrated its sixtieth anniversary. All the models got a new body, except the Challenger. The model sold so badly that it was removed from the program. When the name Challenger was introduced again four years later, the car had nothing in common with its predecessor.

Production numbers:

1970	88,081
1971	29,883
1972	26,658
1973	32,596
1974	16,437

The dashboard of a Challenger from 1971. A counter-revolution was still unnecessary.

Technical specifications

Model:	**Dodge Challenger**	
Years of manufacture:	1970-1974	
Production:	193,656	
Engine:	six-cylinder	V8
Displacement:	225.8 cu. in.	317.3-439.4 cu. in.
Output:	from 230 to 425 hp/rpm	
Top speed:	99-143 mph	
From 0 to 60 mph:	not known	
Wheel base:	9 ft 2 in	
Length:	15 ft 11 in	
Width:	6 ft 4 in	
Height:	4 ft 3 in	
Weight:	3,185-3,659 lb	

Dodge Stealth

A Dodge Stealth. In the nearly identical Mitsubishi 3000GT, the headlight covers were painted in the color of the car.

Compare a Dodge with a Japanese Mitsubishi? Why not? An example of the close collaboration between the firms was the Dodge Stealth sports car, built in the same factory as the Mitsubishi 3000 GT. The two cars left the same conveyor belt and were built in Japan and in America. The car in the photos is a Dodge, as evidenced from the non-panoramic rear window and the positioning of the wing, immediately behind the rear window.

The Challenger was called a 2+2 by Dodge – but only when the front seats were shifted far forward, since the rear passengers had very limited space for their legs.

The dashboard of the Stealth. On the small monitor, information appears about the air-conditioning.

Everybody could recognize it: four camshafts, 24 valves and four-wheel drive.

From a technical point of view, and in particular in regard to the engine, the Dodge Stealth was very interesting. The car was powered by a V6 placed askew in the front part of the car. With one upper camshaft per cylinder row, the 3.0 liter engine gave 166 hp; with four axles and four valves per cylinder, 225 hp. When two turbos were added, the output increased to 324 hp.
In this last case, the car was called the Dodge Stealth R/T. This version of the Stealth had permanent four-wheel drive and an electronically controlled suspension. At a speed of more than 31 mph, the rear wheels supported the steering automatically. Although the Stealth R/T could reach a top speed of more than 155 mph, the car was also very suitable for city driving. At a speed of 31 mph in the fifth gear, the engine made only 1,000 revolutions per minute. The car was also very comfortable and was equipped with ABS breaks, steering servo, two air bags and automatic air-conditioning as well as electronically powered windows and leather finishing.

The headlights had small dimensions, but an enormous capacity.

Technical specifications

Model:	**Dodge Stealth R/T**
Years of manufacture:	1990-1996
Production:	not known
Engine:	V6
Displacement:	181.4 cu. in.
Output:	324/6,000 hp/rpm
Top speed:	155 mph
From 0 to 60 mph:	5.9 sec
Wheel base:	8 ft 1 in
Length:	14 ft 11 in
Width:	6 ft
Height:	4 ft 1 in

Dodge Viper

"Approach with caution!" warns the advertising campaigns for the DodgeViper and you can understand why. The model has been around for a few years now and created quite a sensation when first launched. With its aggressive looks and huge lightweight 8 liter V10 engine, it could be termed the classic American sports car.

Since its introduction as a concept car at the 1989 North American International Auto Show in Detroit, the Dodge Viper has captured the hearts and imagination of car enthusiasts around the world. It has also captured its share of trophies on the track as a three-time FIA GT2 and Le Mans class champion.

As part of the Dodge Viper's complete redesign for 2003, more than 100 changes and improvements have been made to the chassis, brakes, suspension, tires, engine, transmission, cockpit, electronics and more than a dozen body panels. Yet the Viper still retains a traditional front-engine, rear-wheel-drive layout with a six-speed manual transmission. The commitment was made to use a racing-style chassis including fully independent four-wheel suspension, wide tires and wheels for maximum grip and massive brakes for stopping power. A race-derived two-seat cockpit looks over a highly functional instrument panel with centrally mounted tachometer and a 220 mile-per-hour speedometer.

A new version of the Viper's four-wheel, anti-lock disc brake system, originally introduced for the 2001 model year, is enhanced for this next-generation car.

The mean front end and low lines give the Viper a smooth and powerful look. The open road is just what it dreams about.

From this view one can spot plenty of ventilating outlets to keep that V10 from overheating.

With a newly bored and stroked aluminum engine block that increases the Viper's displacement from 488 to 505 cu. in. has been pushed its V-10 power output, to 500 horsepower and 525 lb.-ft. of torque.

With styling cues derived from the Dodge Viper GTS/R concept car first shown at the 2000 North American International Auto Show, the all-new 2003 Dodge Viper SRT-10 convertible packs an outrageous new design into a low-slung roadster shell.

Lowered hood lines, swept-back fenders and deep-cut side scallops take their cues from the classic original, yet bring the Viper into the 21st century. Improved aerodynamics and a partial undertray add functional performance enhancements.

Debuting alongside the Dodge Viper SRT-10 Convertible will be the Viper Competition Coupe.

This new car will emerge as a serious competitor from the first lap with a coupe-shaped composite body based largely on the Dodge Viper GTS/R concept car shown at the 2000 North American International Auto Show and a track-ready chassis based on the new 2003 Dodge Viper SRT-10 convertible.

Though largely based on the SRT-10 convertible, the Competition Coupe develops 20 more horsepower (520 bhp) and 15 more lb.-ft. of torque (540 lb.-ft.) than the street-going version. Power is enhanced via a performance camshaft and tuned exhaust.

Technical specifications

Model:	**Dodge Viper**
Engine:	90-degree V10, fuel injected, liquid-cooled
Displacement:	505 cu. in.
Bore x Stroke:	4.03x3.96 in
Power (SAE net):	500 bhp (372 kW) @ 5600 rpm (60.4 bhp/liter)
Torque (SAE net):	525 lb.-ft. (712 Nom) @ 4200 rpm
Overall Length:	175.6 in
Overall Width at Sill's:	75.2 in
Overall Width at Mirrors:	78.5 in
Overall Height:	47.6 in
Wheel base:	98.8 in
Curb Weight:	(est.) 3,380 lb
Fuel Tank Capacity:	18.5 gal. (70 L)
Body/chassis:	
Layout:	Longitudinal front engine, rear-wheel drive
Chassis Construction:	Backbone tubular steel space frame with separate cowl structure
Body Construction:	Sheet-moulded composite (SMC) and resin injection molded (RIM) body panels

Excalibur

Although the Limited Edition had a cloth top and side windows, the car was intended for countryside with a warm climate.

The Excalibur brand has a long history. It began when the famous designer Brooks Stevens (1912-1995) built a Neo-classical car in 1964 which resembled a Mercedes SSK. Stevens was already a very well known designer at that time and had worked for various automobile factories. He was, among other things, responsible for the bodies of the Studebaker Gran Turismo Hawk, the AMC Hornet and the Jeep Cherokee. In 1986, Brooks Stevens left the Excalibur Company. When his sons David and William lost their interest in the enterprise, bankruptcy was inevitable. Henry Warner bought the company for $ 2.3 million. But he cheated because he failed to state the building years correctly

Thanks to its width of 72.44 inches, the Cobra looked quite massive and dangerous in the frontal view.

When father and son Geitlinger took over the Excalibur firm, they found that all the drawings had disappeared. They had to start over from the very beginning. In the photo, you can see their Roadster.

and thus the name Excalibur was ruined again, for the time being. In 1991, Warner also went bankrupt. Udo and Jens Geitlinger, dealers of second-hand cars, then took over the enterprise. In their Milwaukee factory, the father and son confined themselves to two models: the Excalibur Roadster and the Limited Edition. They also built a replica of the AC Cobra. In 1992, 45 people worked in the enterprise again. The 'Cobra' was assembled from Ford-Mustang components, the Excaliburs from the components of the Chevrolet Corvette. The bodies were of plastic and were painted red, blue, black, green and yellow.

The dashboard of the Limited Edition. The dials were specially made for the vehicle.

The Geitlingers hoped to be able to build fifty Excaliburs and one hundred and twenty Cobras. They never succeeded in attaining these numbers and it is not known whether they are still in business. Even our letter with a request for information was returned undelivered in 1997.

Technical specifications

Model:	**Excalibur**	**J.A.C. 427 Cobra**
Years of manufacture:	1992-unknown	1992-unknown
Production:	not known	not known
Engine:	V8	V8
Displacement:	347.8 cu. in	305 cu. in.
Output (hp/rpm):	306/5,000	215/4,200
Top speed:	146 mph	143 mph
From 0 to 60 mph:	4.7 sec	5.9 sec
Wheel base:	9 ft 4 in	7 ft 10 in
Length:	14 ft 7 in	13 ft 9 ft
Width:	6 ft	6 ft 1 in
Height:	4 ft 4 in	3 ft 10 in
Weight:	3,174	2,500

Facel Vega Facel II

The enterprise of Jean Daninos, Facel-Métallon, has built bodies for Panhard, Simca and Ford for many long years. At the beginning of the fifties, Daninos decided to produce his own car. It had to be a very luxurious vehicle, recalling the times of Hispano Suiza, Delage and Delahaye. Expense was no object if the quality was perfect and the fastidious motorist had everything he wanted.

Note the special location of the blinkers, above the rear mudguards. The spoke wheels could be ordered for an extra charge.

The leather was genuine, but the 'wood' was painted on the metal dashboard.
The heating could be regulated by five levers between the gear lever and the dashboard.

The first Facel Vega came from the factory in Colombes, not far from Paris, in 1954. The car stood on a beautiful tube chassis and was powered by the engine and gearbox of the American De Soto. Daninos was one of the first designers who combined the qualities of the American engine with the gracious lines of a European body, just as Iso Rivolta, Jensen, Monteverdi and others would do later. After about 350 cars had been built, the Facel Vega HK500 appeared on the market in 1958. This model, which remained in production until 1961 and had 548 sales, was the most popular Facel.

According to connoisseurs, its successor, the Facel II, had a still more beautiful body. The stronger 382.5 cu. in. V8 engine from Chrysler had an output of 355 hp/4,800 rpm. For an extra charge, the Facel II could even be delivered with a 390-hp engine, which Chrysler custom-made for the California police. In this case, the engine was equipped with two four-barrel Carter carburetors.

The Facel II resembled its predecessor, the HK500, in many aspects. But now, it was equipped with double headlights behind one convex glass.
Also, the roof rods were thinner, making it possible to enlarge the glass surface.

Most vehicles were geared by an automatic TorqueFlite gearbox from Chrysler. But enthusiasts could instead have a completely synchronized four-speed gearbox from Pont-à-Mousson. Also, the Facel II had a tube chassis. The car was braked by four Dunlop disc brakes. The steering booster was part of the standard equipment. The wheels with their Rudge hubcaps could be exchanged for spoke wheels for an extra charge.

Most Facel II's could be equipped with a "police engine" which was enhanced to 390 hp. In the standard version, the engine had a four-barrel carburetor and an output of 355 hp/4,800 rpm.

The body of the Facel II differed from that of the HK500. The roof line was lowered by 13.15 in, the glass surface and the luggage compartment were enlarged and the automatic gearbox was no longer controlled by pushbuttons on the dashboard, but by a centrally-mounted lever. Though the lower roof looked very good, it also had a serious disadvantage. As the floor of the vehicle was not lowered, the sitting cushions took the rap. They became thinner and thus less comfortable. Due to a larger luggage compartment, the gas tank and the spare wheel were placed farther back with, as a consequence, a worse weight distribution of the car. The Facel II was a large, heavy vehicle. Despite its weight of 3,417 lb, it was able to accelerate in less than 10 seconds from 0 to 60 mph and its top speed was more than 149 mph. However, it was not a sports car, but a genuine touring car which could comfortably cover long distances in a short time.

The Facel II was the last large Facel Vega. The professional journals reproached Daninos regularly for having built a 'bastard:' a European car with American technology. Perhaps under the influence of this criticism, the following model, the Facellia (which was built in 1959) was equipped with a French four-cylinder engine and gearbox. But the car was so bad that the factory nearly perished due to guarantee claims. The mechanical parts of the Facellia were replaced with those of the Volvo Amazon and later by those of the Austin-Healey. But it was too late. The name Facel was ruined and in 1964, Daninos was obliged to close his factory. In total, he had built 2,938 cars over the course of ten years. His regular clients included Pablo Picasso, Ava Gardner, Danny Kay, Tony Curtis, Ringo Starr, Stirling Moss, Maurice Trintingant and the Dutch rally rider Maus Gatsonides.

Technical specifications

Model:	**Facel II**
Years of manufacture:	1961-1964
Production:	184
Engine:	V8
Displacement:	383.6 cu. in.
Output:	390/5,500 hp/rpm
Top speed:	149 mph
From 0 to 60 mph:	10 sec
Wheel base:	8 ft 8 in
Length:	15 ft 7 in
Width:	5 ft 9 in
Height:	4 ft 2 in
Weight:	3,417 lb

Ferrari 166

From this view one can see the large tunnel on the hood which directs cool air straight to the carburettors positioned directly below it.

The first car to bear the Ferrari name was the Tipo 125, a bulky two-seat racer introduced in 1948. This was followed by the 159-really a slightly revised and upgraded 125.

The Ferrari 166 was the first model to be made in volume and was taken up by numerous coachbuilders of the time, who produced various types of bodies for the model. A coupe was presented by Vignale. Touring produced a berlinetta and others, including the 166 Inter saloon, a Formula 2 single seat racer and then of course the formidable 166MM Barchetta, probably the best known of them all.

Most if not all the bodywork on the 166MM Barchetta were beaten to shape. It is easy to see just how much work was involved.

The car used a V12 engine originally designed by Gioacchino Colombo, who had been part of the early Scuderia Ferrari and who had also worked at Alfa Romeo with Vittorio Jano on the 12C car, which was powered by a supercharged V12 engine. Luigi Bazzi, an ex-Fiat man, got the opportunity to work his magic with the Colombo engine.

The 166 Barchetta was given the designation MM because it triumphed for Ferrari for the first time at the grueling 1948 Mille Miglia race and the barchetta description comes from the English translation of 'little boat,' which is how

the Italians described the body. The body was created by the design studio Carrozzeria Touring and nearly completely hand beaten.
The 166 barchetta became a legend in its own time. After the world watched Luigi Chinetti go on to win the 1949 Le Mans in one of these cars, there was no doubting the future of the Ferrari mark and in particular the little barchetta.
In those early days, most cars were used for racing and Ferrari was no exception. In fact, Enzo Ferrari was well aware of the benefits gained from race track experience. Having a car do well in any race meant that it was strong and reliable and therefore gave the company good publicity.

No frills here. A race car needs very little instrumentation and can do without interior door handles. Note the pull cord used to open the doors.

Technical specifications

Model:	**Ferrari 166MM Barchetta**
Engine:	60° V12, front longitudinal
Bore & Stroke:	2.36x2.32 in
Total Displacement:	121.7 cu. in.
Power Output:	130 bhp at 7000 rpm
Fuel system:	3 Weber 32 DFC carburettors
Transmission:	Dry, single-plate clutch, 5-speed gearbox + reverse
0 – 60 mph:	10 sec
Top Speed:	125 mph
Front Suspension:	Independent with transverse leaf spring and hydraulic dampers
Rear Suspension:	Live axle, semi-elliptic longitudinal leaf springs, hydraulic dampers, anti-roll bar
Brakes:	hydraulic drums
Wheelbase	7 ft 2 in
Dry Weight:	1,433 lb
Tyres:	5.50-15

Ferrari 246 GT Dino

In memory of his bright young son, who died at only twenty-four in 1956, Enzo Ferrari named many of his most famous engines Dino.
The Dino road car evolved through prototypes on the racetracks of the world, both in regard to the bodywork and to the engine. Pininfarina showed several prototypes before Ferrari decided on the final production model.
The Dino 206GT made its debut in 1967, the first of the company's road cars to feature an engine amidships, a direction that most of the sports car companies were taking or had taken during this period. Strangely, there was no Ferrari badge to be seen, just the now familiar yellow-backed Dino emblem. It was however a pretty car with a pointed nose and a body sweeping back over the sharply slanting windscreen, back over the roof and down to the vertical reverse curved rear

Clearly a GTS model, the center roof section could be removed for open top motoring.

window. The back was flat and dropped sharply at the rear. Two large air intakes were sculpted behind the doors to feed air into the rear engine compartment, keeping the engine cool and possibly to help the rear brakes also. The bodywork was made by hand at the Scaglietti works using aluminium alloy.

Fiat had been contracted to build the V6 engines and took the opportunity to use it in several of their own cars too. The engine of the Dino was placed at an angle in the rear of the car to save space, which in turn gave room for a small luggage area just behind the engine.

In front of the driver inside the cabin is a full selection of instrumentation, rev counter, speed, oil gauge, water gauge and even a clock. To the left are heater controls and the now familiar gateshift gearchange on the central tunnel.

The 246GT Dino was presented to the general public in 1969 and it varied from the 206 in several areas. The engine blocks were made of cast iron rather than alloy. The light alloy bodywork was replaced by a thin steel body, still hand beaten at the Scaglietti works. Slight changes to the height and other dimensions were made along with a slightly enlarged fuel tank. Although there were minor adjustments to the car, the models changed little subsequently. At the Geneva motor show of 1972, the 246 was shown with an open top Targa style roof, which could be removed and stowed behind the seats. This car was designated 246GTS. Production of the Dino stopped in 1974.

Note the vertical reverse curve rear window just in front of the flat engine bay cover. There was also space behind the engine for a luggage compartment.

Technical specifications

Model:	206 GT	246 GT (GTS)
Engine:	V6	V6
Bore/Stroke:	3.34x3.42 in	3.64x2.36 in
Capacity:	121.2 cu. in.	147.5 cu. in.
Power:	180 bhp/8000 rpm	195 bhp/7600 rpm
Gearbox:	5 speed + reverse	5 Speed + reverse
Brakes:	Servo assisted dual circuit	Servo assisted dual circuit
Front:	11 in ventilated disc	11 in ventilated disc
Rear:	10.5 in ventilated disc	10.5 in ventilated disc
Wheels:	14 x 6 1/2_ J Alloys	14 x 6 1/2 J Alloys
Tyres:	185 x 14 in	205 x 14 inch
Wheel base:	90 in	92.3 in
Length:	163 in	166.7 in
Width:	67 in	67.2 in
Height:	42 in	45 in
Weight:	1984 lb	2380 lb
0 – 50 mph:	5.6 sec	5.7 sec
0 – 100 mph:	19.0 sec	18.0 sec
Top Speed:	140 mph	150 mph

Ferrari 275 GTB

The Ferrari 275 GTB, a fastback coupe and its open top sister, the GTS, S standing for spider, were introduced at the Paris Auto Salon of 1964. They were the first independent suspension chassis models from Ferrari to be equipped with a single overhead camV12 engine positioned at the front of the car, while the transmission was placed at the rear along

This is an early 275 GTB. It has Borani wire wheels fitted, which were an optional extra. Standard wheels were Campagnolo alloys with 10 oblong holes, which helped with brake ventilation.

This is an extremely rare 275 GTB/4 of which only a handful were built for racing by private owners.

with the differential. This configuration also helped to distribute the weight more evenly. The engine was a competition proven Colombo V12 design, which was enlarged from 3 liters to 3.3 liters.

The 275 GTB and GTS were designed by Pininfarina, with the GTB being built by Scaglietti in Modena and the GTS by Pininfarina themselves.

Although a few refinements were made to the original GTB by early 1966, the GTS had been superseded by the 330 GTS and the GTB was given series II status due to the changes. The car was also fitted with a torque tube, which rigidly united the front mounted engine with the rear-mounted transaxle, eliminating worrying vibrations. Today's owners of these models usually refer to their car as a torque tube model, thus distinguishing it from the earlier model.

This is the engine of the 275 GTB/4. A host of carburetor trumpets nestles between the cylinder heads of the Colombo 3.3 liter V12.

The bulge in the hood identifies this car as a 275 GTB/4. Shown at the 1966 Paris Salon, the car still used the Colombo V12 but gained an extra camshaft per engine bank.

In late 1966, the GTB was given twin cam cylinder heads and became known as the 275 GTB/4. Six carburetors were now standard and the car could be identified by the bulge in the centre of the hood.

During this same year, a competition model was introduced: the GTB/C. This was a greatly lightened version, which could be used for private entry racing. It used thin gauge aluminum bodywork, plastic side and rear windows, lightened chassis parts and also had mechanical changes to boost power. One of these cars won the GT class at Le Mans and came in eighth place overall in that same race.

An American importer, Luigi Chinetti, modified some GTB's for the American market by turning them into open tops, which he called NART spiders (North American Racing Team), one of which was raced at Sebring in 1967. Production of the 275 ended in 1968 with the introduction of the Daytona.

Technical specifications

Model:	**Ferrari 275 GTB/4**
Engine:	V12 dohc
Displacement:	201.4 cu. in.
Fuel system:	6 carburettors
Power:	300 hp / 8000 rpm
Transmission	5 speed manual
Wheel base:	94.5 in
Weight:	2,663 lbs
0 – 60 mph:	6.2 sec
Top Speed:	155 mph

Ferrari 288 GTO

The first GTO (Gran Turismo Omologato) car produced by Ferrari in the 1960's was fitted with a V12, 3 liter engine. It was an awesome car and remains a legend today. The new GTO was officially named the 288 Gran Turismo Omologato in honor of the new V8, which had a displacement of 174.2 cu. in..

The 288 GTO, produced to comply with Group B regulations, was a completely different animal. To participate in this Group, it was stipulated that a minimum of 200 cars would have to be produced for homologation. Ferrari had also planned to build a GTO 'Evoluzione' to be the pure race version for use in this category. Unfortunately these cars were never raced in the Group B category because several fatal accidents led to the termination of the Group by the FIA.

Looking at the new GTO, you could be forgiven for mistaking it for the 308 as they are very similar, in fact. The engine was a quadcam V8 like the 308, but the GTO had two turbochargers added. The engine positioning was also changed from transverse location to longitudinal. In addition to the advanced engine technology, the GTO used modern structural materials such as aluminum honeycomb and carbon, Kevlar and Nomax composites. These were used in the bodywork and refined in the Pininfarina windtunnel. The car's wheelbase was lengthened by four inches to accommo-

From above you can see where the body has had to be widened to accommodate the extra large tyres on this GTO.

Everything neatly in its place on the mean front end of this GTO. Note the stick up type door mirrors.

date the new engine positioning and the width of the car was enlarged to accommodate the bigger tires. This did not entail adding bits to the sides of the wheel arches, but in fact, the whole top area was enlarged to accommodate the extra width.

Because the car was designed to compete as a sports race car, it needed a cabin where two people could sit comfortably and had to have instrumentation, lighting, mirrors, and windscreen wipers to make it usable on public roads and to make the cabin well stocked and comfortable. One way to recognize the GTO is to look out for its very familiar stick-up mirrors fitted to the top of the doors.

At the end of its life, over 260 GTO cars were made, surpassing the originally planned 200, and the last was delivered to the factory F1 racing legend Niki Lauda.

Technical specifications

Model:	**Ferrari 2888 GTO**
Engine:	Longitudinal, mid-rear mounted 90° V8
Bore & Stroke:	3.14 x 2.79 in
Displacement:	174.2 cu. in.
Power Output:	400 bhp at 7,000
Brakes:	Ventilated discs, servo assist.
Length:	14 ft
Width:	6 ft 3 in
Height:	3 ft 8 in
Wheel base:	8 ft
Weight:	2,557 lb
0 – 100 mph:	11.0 sec
Top Speed:	191.2 mph

Ferrari 308 GTB

308 GTB Quattrov: This is a side view of a 1982 308 GTB Quattrovalvole. The engine in this car has four valves per cylinder, hence the Quattrovalvole designation.

The true successor to the Dino 246 GT was the Ferrari 308 GTB, which was also Ferrari's first two-seat V8 road car. Alhough the 308 GT4 was Ferrari's first mid-engined V8 road car and followed on from the 246 GT, the designers Bertone were given little time to create a 2+2 mid-engined car which could follow the lines of the Pininfarina model. Even though the 308 GT4 was a fine design, it was not popular.

The new 308 GTB was designed by the Pininfarina studios in Turin, Italy. The first models were bodied in fibreglass over their oval-section tube frame chassis. The front hood was made of aluminium; their inner floorpans, wheel arches and the front firewall were also formed from fibreglass, while most of the remainder of the car was steel. Although some European units were fabricated from fibreglass up to 1977, to speed up construction, Ferrari started producing the bodies from steel in 1976.

308 GTS: This is a shot of the cockpit of a 308 GTS, note the targa style top has been removed.

The heart of the 308 series is its three-liter V8 engine. The 308, 308i and 308qv can be identified mainly by the developments of the engine. Along with the body change came changes to the engine also, made primarily to improve power and reliability in the face of increased emission controls. Unfortunately this also affected the power output and general performance of the car.

1981 saw the introduction of a new design for the engine. Ferrari developed 4 valve heads for the 3 liter V8 and although this car was heavier than the original glassfibre cars, its performance was restored. The cars were now known as the 308 GTB/GTS Quattrovalvole (four valve).

A 208 GTB turbo was manufactured for the Italian market, purely to dodge taxes on cars over two liters. This used a 121.5 cu. in. V8 with a turbocharger and looked much like the 308 GTB, but with minor changes.

308 GTB fiber 2: The gold wheels of this fiberglass bodied 308 GTB compliment the black paintwork.

The 308 saw its greatest structural changes when the open top GTS model was introduced. Apart from a new removable fibreglass roof section, the body was strengthened with a roll bar extending through the B pillars and the roof. In 1985, the first major redesign emerged with the 328 GTB/GTS. Engine capacity was increased to 194.4 cu. in. and power to 270 bhp, making the 328 the fastest of this series of Ferraris.

Technical specifications

Model:	**Ferrari 308 GTB**
Engine:	Transverse, mid-mounted 90° V8
Bore & Stroke:	3.2 x 2.8 in
Displacement:	178.5 cu. in.
Power Output:	255 bhp at 7,700 rpm
Fuel system:	4 Weber 40 DCNF carburettors
Transmission:	Dry single-plate clutch, 5-speed gearbox + reverse
Front Suspension:	Independent, double wishbones, coil springs
Rear Suspension:	Independent, double wishbones, coil springs
Brakes:	Ventilated discs
Length:	14 ft 10 in
Width:	5 ft 7 in
Height:	3 ft 8 in
Wheel base:	7 ft 8 in
Dry Weight:	2,403 lb
Top Speed:	157.5 mph

Ferrari 360 Modena

This is the instrument cluster of the 360 Modena, which is positioned directly in front of the driver, all dials and gauges in clear view with the rev counter in the middle.

The Ferrari 360 Modena was unveiled at the Geneva Motor show in 1999. Pininfarina designed the car and it was the 163rd model they had designed for the Ferrari Company.

Today's car has taken full advantage of new materials and has a significant weight loss. Aluminum was used by Ferrari for the first time on a road car to build the entire frame, body shell and chassis components.

The lines of the body flow very distinctly and air passes over it with ease. The two large air intakes incorporated at either side of the front of the car act as channels directing the air flow beneath the vehicle to the two rear diffusers. This system provides ground effect solutions without compromising the design and style of the bodywork; no nasty protruding wings or scoops here. In fact, 5,400 hours were spent testing in a wind tunnel to achieve the needed results, thereby giving the car the correct down force properties to make its merry way to a 183 mph speed.

Once inside the cabin of the 360 Modena, the driver is confronted by all the main instrumentation; the rev counter in the center and the speedometer to the right of it. These are grouped dirrectly in the driver's line of vision. On the cars fitted with the F1 style gearchange, the rev counter has a gear engagement readout incorporated into it. There are airbags for safety including a standard fitting for the passenger also. The trim is natural Connolly leather in which again a certain amount of aluminum parts are added. Behind the seats is a small bench seat big enough to take a golf bag or some small cases. The front trunk area is the main baggage storage area. The car has been designed for space and comfort and the doors are big, allowing good entry and exit.

Adding an individual feel to your Ferrari 360 is simple. Carrozzeria Scaglietti runs a personalization program, which allows you to personally add some distinctive sporting accessories to the car.

Clearly visible at either side of the front of this 360 Modena are the two large intakes that channel the air under the car and back to the radiators, helping not only to cool the engine but act as an aerodynamic aid also.

No nasty wings on the back here. Everything is kept neat and tidy, twin light pods either side, twin exhaust outlets and the distinctive prancing horse emblem in the middle.

It wouldn't be right not to mention the 360 Modena Challenge. This is the racing version of the 360 for Ferrari customers wanting to compete in the Ferrari Challenge Trofeo Pirelli Championship. It's based on the 360 Modena and the target of the Challenge version was to develop a racing package attractive to customers

Technical specifications

Model:	**Ferrari 360 Modena**
Engine:	V8. 4ohv. 5vpc
Bore/Stroke:	3.34 x 3.11 in
Displacement	218.8 cu. in.
Power:	400 bhp / 8500 rpm
Transmission:	6 gears + reverse or F1 electro hydraulic system
Wheel base:	8 ft 6 in
Length:	14 ft 8 in
Width:	6 ft 4 in
Height:	4 ft
Weight:	2,843 lb
0 – 62.5 mph:	4.5 sec
Top Speed:	184.4 mph

Ferrari 575

Clearly visible here is the changed front end of the 575M with its different shape and size air intakes, new spoiler and modified light clusters.

There is no doubting that the 550 Maranello is an awesome car both in looks and power. Now, however, it is superseded by its upgraded brother, the 575M Maranello.

The numbers and letters are just part of the upgrade story. The Maranello has a new code number of 575 because the engine capacity has been increased to 351 cu. in. (5.75 liters) to the previous 335.6 cu. in (5.50 liters). The letter

This side view shows off the sleek lines of the 575M and the new 19 inch tires and wheels.

M stands for 'Modified' underlining all the changes that have taken place since the 550 Maranello. Apart from the engine upgrade, the 575M introduces the F1 type gearchange, used for the first time on a road – going 12 cylinder Ferrari. So now the driver has the ability to change gear with paddles positioned behind the steering wheel.

The majority of changes made to the car have been on the technical side. Therefore, the styling has been modified only to compliment those changes. The front end, for example, has been given new style air intakes and a new front spoiler. The light clusters have been redesigned to incorporate xenon technology headlamps and the wheels too have been. The new F1 style gearchange system allows the driver to choose between sport and comfort, both of which are tied into shock absorber control. A choice of automatic and low grip can be activated. The tires are now fitted with pressure sensors and can be checked while travelling.

Ferrari has restyled the interior to make the cabin sportier. All the dials have been grouped together in one single panel in front of the driver with the rev counter sitting right in the middle. The owner now has the ability to choose his or her own features from the Carrozzeria Scaglietti personalized program, which allows buyers to specify their own styling and equipment and alters the functionality of the vehicle to suit their personal taste. Racetrack options, exterior changes, color and the treatment of the interior can all be pre-ordered.

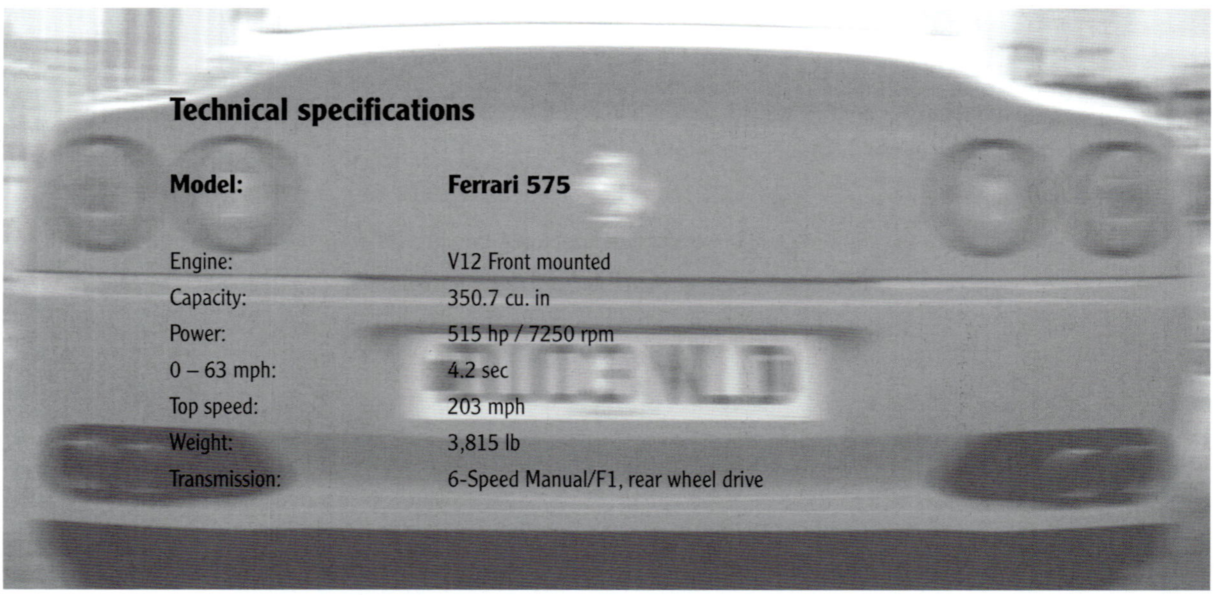

Technical specifications

Model:	**Ferrari 575**
Engine:	V12 Front mounted
Capacity:	350.7 cu. in
Power:	515 hp / 7250 rpm
0 – 63 mph:	4.2 sec
Top speed:	203 mph
Weight:	3,815 lb
Transmission:	6-Speed Manual/F1, rear wheel drive

Ferrari F40

This rear view of a 1988 Ferrari F40 shows off the large rear wing and large round lights.

What better way to celebrate Enzo Ferrari's forty years of car manufacture than by designing a car to suitably represent all the achievements of many years of racing?

The idea was born in 1986 and one year later the prototype was being driven at the home test circuit of Fiorano. The F40 was born.

At this stage, the prototype was merely a test. Different elements were tested: fatigue on composite materials, competition engines and their components and advanced four-wheel drive solutions. Hours and days of testing were carried out both on the test track and on normal roads to verify the building of a super car.

The F40 has a very sporty appearance of which the main features are the central passenger cell, the low front end, the aerodynamic rear spoiler and a clean smooth underside.

The interior was designed to give a real feeling of sportiness and functionality, hence the sliding side window glasses and the sports pedals as used in race cars. The dashboard is the same as in competition cars and the composite materials from which it is made are visible. Instrumentation has deliberately been kept to a minimum and can be easily read, thus detracting from potential distraction for the driver. The seats are wraparound sports style for maximum hold.

The aerodynamics of the car have been tested in a wind tunnel, requiring many hours of computer monitoring of airflow measurements. The idea of Pininfarina was to create a car which could aesthetically arouse the desire

The power plant of the F40, mid mounted V8 with two IHI turbo chargers with intercoolers.

The interior of the F40, functional but somewhat scarce. Note the racing pedals and gate lever gearchange.

to own a racing car, but which could also be used on ordinary roads. The concept dates back to the 1950s when customers with everyday cars could also dominate the racetracks of the world.

As far as the power plant was concerned, many hours of experience gained from the prototype – GTO Evoluzione, constructed and based on Group B race cars – provided the solution for what kind and size of engine was needed: a rear, central mounted V8 configuration with twin turbo chargers. The gearbox has five forward and reverse positions and therefore allows the owner to choose a traditional box with synchronisers or a sports box with dog clutches.

Much care was taken in choosing special aeronautically derived rubber fuel tanks, fitted with race style rapid filler caps.

The outcome of all this is an incredibly fast sports car with all the character of the past, but which uses all the latest technology. Ferrari was forty years old in 1987. It has come a long way since the very first volume car, the 166, was raced.

Technical specifications

Model:	**Ferrari F40**
Engine:	90 degree V8. Two IHI turbo chargers.
Bore/Stroke:	3.2 x 2.7 inch
Power:	478 hp / 7000 rpm
Top Speed:	201.3 mph
0 – 124.3 mph:	12.0 sec
Standing kilometer:	21.0 sec
Length:	174.4 inc
Width:	78.0 in
Height:	44.5 in
Wheelbase:	96.5 in
Gearbox:	5 Speed manual

Ferrari F50

From this angle it is easy to see how well the little roof section fits, just in front of the rollover bars on both passengeres and drive sidee.

The Ferrari F50 was the costliest Ferrari ever made when it was introduced to the general public. It mixed Formula 1 mechanics with lightweight construction, creating an awesome combination of lightweight power. Many wondered how Ferrari could improve on the technology and power of the F40, but the F50 did not fail to deliver. A radically different construction design was used and materials such as titanium, magnesium and carbon fiber meant that the car was able to take four seconds off the F40's best lap time at the Ferrari home test track of Fiorano.

Ferrari had taken a Formula 1 race car and built a roadster around it. The starting point had been Alain Prost's 1990 641/2 race car. The 3.5 liter engine was compact enough so as not to give too long a wheelbase and it could be fitted neatly into the rear of the new car. It would be of little surprise to anybody to mention that the body was designed by Pininfarina. CAD and normal methods were combined for the design and after various proposals the final result emerged.

The final styling model was completed in 1991 and although it looks all but identical to the production car, three important modifications were carried out.The front air intakes were made larger, a small spoiler was fitted just under the front bumper and two small wings were added to the A-pillar.

The Ferrari F50 was introduced at the 1995 Geneva Motorshow, in anticipation of the 50th anniversary in 1997 of the founding of the Ferrari Company. The launch of the F50 was greeted with huge enthusiasm and it took the show by

The beautifully sculpted front end of the F50 – You will not often find this kind of machinery parked in a public parking spot.

The wing at the rear of the F50 is an integral part of the side panels and stretches right over the extreme end of the engine bay.

storm. The F50 can be both a berlinetta and a spider. A removable roof allows owners to switch from one type to the other. This is not a quick transition however; the job takes over half an hour, so it is unlikely to be attempted by the road side if rain starts to fall.

The F50 was restricted to a mere 349 units, setting a precedent for the low-volume supercar production that Ferrari is continuing with the current Enzo.

Technical specifications

Model:	**Ferrari F50**
F50 Engine:	Longitudinal 65° V12,
Bore & Stroke:	3.35 x 2.72 in
Displacement:	286.7 cu. in.
Dry sump Engine Weight:	436.5 lbs
Transmission:	Dry, twin-plate clutch, 6-speed gearbox + reverse
Width:	78.2 in
Height:	44.1 in
Wheel base :	101.6 in
Dry Weight:	2,976 lb
Front Tyres:	245/35 ZR 18
Rear Tyres:	335/30 ZR 18
Top Speed:	202 mph
0 - 60 mph:	3.2 sec

Ferrari Testarossa

An impressive view of the wide rear end of the Testaross, in fact some six and a half feet (two metres) from side to side.

If you see it on the road, you will definately recognize it. The low, sharp front which swoops backwards over the highly finned doors and then out and over the very wide rear end is quite unique. The back of the car is expansive, but very neatly designed and finished. The designer, as with many Ferraris, is Pininfarina, based in Torino, Italy. He has been designing cars for Ferrari for many decades.

The car is known as the Testarossa (Redhead) due to the red-painted engine cam-covers, which distinguish the engines from the less powerful models. The name Testarossa has been in the Ferrari vocabulary since the 1950's and is only given to the most impressive of their models.

The side shot of the Testarossa is like no other car. The huge fins built into the side doors are clearly visible from this angle.

This shot of the interior of the Testarossa shows that limited accessories were fitted, enough though to keep the driver informed of what was going on.

The large slats in the doors serve as air intakes for the vast 12-cylinder engine that sits at the rear of the cockpit and the intake at the front helps to keep the front brakes ventilated.

The car was introduced at the Paris Motor Show in 1984 and was upgraded to the 512TR (denoting 5-liter engine in a flat 12 configuration) from 1992 onwards. This configuration is very different from any of the previous testarossa layouts, which tended to be straight fours or V12 format. There are twin camshafts per cylinder bank and 48 valves. A Bosch Motoronic engine management system controls the fuel injection and electronic ignition.

The cabin of the Testarossa is not exactly bulging with instrumentation, but does equip the driver with all the essentials. Three dials sit neatly in front of the steering wheel encased in Conolly leather, the seats too are leather and the infamous gated gearlever is placed between the driver and the passenger seats.

Ferrari supplies made-to-measure leather luggage, neatly embellished with the prancing horse insignia, to fit snugly in the pointed front end of the car.

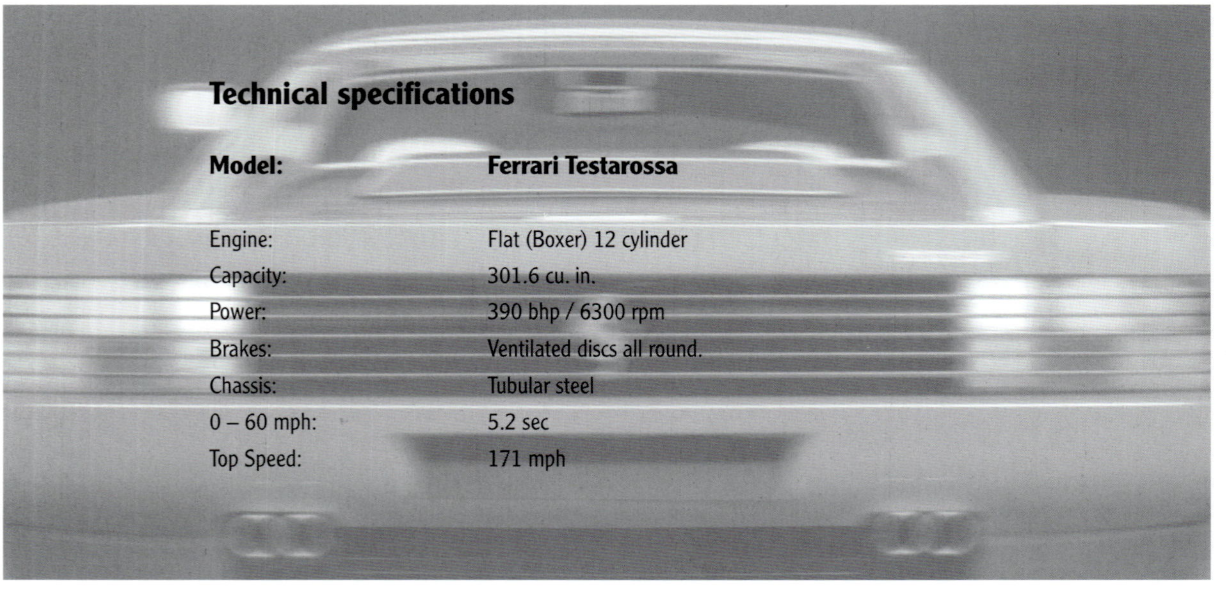

Technical specifications

Model:	**Ferrari Testarossa**
Engine:	Flat (Boxer) 12 cylinder
Capacity:	301.6 cu. in.
Power:	390 bhp / 6300 rpm
Brakes:	Ventilated discs all round.
Chassis:	Tubular steel
0 – 60 mph:	5.2 sec
Top Speed:	171 mph

Fiat Nuova 500

A Topolino from 1947. Between 1936 and 1955, 517,370 were sold.

When Henry Ford built his T-Ford in 1909, he wanted to give as many people as possible the opportunity to buy a car. With this idea, the German Volkswagen Beetle, the English Austin Seven, the Dutch DAF, the French 2CV, and of course, the Italian Fiat 500 were also designed. The latter model was presented to the press on June 15, 1936. Wages were low and steel and gasoline rare in those days. But everyone still wanted to possess their own car. Giovanni Agnelli, the big boss of Fiat, gave Dante Giacosa the order to develop a car which would be cheap to maintain, but which could be sold at a profit for less than 5,000 lira. It was not a simple task. The cheapest Fiat up to that moment, the 508 Balilla, cost more than 11,000 lira. But Giacosa, only thirty years old at the time, succeeded in achieving the task. The result was the Fiat 500, known as the Topolino, or 'little mouse,' in Italy. Immediately after the war, production of the 500 restarted.

Only in 1955 was the model succeeded by the Fiat Nuova 500. Even though this car was designed by Giacosa, the model differed in every aspect from the Topolino. It now contained an air-cooled two-cylinder engine mounted in the rear, instead of a water-cooled four-cylinder engine in front. The Nuova 500 provided more interior space than its

In the first models, here a car from 1960, the cloth top protruded as far as the engine hood. This changed with the 500D in 1961.

This 500L from 1972 was one of the last cars of its series.

predecessor and was thus more appropriate as a family car. The engine of the Nuova was further enhanced and enlarged, from 29.23 and 30.45 to 36.24 cu. in., while the output increased from 13 to 18 hp. Until 1965, the vehicle had doors opening "the wrong way," but in the Fiat 500F, the hinges were mounted in the front for the first time. In 1960, the 500 was also available as a station wagon. In the so-called Giardiniera, the rear seat could be tilted down to a horizontal position. The loading platform which was then created could be accessed through the "third door." The engine, situated under the floor, was rotated by 90 degrees due to space shortage. The Giardiniera had a wheel-base which was 3.9 in. wider and a body 9.4 longer and 1.18 in higher than the 500.

Technical specifications

Model:	**Fiat Nuova 500**			
Years of manufacture:	1957-1975			
Production:	about 3.7500,000			
Engine:	two-cylinder			
Displacement:	29.23 cu. in.	30.45 cu. in.	36.24 cu. in.	
Output (hp/rpm):	13/4,000	18/4,600		18/4,500
Top speed:	56 mph	62 mph		65 mph
From 0 to 60 mph in sec:	not known			
Wheel base:	6 ft			
Length:	9 ft 9 in			
Width:	4 ft 4 in			
Height:	4 ft 5 in			
Weight:	1,146			

Ford Thunderbird

In the first half of 1997, Ford's prospects in Dearborn were very bad. Many models had to be subsidized. Management decided to cancel some models from the range. The first victim was the Aspire, a car smaller than the Ford Escort, built at Kia in Korea. The Probe coupe and the Aerostar, a minivan, followed. Mercury Cougar too was forced to clear the gangway, as well as the Lincoln MkVIII. And at last, theThunderbird disappeared. In 1977, Ford was still able to build 325,153Thunderbirds, but by 1996, it was only able to offer less than 80,000 cars. However, theThunderbird is too well-known to disappear forever and must surely reappear.

In 1957, the dashboard looked a bit more orderly. The air-conditioning was placed, a little bit strangely, under the radio.

The Thunderbird began its existence in September 1954, less than two years after Chevrolet had presented the Corvette. The Corvette had a light plastic body, but with its lazy six-cylinder engine and automatic two-speed transmission, it could hardly be called a sports car. And in 1955, with a selling price of $2,934, the model was surely not inexpensive. The Thunderbird was $10 more expensive, but the client got a two-seater with a V8 engine with a capacity of 4.8 liters and almost 200 hp as well as a sporty, manually geared two-speed transmission.

Since the beginning of their existence, the Ford and Chevrolet brands have been engaged in a tenacious struggle. When Chevrolet presented the Corvette in 1953, Ford hastily began to develop a comparable vehicle and a wooden model of the future Thunderbird was presented on February 20, 1954. Little more than a year after the introduction of the Corvette, this model turned heads at the Detroit automobile show. The wooden

The Thunderbird, here a car from 1955, could be used even in the winter with its plastic hardtop.

In the 1956 Thunderbird, the spare wheel was placed on the rear bumper, unfavorably influencing the road stability.

Thunderbird was presented in all the big American cities. Perhaps due to this fact, sales of the Corvette were very low.

After Ford had made a series of prototypes, the first production Thunderbird rode down from the conveyor belt on September 9, 1954. By the end of 1954, 3,546 cars had been built, more than the total production of Corvettes over the whole year.

The T-bird, as the vehicle was immediately christened, offered more than the Corvette. For a modest surcharge, you could add an automatic, electric windows, power steering, a brake booster and heating. For those who wanted to use the vehicle during the winter, there was a plastic hardtop available. The body was made of steel, but this was more an advantage than a disadvantage in 1955. Not all coachbuilders were yet able to repair a plastic body after a collision.

The two-passenger T-bird did not change much in the following years. In 1956, the model got ventilation windows in the doors and ventilation valves in the front mudguards. The "Continental Look" consisted of a spare wheel mounted behind on the luggage compartment lid. The latter looked very sporty, but also had its disadvantages. The car became 9.9 in longer and the center of gravity shifted further back, so that road stability deteriorated. By the summer of 1956, the client could also have a stronger engine built in, with a capacity of 312 cu. in.. With its two four-barrel carburetors, this V8 engine had an output of 228 hp.

The dashboard of a Thunderbird from 1956. The revolution counter was placed to the far left.

The standard engine of the T'bird from 1957 gave 269 hp/4,800 rpm and could do (on a straight road) a top speed of 130,5 mph.

The Thunderbird from 1955 in a special version with chromed headlight frames, wheel hubcaps with "spokes," and partially covered rear mudguards.

In 1957, the two-seater was built for the last time. The spare wheel got a place in the luggage compartment. For this purpose, the rear side of the vehicle was extended a little bit. The filler inlet cap was now in the right mudguard and there were fashionable small fins above the mudguards. On the front side, there was a new bumper with small overrides. The grill was placed in the nose, a little higher than before. The 312 cu. in. engine was now standard, and the vehicle stood on 14" instead of 15" wheels.
Many clients missed their familiar two-seater, but Ford believed a four-passengerThunderbird would be more lucrative. And they were right, as the production numbers prove.

Technical specifications

Model:	**Ford Thunderbird**	**2-seater**
Years of manufacture:	1955-1957	
Production:	53,166	
Engine:	V8	
Displacement:	292 cu. in.	
Output:	193/4,400 hp-rpm	
Top speed:	118 mph	
From 0 to 60 mph in sec:	not known	
Wheel base:	8 ft 6 in	
Length:	14 ft 7 in	
Width:	5 ft 10 in	
Height:	4 ft 4 in	
Weight:	3,141	

Heinkel Kabinen-Roller

Professor Ernst Heinkel was one of the best-known German aircraft designers of his time. In his factory, more than 10,000 fighters and bombers were built. Together with Werner von Braun, Heinkel had already developed a rocket-powered aircraft in 1935. His first jet fighter, the HE 178, dated back to 1939. His small jet fighter, the Volksjäger, was used by the Hitler Jugend in the fight against Allied bombers in the last months of the war.

Immediately after the war, it was forbidden to build aircraft in Germany. Ernst Heinkel was allowed to enter his only remaining factory in Zuffenhausen near Stuttgart in 1950. Heinkel's other factories were in the Russian zone, or had been razed to the ground by the Allied bombers. Of the 50,000 (forced) laborers, only 200 were left. They spent their time repairing vehicles, but engines were also built there, such as the first three-cylinder two-stroke engines of Saab, the engine of the Tempo three-wheelers and the engines of Veritas sports vehicles. Additionaly, most gearbox housings for Porsche were also cast at Heinkel. In 1953, Heinkel decided to build a new type of motorbike. The engine was built in so that the rider had no problems with oil spray, and a metal shield protected him/her against the wind and rain. The scooter was a success and Heinkel was able to sell more than 100,000.

In 1956, Heinkel began to construct his first car. As the factories in Stuttgart and Karlsruhe concentrated on the production of scooters, he bought an abandoned factory in Speyer. The new car looked very much like the BMW Isetta, but was powered by the one-cylinder engine from the scooter. Thanks to Heinkel's experience as an aircraft designer, his "cars" were much lighter than the BMWs. They weighed only 540 lb and thus they were able to surpass the 53 mph limit, even with their small engines. Two models were made, the Kabine 175 and 200, the numbers referring to the displacement in cubic centimeters. These four-cycle engines gave 9.3 and 10 hp/5,500 rpm, respectively. The engine made an infernal noise at full throttle and was therefore placed in the rear of the vehicl. Consequently the exhaust pipe had to be very short. The four-speed gearbox was equipped

The three-wheelers were mostly exported. Germans preferred the four-wheel version.

Unlike the BMW Isetta, the steering column of the Heinkel was fixed. When getting in, the driver had to squeeze himself past the steering wheel.

with a reverse gear. Gears were shifted with a lever placed on the left side of the driver. The suspension was independent: in front with a rubber ring and behind with springs. The foot brake was hydraulic, but was only provided for the front wheels. The mechanical hand brake worked on all the wheels.

The car could also be delivered with four wheels. But in this case, the rear wheels were located so near to each other that, according to the law, they were considered as one wheel. Unlike the BMW Isetta, in which the steering column hinged outward with the door, the steering wheel of the Heinkel was mounted firmly to the floor of the vehicle. This did not make getting in and out any easier. BMW had had its system patented, and was not going to allow Heinkel to profit from it. In the rear of the Heinkel, there was a bench for two small children, but they had to climb over the front seat backrest backwards. This acrobatic exercise was also necessary, by the way, when you needed to measure the oil level in the engine. The dip-stick was accessible solely through a hole under the rear window. In the four-wheeler version, no spare wheel was included. When a front tire went flat, one of the rear wheels could be screwed off, and the journey continued on three wheels.

When German prosperity began to rise thanks to the Wirtschaftswunder, the demand for dwarf cars diminished strongly. Now there was enough money for a "real" car. Although Heinkel had plans ready for a big model, he

In the frontal view the car appears massive, but the Heinkel was, in fact, a dwarf. It stood on a wheel-base of 5 ft 9 in and had a length of 8 ft 4 in.

With a Heinkel, drivers nearly always drove at full throttle. It could reach a speed of 53 mph.

decided to stop the production of cars. His interest was concentrated, as before, on aircraft. In the 1950s, he built, among other things, the French Fouga-Magister, a two-engine jet-trainer.

Ernst Heinkel died on January 30, 1958, at the age of seventy-one. His death signaled the end of production for his Kabinen-Rollers. The components and tools were sold to the English company Trojan, which brought the three-wheelers to the market under the name Trojan 200 until 1966.

Technical specifications

Model:	**Heinkel Kabinen-Roller 175**	**200**
Years of manufacture:	1956-1958	1956-1958
Production:	6,438	5,537
Engine:	one-cylinder	one-cylinder
Displacement:	10.6 cu. in.	12.44 cu. in.
Output (hp/rpm):	9.3/5,500	10/5,500
Top speed:	53 mph	53 mph
From 0 to 60 mph in sec:	not known	not known
Wheel base:	5 ft 9 in	5 ft 9 in
Length:	8 ft 4 in	8 ft 4 in
Width:	4 ft 6 in	4 ft 6 in
Height:	4 ft 4 in	4 ft 4 in
Weight:	540 lb	540 lb

Honda NSX

In March 1989, the prototype of the Honda NSX was presented at the Chicago Automobile Show. Two years later, the model already stood in the showroom. Honda was especially famous for its passenger cars. And although the Formula One vehicles won important races with Honda engines, the factory delivered no sports vehicles. In the 1960s, they tried

The cockpit of the vehicle was placed very far in the front, which enhanced stability against side winds.

once unsuccessfully with the Honda S 600 and S 800. Admittedly, the Honda CRX was also a fast vehicle, but it could never be a match for a Ferrari, Porsche or Lamborghini. With the NSX, Honda wanted to produce a true sports car.
Honda approached the matter professionally and invested 125 million guilders ($70 million) in a new factory in Tochigi, Japan. 25 cars per day were to be assembled there. The 200 employees for the new production line were selected very carefully. Each employee was supposed to have at least ten years of professional experience.
The NSX was not a simple vehicle. In the design, the car evidently profited from the Formula One experience. But comfort was not forgotten. The engine was placed askew in front of the rear axle and the gas tank (one of the few steel parts) was mounted between the engine and the seats. Thanks to this, the car had a nearly ideal weight distribution, with 42% of the weight on the front and 58% on the rear wheels. The self-supporting aluminum body had

In the front "luggage compartment," there was no space for luggage. A small electric compressor was part of the standard equipment by which the reserve wheel could be pumped up.

In model year 1998, the NSX got a small facelift and a larger 3.2-liter engine.

an excellent aerodynamic shape. The engine had two upper camshafts per cylinder row, servicing four valves per cylinder. The engine block and the cylinder heads were made of aluminum and the connecting rods, just as in a Formula One engine, were made of titanium. The client could choose a manually geared five-box or an electrically controlled four-speed automatic. The four ventilated disc brakes were large enough for a Formula One vehicle. In order to reduce weight, the wheel suspensions were cast of alloy.

The 3.0 liter V6 gave more than 270 hp, even without a turbo or a compressor.

The dashboard of the 3.2 liter NSX. The red strip begins at 8,000 rpm and the odometer reaches 174 mph.

The NSX has been constantly perfected over the years. In November 1992, a special racing version arrived, the NSX-R, the engine of which gave about 410 hp at 8,500 rpm. In 1995, a version with a T-roof was presented, and in January 1997, the NSX could also be ordered with a 3.2 liter engine with 294 hp. This vehicle needed only 6 seconds to accelerate from 0 to 60 mph and attained a top speed of more than 171 mph.

Technical specifications

Model:	**Honda NSX**
Years of manufacture:	1990 – present
Production:	not known
Engine:	V6
Displacement:	181.7 cu. in.
Output:	273/7,300 hp/rpm
Top speed:	168 mph
From 0 to 30 mph:	6.2 sec
Wheel base:	8 ft 4 in
Length:	16 ft 6 in
Width:	5 ft 11 in
Height:	3 ft 10 in
Weight:	3,020 lb

Hudson Commodore

After the war, Hudson was one of the first factories in Detroit to resume production of passenger cars. On February 5, 1942, the last passenger car left the conveyor belt. The first post-war car already stood at the dealers on October 1, 1945. These cars were of the 1942 model and got only a small facelift after the war. But there was so much demand for new cars that no one minded and there was no big hurry to design completely new models. However, designers kept working behind the scenes. The design department at Hudson was managed by Frank Spring. Under his lead,

The new Hudson achieved a yearly production of 142,454 cars. But in 1947, only 100,393 cars could be sold.

a completely new model was born which would make history as a Step-Down Design. By then, it was usual that the body was placed above, on the chassis. Also, with a car with a self-supporting body, the body was placed on the braces in the floor. Spring chose another solution and drew the floor of the vehicle under the chassis beam. The consequence was that the whole car was now reclining.

The difference between a Hudson and a car of another brand was striking. The height of the new Hudson was only 5 ft 2 in. A Chevrolet was 4.7 in higher, and a Ford no less than 8.6 in. Though the differences in height seem to be small, they are clearly visible when the cars stand parked side by side.

The Hudson was a relatively safe vehicle. The self-supporting body was reinforced with beams in the longitudinal direction of the car. These beams run up to the rear part of the vehicle and the tread width of the rear axle was about 3 in narrower than that of the front wheels. Since the center of gravity of the vehicle was much lower than usual, the Hudson had excellent road stability. The new Hudson was presented to the public in the MasonicTemple in Detroit in December 1947, and accepted with much enthusiasm. Car journalists also praised the new design.

All Hudsons had the same wheel-base of 12 ft. They were 20.5 ft long and extraordinarily broad (6.43 in), so that the factory could advertise that the front seat of the car was broader than the height. The Hudsons had a super-modern appearance, but nevertheless, under the engine hood there was still an antiquated side-valve engine. The six-cylinder 260.3 cu. in. and the eight-cylinder 254.2 cu. in. engines had an impressive output. There was no other American engine which was able to give so many hps with such a small displacement except the small Crosley engine with the upper camshaft. Even the six-cylinder engine was stronger than that of the competitors. Chrysler, Packard, Cadillac and theV12 of Lincoln had, of course, a bigger displacement, but in 1948, the six-cylinder engine of the Hudson was the strongest engine built in Detroit.

Despite their light bodies, the vehicles were heavy. A sedan with an eight-cylinder engine weighed 3,682 lb and the cabriolet version even 265 lb more, which explains why the top speed was only about 87 mph. Fuel consumption was high, at about 15 mpg.

The Commodore was available with three different bodies in 1948.The cheapest was the two-door Club Coupe, followed by the four-door sedan, and finally there was the two-door cabriolet with an eight-cylinder engine for $3,138 in the catalogue. This cabriolet was relatively expensive, so only 48 six and 65 eight-cylinder cabriolets were sold in 1948.

Technical specifications

Model:	Hudson Commodore Six	Eight
Year of manufacture:	1948	
Production:	27,159	35,315
Engine:	six-cylinder line engine	eight-cylinder in-line engine
Displacement:	260.3 cu. in.	254.2 cu. in.
Output (hp/rpm):	122/4,000	130/4,200
Top speed:	84 mph	87 mph
From 0 to 60 mph in sec:	not known	not known
Wheel base:	12 ft	12 ft
Length:	20 ft 6 in	20 ft 6 in
Width:	4 ft 5 in	4 ft 5 in
Height:	5 ft 1 in	5 ft 1 in
Weight:	3,637 lb	3,682 lb

Innocenti Turbo De Tomaso

The Innocenti Turbo de Tomaso was a dangerously fast car. The model was presented at the Torino motor show in 1974. The mechanical parts originated from the Mini of British Leyland. The chassis was designed by Bertone, the famous Italian designer. In 1976, Alejandro de Tomaso took over the factory from Innocenti. The 49-hp engine was replaced by a model with 74 hp.

Innocenti Turbo de Tomaso was dangerously fast. It had a small acceleration and front-wheel span, which could cause surprises on a smooth road.

The rear lid served as the third door. The luggage compartment had a capacity of 280 liters. When the back bench was tilted down, you were disposed of 900 liters.

The car sold well, but the transport of spare parts from England tended to stagnate due to frequent strikes. De Tomaso decided to switch over to the three-cylinder engine from Daihatsu. In 1982, the factory presented the Innocenti 3 Cilindri. The 60.5 cu. in. engine gave 52 hp, enough for a top speed of 145 km/hour. A year later, a very special version of the small Innocenti was presented in Torino. This car was equipped with a turbo engine, which enhanced the output to more than 70 hp. Since the small car performed like a full-blooded racing car, the expression "a wolf in sheep's clothing" was very appropriate indeed. The engine had an upper camshaft in an aluminum cylinder-head, the compression ratio was 9.1:1 and a double Asian carburetor sucked in the proper air-gas mixture. The small three-cylinder engine ran like clockwork, and the sound of it at high revolutions recalled the three-cylinder DKW engine enhanced by Henk van Zalinge. The vehicle stood on aluminum wheels with 160/65 R 315 tires. With a stabilizer, very good road stability was ensured. Appropriately, there was no shortage of comfort in the four-seater. The glass of the windows was opaque and the doors were electrically controlled. The outside mirrors were adjustable from the inside and halogen lamps burned in the headlights.

In 1990, Fiat took over the factory from de Tomaso, and the fun ended. New models arrived, with Fiat engines, of course.

The Japanese engine was situated askew under the engine hood, and drew the front wheels.

Technical specifications

Model:	**Innocenti Turbo De Tomaso**
Years of manufacture:	1983-1990
Production:	not known
Engine:	three-cylinder
Displacement:	60.5 cu. in.
Output:	72/6,200 hp/rpm
Top speed:	106 mph
From 0 to 60 mph:	18.8 sec
Wheel base:	6 ft 8 in
Length:	10 ft 4 in
Width:	5 ft
Height:	4 ft 5 in
Weight:	1,543 lb

Jaguar Mk V

When the Germans invaded Poland in 1939, it was clear that a world war was inevitable. Before that time, a special division of S.S. Cars Ltd. (S.S. indicates Swallow Sidecars) had already been occupied with the production of aircraft components. Due to the threat of war, the production of passenger cars completely ceased and the conveyor belts were adapted for the assemblage of trailers, which left the belt in all dimensions, equipped for loads from 550 to 13,228 lb. Additionally, a type of Jeep was developed which could be dropped from an airplane using a parachute. Nevertheless, it remained highly experimental since the quality of the genuine American Jeep proved unbeatable.

Impressive: the dashboard of a Mk V. Note the revolution counter, which rotates counterclockwise. The cigarette box was handy perhaps, but the ashtray was a bit too small.

Coventry was one of the most heavily bombed cities in England and the factories of S.S. Cars Ltd. were not spared. By November 1940, the six factory halls had been turned to ashes. Very expensive equipment was destroyed. In March 1945, William Lyons decided, for obvious reasons, to remove the name 'S.S.' from his stationery. The enterprise was called Jaguar Cars Ltd. after a model built before the war. During the war, Lyons bought the machines with which the Standard Motor Company had made engines for S.S. Cars Ltd., thus ensuring the independence of the new enterprise after the war.

On May 8, 1945, Germany surrendered. By July, Jaguar Cars began to re-adjust the conveyor belts for the production of the four-door passenger vehicle. During the war, William Munger Heynes, the former head designer for Humber, and his collaborators were drawing new models. A beautiful engine with two upper camshafts had also been developed. But since the demand for new vehicles was enormous and the pre-war machines for the pressing of bodies had survived the war, the models from 1940 were leaving the conveyor-belt first. Lyons would have preferred to present his new car, but the Pressed Steel Company, which produced the bodies, lacked the templates and the tools. Jaguar could

Unlike the previous models, which could also be delivered with a 1.5 liter four-cylinder engine, the Mk V was equipped with a six-cylinder engine.

The first post-war cars, here a 3.5 liter from 1947, could be externally distinguished from the pre-war models only by their emblems.

have built the new engine into the old body, of course, but Lyons considered it wasteful. He wanted to wait until he could offer a completely new car to the market.

The post-war models were identical to those produced before the war. Six-cylinder engines were produced in their own factory now, but the four-line engines were ordered at Standard. The Standard enterprise had been taken over by Triumph in the meantime. The Jaguar engine was specially developed for the new sports car, the Triumph 1800. The pre-war body was adapted in some aspects. The tiltable tables disappeared from the front seat backrests. Technical novelties differed too, and along with other things, a new, though still mechanical, brake system emerged.

Almost all of the production was exported. England needed foreign exchange badly in order to pay back its debts to America, and the government thus gave raw materials only to factories which were able to export. However, the average European motorist, with the exception of those in Switzerland, Sweden and Belgium, had no money for

With the Mk VII, Jaguar finally presented the first real post-war model. The car had a modern body and a super-engine, which would be used for many years to come.

a Jaguar. The Belgian importer of Jaguar, Madame Bourgeois, had already ordered five four-door Jaguars by March 1946. The cars were destined for Belgian ambassadors.

At the London Motor Show of 1948, the new cars of model year 1949 were presented. The big hit was the XK120 sports car, standing on a shortened chassis of the MkV. Because of this model, the "genuine" MkVs were nearly overlooked. The new range consisted of a limousine and a cabriolet designed for export. In the sports car, the new six-cylinder engine with two upper camshafts was built in. But the new bodies for the passenger vehicles could not be produced yet. So Lyons equipped the MkV with the old six-cylinder valve-in-head engines again. There were two versions, with 2.5 or 3.5 liter displacements, giving 104 and 126 hp, respectively. A technical novelty was the completely new chassis of the MkV, with independent front wheel suspension with torsion bars. Externally, the MkV was nearly identical to its predecessor. The model could be recognized by its built-in headlights, which replaced the independent and imposing, but not very functional, Lucas P 100 lamps. Also, the bumpers were new, and possibly even more robust than before.

The Mk V cabriolet is a very special car. Only 29 with a small engine were sold. The cabriolet with the large six-cylinder engine changed owners 972 times.

More and more often, the Jaguar was called the "Bentley for the ordinary man and woman" with good reason because a Bentley MkVI cost £2,595 in its cheapest version in 1948, whereas a Jaguar MkV with the big 3.5 liter engine was available for only £988.

The MkV was not granted a long life. Two years after its introduction, it was removed from production as the last Jaguar having an engine without upper camshafts, and the long awaited MkVII could finally be presented. With its completely new body and the XK engine, the period of footsteps and independent mudguards was definitively ended for Jaguar. An MkVI never existed, as there was already a Bentley with this type of designation. When Bentley wanted to replace the MkVI with a new model, this model could not use the familiar Jaguar model name MkVII. The new offspring was thus christened the Bentley R-Type.

Technical specifications

Model:	**Jaguar Mk V 2.5 Litre**	**3.5 Litre**
Manufacture years:	1948-1950	1949-1951
Production:	1,690	8,803
Engine:	six-cylinder	six-cylinder
Displacement:	162.5 cu. in.	212.7 cu. in.
Output (hp/rpm):	104/4,600	126/4,250
Top speed:	90 mph	96 mph
From 0 to 60 mph in sec:	not known	14.9
Wheel base:	10 ft	10 ft
Length:	15 ft 6 in	15 ft 6 in
Width:	5 ft 8 in	5 ft 8 in
Height:	5 ft 3 in	5 ft 3 in
Weight:	3,582 lb	3,582 lb

Jaguar XK 120, 140 and 150

During World War II, S.S. Cars Ltd. was already making plans for a post-war car. The Jaguar XK 120 would become one of the most beautiful sports cars in automobile history. The project was naturally led by William Lyons, who drew the body. William M. Heynes and Claude W. Baily designed the engine, Walter Hassan was responsible for the independent front-wheel suspension and Bob Knight took care of the chassis. The engine, which was improved by Harry Weslake, formed the heart of the new vehicle. The design would be used until the arrival of the V8 in 1997. The XK 120, with its six-cylinder engine, was presented at the London Motor Show in 1948. The car stood on the chassis of an Mk V shortened by 18 in for this purpose. The entire

The XK 120 was the fastest production sports car of its time.

body was hammered from an aluminum plate. Lyons christened the vehicle XK 120, as he presupposed that the two-seater would reach a speed of 120 mph.

In 1948, the competitors were only able to offer very out-of-date-looking sports cars. The Jaguar was thus not only ultra-modern but with its price of less than $1,000 it was also quite inexpensive. Lyons expected to reach sales of about 200 of the XK 120 in total, but this number had already been achieved after two days.

It was, of course, impossible to make so many bodies by hand and Pressed Steel in Oxford got the order to produce the series of steel bodies. By the end of 1949, the first sixty cars had been shipped to America and by the end of April 1950, the last of the 240 vehicles with aluminum bodies left the factory. In the meantime, the question arose as to whether the XK 120 would indeed be able to attain the promised top speed of 120 mph. To prove this, the factory sent a vehicle to Belgium in order to furnish evidence on a section of freeway at Ostende. The car was driven by the racing driver Ron Sutton. In the first drive, the vehicle was able to attain a speed of 126 mph. When the cloth top and the side windows were removed, the car was even able to reach a top speed of 132 mph. Everybody at Jaguar could be content.

Sir William Lyons, the founder of the Swallow Sidecars, later Jaguar Ltd., had drawn the body of the XK 120.

The XK 140 differed externally from its predecessor in its broader bumpers and a different grill.

In March 1951, a coupe version designed specially for the export market was presented. In order to prove that such a vehicle was reliable and fast, Stirling Moss went driving with three assistants for 7 days and nights on the circuit of Montlhéry. They covered 17,000 miles in total, with an average speed of 99.5 mph. In April 1953, a third version of the XK 120 was marketed, the Drophead coupe. With its movable windows in the doors, and a "genuine" cloth top, this model provided more comfort to its driver than the roadster.

In October 1954, the last XK 120 left the conveyor belt, to be succeeded by the XK 140 which, as the number indicates, was 20 miles per hour faster. The cars bore an unmistakable resemblance to each other except the

A 3.8-liter XK 150 S roadster. Only 36 were built of the rare model.

As the XK 140 was a little longer than the XK 120, the passengers on the rear bench had some more space.

bumpers of the XK 140 were more massive, as the Americans found those of the 120 too fragile. But the steering was also improved, and as the engine was mounted 3 in forward, the model had better weight distribution than its predecessor. The XK 140 could also be ordered with an electrical overdrive. For the (American) driver, an automatic gearbox was added to the options in 1958. In the closed model of the XK 140, the rear passengers had some more space, so that adults could also ride.

Some special models were produced for the American market. There was, for instance, an XK 140 C with the cylinder head of a C-type racecar and an XK 140 M with two exhausts, spoke wheels and fog lamps. And a car with all

The grill of the XK 140 had fewer staves than that of the XK 120.

The interior of the 120. Note the revolution counter (on the left), the pointer of which ran counterclockwise.

these accessories was called the XK 140 MC. In these cases, the chassis number always ended with an S (which meant Special Equipment).

In March 1958, nearly ten years after the fastest production sports car in the world was first presented, the last model of this type appeared, the XK 150. The car didn't look as aggressive as its predecessors, but was much faster. The windshield was made of one piece of glass, and the car seemed to be broader and larger. But the dimensions of the

The XK 150 S-engine with three S.U.-carburetors. The output was 265 hp/5,500 rpm.

XK 150 were the same as those of its predecessor, the XK 120. There were not many mechanical changes either. The vehicle was powered by the 3.4 liter engine from the XK 140. Now, there was even an S model for export to America, with three S.U. carburetors – instead of two. In fact, only the brake system was new. The XK 150 was the first serial car to have four Dunlop disc brakes. This system had been tested in the C-type racecar. As the race drivers could brake later than their rivals, an XK 150 won the 24-hour race of Le Mans.

In October 1959, the XK 150 could also be delivered with a 3.8 liter six-cylinder engine. The promised top speed of 143 mph was not unrealistic. At that time, the Jaguar was not the fastest sports car in the world anymore, but indeed it was one of the cheapest in its class.

Regarding the XK 120, it has been said that such a car could have cost twice as much without problem. With the XK 150, it was much the same. Its successor, the Jaguar E-type (in America, it was called the XK-E) heralded a completely new period for the Jaguar.

Technical specifications

Model:	**Jaguar XK 120**	**XK 140**	**XK 150**
Years of manufacture:	1948-1954	1954-1957	1957-1961
Production:	12,055	9,051	9,398
Engine:	six-cylinder	six-cylinder	six-cylinder
Displacement:	208.8 cu. in.	208.8 cu. in.	208.8/230.7 cu. in.
Output (hp/rpm):	160/5,000	190/5,500	190/265
Top speed:	124 mph	127 mph	130/143 mph
Wheel base:	8 ft 6 in	8 ft 6 in	8 ft 6 in
Length:	14 ft 5 in	14 ft 8 in	14 ft 9 in
Width:	5 ft 2 in	5 ft 4 in	5 ft 4 in
Height:	4 ft 4 in	4 ft 5 in	4 ft 6 in
Weight:	2,469 lb	2,679 lb	2,998 lb

Kleinschnittger

The Kleinschnittger certainly looked very sporty.

Immediately after the war, the transport problem in Germany was bigger than ever. Cars were only sold with a special license and you had to be a country physician to be considered eligible. Motorbikes were a little more accessible, but this means of transport was much less in demand. The engineer Paul Kleinschnittger looked for and found the solution in a sort of "covered motorbike," the prototype of which he built for himself in 1947. It was a minicar powered by a small 6 cu. in. DKW RT motorbike engine and provided enough space for two people.

When the new car attracted a lot of interest, plans were immediately made to produce the vehicle in a series. In 1949, Kleinschnittger succeeded in attracting a businessman from Hamburg to finance his project. With his investment of 20,000 DM, the production could start. The new car – the model was baptized the F 125 – was powered by a 7.5 cu. in. Ilo engine with 5.5 hp which, unlike the prototype, was equipped with front-wheel drive. The gearbox was also taken from a motorbike, and had three forward gears and no reverse, but no substantial difficulty was caused since the F 125 weighed only 286.5 lb and could be pushed backwards very easily. The vehicle looked outwardly sporty, with a long engine hood and a tiny engine placed at the very end of the front, ahead of the axle.

The Kleinschnittger had no doors. After all, the car was not designed for old ladies! But as the bottom of the vehicle lay close to the ground, you could get in very easily. The size of the luggage compartment was limited, surely because most owners had an additional gas tank mounted behind the seats. Normally, the Kleinschnittger was equipped with a tank containing only 5 liters.

A cap and tie were indispensable accessories, as the roof and side windows were missing.

Even from the rear view, an elegant car.

In total, about 2,000 Kleinschnittgers were sold. Kleinschnittger also wanted to build bigger cars. In 1954, he built his first prototype, with a 15.3 cu. in. two-cylinder engine. The car was planned in three variations: as a four-passenger family car, a 2+2-coupe and a two-passenger sports cabriolet. Production was planned to start by the beginning of 1957. The components for the new F 250 were ready, but the financiers backed out. The one hundred employees were fired and Kleinschnittger went bankrupt.

Technical specifications

Model:	**Kleinschnittger F 125**
Years of manufacture:	1950-1957
Production:	2,980
Engine:	one-cylinder
Displacement:	7.5 cu. in.
Output:	4.5/5,000 hp/rpm
Top speed:	43.5 mph
From 0 to 60 mph in sec:	not known
Wheel base:	5 ft 6 in
Length:	9 ft 6 in
Width:	3 ft 11 in
Height:	4 ft
Weight:	330.5 lb

Lagonda 2.6 Liter

The engine was a jewel. The two overhead camshafts (nothing unusual nowadays) were to be found only in race and sports cars.

In 1897, thirty-eight year old Wilbur Gun moved from Springfield, Ohio to England. He had worked in America as a mechanic on sewing machines for Singer. He sang opera in his free time. Some say that Gun went to England for singing lessons, but he became better known for his automobiles. He built his first motorbike in 1900. This was followed by motorized, three-wheeled vehicles and finally by real cars, which were placed on the market as Lagondas, named after the river that flows through Springfield. Lagonda built mainly fast sports and racecars. Four cars participated in the 24-hour race of Le Mans in 1935. Johnny Hindmarsh and Louis Fontes won at Le Mans with their 4.5 liter Lagonda. Two cars passed the finish line in third and fourth place in 1939.

W.O. Bentley became the technical director at Lagonda in 1939. He deserves great credit for his beautiful engines. Bentley designed a V12 and six-cylinder engine with overhead camshafts, which would still be used in the fifties for Lagondas and Aston Martins. The engine was used in the 2.5 liter Lagonda-Bentley, announced in September 1945. However, the model did not get this name because Rolls-Royce had taken over the Bentley factory in 1931, and did not consent. At Lagonda, they tried to get their way through a lawsuit. They invested £10,000, but lost. Advertisements announced the car therefore like this: "The new 2.5-liter Lagonda, designed under the supervision of W.O. Bentley."

Technically, the new Lagonda was as good as the pre-war vehicles. Under the hood, there was the 157.4 cu. in. six-cylinder engine with an aluminum engine block, a light metal cylinder head and two overhead camshafts. The undercarriage was made of 6.3 in-thick steel beams, which formed a cross in the middle of the car. The brakes were placed directly beside the differential, not to the rear wheels, in order to lessen the unsprung weight of the wheels. The front as well as the rear wheels had independent suspension, a novelty for the English automobile industry.

The 2.5 liter engine was not a successor of a pre-war model. Nevertheless, the vehicle has a conservative appearance.

The 2.5 liter Drophead Coupe was a spacious car. Two people in the front seat and three in the rear caused no problems whatsoever, and everyone sat on leather seats.

The demand for the Lagonda was very great. However, the amount of steel appointed by the government was sorrowfully little. Lagonda was not able to build enough vehicles to meet the demand, nor enough to survive. The future was looking very grim and the directors of Lagonda could not say no when David Brown, the English "king of the tractors," made an offer in 1947. Brown became the owner of the drawings, the components and three existing prototypes. When Brown also acquired Aston Martin, Aston Martin Lagonda Ltd. became a fact. The company found a new residence in Feltham, but W.O. Bentley did not move along with the company. The sale of Lagonda was a reason for him to retire. In 1948, two prototypes drove several thousand miles through all of Europe. David Brown wanted to be convinced of the quality before he produced the model. The engine, the undercarriage and the gearbox were manufactured in Brown's factory near Leeds. Then the parts were transported to Feltham for final assembly. The first post-war

The rubber knobs in the bumpers could be removed for the placement of the jack.

Notice the little details: the Lagonda had a gas tank of 86 liters, with two beautiful fuel lids, one on the left and one on the right.

The gear handle at the steering wheel was modern directly after the war, but was only offering an advantage if a continuous seat was installed. The Lagonda, however, had two separate seats in the front.

Lagondas could be admired at the Earls Court Motor Show in London in the spring of 1949. The Lagonda was continuously improved upon. When the undercarriage was widened by 4 in in 1952, people talked of it as the Mk2. This model had far more space for passengers in the rear seat.

The English trade magazine,The Autocar, tested a Lagonda Drophead Coupe in February 1951. The test drivers of this cabriolet were impressed. The vehicle accelerated in 18.8 seconds from 0 to 60 mph and reached a top speed of 84 mph. Lagonda had equipped the prototypes with semi-automatic Cotal gearboxes, but Brown preferred the boxes of his own make. The test drivers from *The Autocar* received this gearbox enthusiastically. The box functioned outstandingly, even when switching to a lower gear. Actually, nothing less could be expected, because the automobile cost £1,970 in England, with £547 for the sales tax. One was able to buy a small cottage for this amount of money.

Technical specifications

Model:	**Lagonda 2.6 Litre**
Years of manufacture:	1947-1953
Production:	550
Engine:	six-cylinder
Displacement:	157.4 cu. in.
Output:	105/5,000 hp/rpm
Top speed:	90 mph
From 0 to 60 mph:	18.8 sec
Wheel base:	9 ft 5 in
Length:	15 ft 8 in
Width:	5 ft 5 in
Height:	5 ft 4 in
Weight:	3,247 lb

Lamborghini Espada

Ferruccio Lamborghini.

Is Lamborghini a passenger automobile? No, certainly not. Or is it? Like Enzo Ferrari and the Maserati brothers, Ferruccio Lamborghini also built a family car, a full-size four-seater, or the Espada, which like almost all the vehicles made by Lamborghini, came to life on the drawing board of Bertone. The Italian designer also had the privilege of building the bodywork of the entire automobile, except for the engine, the gearbox and the front and rear axle. The company in Thuringia manufactured and painted the bodywork, installed the interior, including the chairs and floor mats, assembled the electric wiring as well as the headlights as well as rear lights.

Bertone had already wanted to build a four-person car for Lamborghini earlier. The company had even made a prototype, drawn by Marcello Gandini, which was very successful at different automobile exhibitions under the name Marzal. When the car celebrated its world premiere in March 1966 at the Exhibition of Geneva, it was equipped with a six-cylinder engine (a bisected V12 Miura engine) which was placed sideways in the rear. There was still enough space for four adults. The Marzal had four enormous gull-wing doors, hinged from the roof, according to the same principle that was applied by Mercedes in its 300 SL. Most prototypes are not able to operate, but the Marzal was an exception to this rule. Prince Rainier and Princess Grace of Monaco even opened the Grand Prix of Monaco in 1967 with this car.

Ferruccio Lamborghini found the Marzal much too conspicuous. Nevertheless, he decided to take the car into production after Bertone had showed him the altered drawings. The new four-person vehicle became a hybrid of the Marzal and the Jaguar Pirana, which Bertone had built as a prototype in 1967. The so-called Espada was driven by

The Marzal was too extreme even for Ferruccio Lamborghini.

An open drawing of the Espada of the first series.

the well-known 4.0 literV12 engine placed in front. The model turned out to be a lucrative business, as was indicated by the amount of orders which came in after the model had been introduced for the first time at the Geneva Salon in 1968. At that moment, the Espada was the fastest four-seater in the world. But the vehicle had a great defect: because of the great weight on the front wheels, it was very difficult to steer at low speeds. Power steering seemed to be a necessity, and indeed, it was offered shortly after.

Pietro Frua tried to sell this four-door model to Lamborghini. It remained a prototype.

This vehicle stood in 1972 at the Geneva exhibition: an Espada from the second series.

The Espadas of the third generation were not only equipped with a steering servo as part of the standrd equipment, but also with air-conditioning. The motor was boosted slightly in 1969, which resulted in a 25 horsepower increase. The performance was quite remarkable. The aluminum engine, with its four overhead camshafts and six double Weber carburetors, transferred approximately 350 horsepower to the rear axle.

The Espada remained in production until 1978. Carrozzeria Frua tried the same thing later with another four-door version, but this.was not a successful project. The Lamborghini of Frua was presented inThuringia, but it always remained a prototype.

Technical specifications

Model:	**Lamborghini Espada**
Years of manufacture:	1968-1978
Production:	1,217
Engine:	V12
Displacement:	239.8 cu. in.
Output:	350/7,500 hp/rpm
Top speed:	155 mph
From 0 to 60 mph:	6.9 sec
Wheel base:	8 ft 8 in
Length:	15 ft 6 in
Width:	6 ft 1 in
Height:	3 ft 11 in
Weight:	3,582 lb

Lamborghini Miura
Spider

There were a lot of novelties and world premieres at the Brussels Autosalon in 1968. Alfa Romeo presented the new 1750 series, BMW arrived with the new 2002, and Ford introduced its Escort. However, the most important news this time came from Carrozzeria Bertone. They brought a Miura cabriolet! The undercarriage, sent by Ferruccio Lamborghini

The Spider, as presented by Bertone in Brussels.

especially for the automobile exhibition, had many holes in order to lower the weight. The V12 engine was positioned sideways in front of the rear axle. Without Lamborghini´s knowledge, his technicians Gianpaolo Dallara, Paolo Stanzani and Bob Wallace built the rolling chassis in their free time. Was it a race car? Lamborghini claimed it was not. He himself had driven a boosted Fiat 500 Topolino in de Mille Miglia, but he had refused to build any more race vehicles since then. So did he change his mind? No, because when the chassis stood at the show in Geneva a few months later in March 1966, it seemed to be designed as an "ordinary" passenger automobile. Marcello Gandini, the chief designer of Bertone, designed the bodywork for the two-seater. The design had a certain surreal touch. It looked like a vehicle

All the shiny parts were made of ZN-75, a new alloy from ILZRO.

The front window was placed at a smaller angle than in the Miura coupe.

which would be driven by little green creatures from Mars. Lamborghini managed to overshadow Ferrari and Maserati in Geneva. Orders arrived in large numbers.

Gandini had designed an open model of his Miura for the Brussels exhibition. Bertone hoped to produce the vehicle in a series, but when Ferruccio Lamborghini heard about the cost, he lost interest. The Miura Spider went to Belgium, therefore, as a dream car and abstract concept. Unlike most of the other dream cars, the Spider was a complete prototype. Bertone had adjusted the bodywork of the Miura, strengthened the roll bar and installed it three centimeters lower than in the coupe. The front window was designed to be more flat than in the closed version, in order to reduce turbulence in the car. The switches, located on the roof in the model, were now positioned in the console between the front seats. The vehicle had a light-blue metallic color and the interior was finished with white leather. The trade magazines and the visitors agreed on one thing: the Miura Spider was the most beautiful car at the Brussels exhibition. The prototype was already sold within a few minutes!

The American company International Lead Zinc Research Organization (ILZRO) developed a zinc and lead alloy that they were eager to sell to the automobile industry. Although the board of ILZRO operated from New York, they had offices and laboratories in several European countries. The best way to present the material would obviously be to built an unusual automobile. Schrade Radtke, the President of ILZRO, contacted the designer John Foster of Ford in Detroit.

Additionally, the bumpers, the license plates, the casing for the rear lights and the grill were made of zinc.

In this picture as well, everything is made of ZN-75. In the doors and under the floor mats, they used lead to ensure newer and better sound insulation.

Foster would have liked to try using a Mustang as a guinea pig, but the big bosses forbade the experiment. In the beginning of 1968, Radtke heard about Bertone's Spider. He went to the exhibition in Brussels and bought the prototype. There was, however, one condition: Bertone had to completely disassemble the car and rebuild it with the new material of ILZRO. When the exhibition in Brussels was over, an employee of ILZRO, Ken Altdorfer, was transferred to Thuringia to supervise the activities. They performed their work thoroughly. The Spider was taken apart down to the last bolt. The different branches of ILZRO manufactured the different parts again. Naturally, the project included hundreds of components: for instance, the six carburetors with "velocity stags" and an induction manifold, as well as a complete exhaust system. Even the V12 engine received a plate of zinc on the outside and the new ZN-75 was used to produce a new gear cover, an oil sump, water tubes, a cylinder-head cover and the casing for the water and oil pump. But also the steering wheel, the ashtray and the gear lever were to be made of zinc. All the instruments were taken apart

A beautiful automobile from whichever angle you look at it.

A photo from the time, as evidence that Schrade Radtke still made (private) use of the vehicle. The license plate number was Connecticut LB 3100.

and the visible parts were reproduced. Finally, they also duplicated the bumpers, the grill, the ornamental edges, the wheel nuts, the window frames, the rings of the headlights and the edges around the license plate.

However, ILZRO had more on the agenda than the zinc alloy. There was also the lead alloy. Altdorfer insulated the doors and the floor with it to show the industry that lead could also be used for other purposes than batteries. They also produced the brake and gasoline pipes of the new material. After the ZN-75, as it was now being called, was painted over with a special color of metallic golden green on a black base, it was sent by airplane to Detroit, where it was meant to be presented to a number of invited people. The ordinary public saw the car for the first time in 1970 at the Montreal Motor Show. Just as in Brussels, the vehicle was chosen as the most beautiful automobile of the show. The prototype traveled from Canada to England, Japan and Australia, where automobile manufacturers were given the opportunity to take a close look at the car and the new material. After several years, the ZN-75 had fulfilled its duty as an advertisement car. The Lamborghini was put up for auction in America. Schrade Radtke, still president of ILZRO, bought the car for daily usage. It is not known how much Radtke paid for the car. We do know that the calculations of Bertone far exceeded the amount of $200,000. At present, the vehicle is standing in the Boston Museum of Transport.

Technical specifications

Model:	**Lamborghini Miura Spider/ZN-75**
Year of manufacture:	1968
Production:	1
Engine:	V12
Displacement:	239.8 cu. in.
Output:	380/7,350 hp/rpm
Top speed:	174 mph
From 0 to 60 mph in sec:	not known
Wheel base:	8 ft 2 in
Length:	14 ft 4 in
Width:	5 ft 9 in
Height:	not known
Weight:	not known

Lamborghini Murciélago

In the late afternoon of October 5, 1879, after a fiercely fought contest in the arena of Cordoba, a bull named Murciélago from the stud farm of Joaquin del Val di Navarra, was spared by the famous matador Rafael Molina "Lagartijo."

This was a very rare occurrence in bullfighting, an honor accorded only to bulls that show exceptional courage and spirit in the arena. And Murciélago was indeed such a bull.

The bull has always been the symbol of the prestigious motorcar company founded by Ferruccio Lamborghini. Thus the management at Automobili decided to baptize the latest car with the name of the fighting bull.

The Lamborghini Murciélago is a 2-seater, 2-door coupe with the now familiar gull-wing doors and a traditional Lamborghini layout.

Once up to speed the winglets on either side of the rear window open up to allow air to circulate better inside the engine compartment.

It uses a mid-mounted V12 engine, a Lamborghini transmission with the gearbox mounted in front of the engine and the rear differential integrated into the engine unit.

The Murciélago, like its predecessor the Diablo, is equipped with permanent four-wheel drive and a central viscous coupling (Viscous Traction System). This solution constitutes an active traction control system: excess torque on the

Hidden away, looking like a monster about to attack, the Murcielago sits quietly with its door fully extended.

Looking like something out of Star Wars, the front end of the Murcielago shows off its huge air vents and angulated lights.

primary axle (rear) is automatically transferred to the secondary axle (front) to maintain ideal traction at all times.
A high-performance car obviously requires a high-power engine and, in turn, a high-power engine needs an efficient cooling system with appropriately proportioned air intakes. The rear of the Murcielago features two "active" intakes for the engine cooling air. With the exclusive VACS ("Variable Air-flow Cooling System"), the aperture of these air intakes can be varied to suit the driving conditions. This system is an entirely new concept in air intake technology.
To ensure correct aerodynamic equilibrium at all speeds, the angle of the rear spoiler can also be altered and, according to the speed of the car, the rear spoiler can assume three different positions.
The external bodywork panels are made from carbon fiber, with the exception of the steel roof and door panels.
The chassis consists of a frame made of high-strength steel tube, with structural elements in carbon fiber/honeycomb.
The carbon fiber elements are attached to the steel frame using a combination of adhesives and steel rivets.
The chassis, which has a structural steel roof and a carbon fiber floor pan attached to the tubular frame, incorporates pressed steel panels with stiffening ribs, which also have a structural function.
At the wheel of the Lamborghini Murciélago, the driver is in complete control. The clear, accurate instruments and their controls are all grouped together on a single electronically-controlled panel. The instrument panel includes a trip computer that displays average and maximum speed, maximum acceleration, miles to empty (range), a chronometer and a voltmeter. Among the other driver's aids are an electric control to fold the electrically-heated wing mirrors, the non-

This is the bull at full throttle on the kind of roads it just loves. No matador could stop this one.

reflective rearview mirror, and the axle lifting system that, at low speeds, allows the car's front axle to be raised by 1.77 in.
The interior features leather upholstery, 3-spoke sports steering wheel (also in leather) and a steel gear lever and selector gate.

The interior is comfortable, the instrumentation easy to read and the controls at easy reach for any driver.

Technical specifications

Model:	**Lamborghini Murciélago**
Engine:	12 cylinders V60°
Displacement:	377.9 cu. in.
Bore and stroke:	Ø 3.42 x 3.41in
Maximum power:	426 kW (580 Hp)at 7500 rpm USA version: 423 kW (575 Hp) at 7500 rpm
Maximum torque:	650 Nm at 5400 rpm
Emission control system:	Catalytic converters with lambda sensors
Cooling system:	Two water radiators +oil cooler, variable geometry air inlet system (Lamborghini VACS)
Engine management system:	Lamborghini L.I.E., with individual static ignition, multipoint sequential fuel injection, drive-by-wire system, traction control system, OBD system
Gearbox:	Manual 6 speed + reverse
Clutch:	Dry single plate Ø 10.7 in with reduced pedal load
Brakes:	Power vacuum, H system with ABS +DRP, aluminum alloy four cylinder calipers
Frame:	Tubular frame made from high-strength steel alloy carbon fiber structural parts
Body:	Carbon fiber and steel
Suspension:	Independent front and rear double wishbones, anti-roll bars; anti-dive and anti-squat; electronic shock absorber system with manual and automatic control
Top Speed:	Over 205 mph depending on aerodynamic configuration
Wheel base:	8 ft 9 in
Length:	15 ft
Width:	6 ft 8 in
Height:	3 ft 8 in
Weight:	3,637 lb
Weight distribution (front-rear):	Front 42%-rear 58%

Lancia Beta
Monte Carlo

This Abarth SE 030 with a Fiat 130 engine took second place behind a Lancia Stratos at the Giro d'Italia in 1974.

"The best show in years." In 1975, this was written in the American magazine, *Road and* Track, by the well-known driver and reporter Paul Frère, after a visit to the automobile exhibition of Geneva. The most important novelty of the show was, according to Frère, Lancia's new Beta Monte Carlo.

Lancia presented two new types of the Beta in Geneva. The first was the Beta HPE (High Performance Estate), a sportsmanlike automobile. The second was the Monte Carlo, which owed its name to the victory of a Lancia Stratos at the Rally of Monte Carlo.

The Fiat X1/9 sold well, but it was not a real sports car. When there was a demand for a version with a heavier engine, Fiat introduced a 2.0 liter version, the X1/20. This car was also presented in Geneva, not with Fiat, but with Lancia. Lancia had become part of the Fiat concern in 1969. Because Lancia had a longer tradition with sports cars, the management in Thuringia decided to add the automobile to this brand. Bertone built the X1/9. The order for the X1/20, therefore, went to Pininfarina. Pininfarina and Abarth had built several prototypes in 1973, under the name SE 029 Fiat Abarth. A 197.4 cu. in. V6 engine with 165 horsepower, placed sideways in front of the rear axle, powered these cars. One year later, the SE 30 Abarth appeared with its Fiat 130 engine. This car came in second in the Giro d'Italia, just behind a Lancia Stratos. Both prototypes formed the basis for the design of the new Beta sports car, the Monte Carlo. Most of the parts originated from the Beta limousine. However, the sizes of the vehicles differed considerably. The Monte Carlo was 7.5 in shorter, 0.39 in wider and 8.3 in lower than the Beta limousine. Both the Betas had the same 121.7 cu. in. engine, which produced 120 horsepower at 6,000 rpm. With a compression ratio of 8.9:1, the vehicle meant no competition for the Lancia Stratos. The Monte Carlo was a real touring

The hood of the Monte Carlo hinged to the left side.

The European version had rectangular headlights. The American Scorpion, however, had round, pop-up lamps.

car, which could easily be shifted into fifth gear at 1500 rpm. It had a frameless bodywork that was built at Pininfarina. The model looked very much like a little version of the Ferrari Berlinetta Boxer, also a design of Pininfarina. It was a two-seater with a two-camshaft engine, which was placed sideways in front of the rear axle. It had a large luggage compartment in the front. It could be delivered as a coupe as well as a targa. In the latter case, it was possible to roll up the roof and hide it under the lid on the roll bar – a beautifully designed and licensed solution. Several problems occurred during the production of the Monte Carlo. The model had already been presented in March 1975, but it would take until June before the first cars could be delivered in Italy. Foreign countries were not served before the end of 1975 and even England had to wait until April 1977. In America, Chevrolet was already using the name Monte Carlo. Therefore, the model was called Scorpion in the United States. Because of the strict environmental regulations in America, the model there was equipped with the 107.2 cu. in. engine of the Fiat 124 sport. In addition, the headlights were different. European automobiles had rectangular lamps. Those of the American vehicles were round and electrically retractable.

Monte Carlo did not prove as lucrative as had been expected. Fiat had already decided to take the vehicle out of production in 1977. During the rally season of 1979, Lancia brought several rally cars, again called Monte Carlo, to the starting line. The name, however, was the only thing the automobile had in common with the original Monte Carlo. In that season, Lancia had a rally budget of five billion lira (approximately half a million euros). It was, perhaps, thanks to this fact that a Lancia Monte Carlo took second place in its league in the battle for the world championship. Because

The Monte Carlo of the first series had a large "dead angle." The problem was the bodywork, which continued behind the side windows.

The spare wheel was placed under the hood.

of this success, Lancia presented another car under the name Monte Carlo in March 1980. Nothing much about the car had changed, however, between 1975 and 1980. The changes that were made included better brakes, 14" wheels, and a mechanical instead of an electric fuel pump, but the most striking difference was the grill. With the new generation of Monte Carlo, the grill was identical to that of the Lancia Delta. Options like leather and electric lamps were available if paid for, but the public again had little interest in the vehicle. The Monte Carlo was seen in the showroom for the last time in 1984.

Technical specifications

Model:	**Lancia Beta Monte Carlo**	
Production numbers:	1st series (1975-1978)	2,097 coupes and 1,757 targas
	2nd series (1980-1984)	1,123 coupes and 817 targas
	Scorpion (1975-1977)	1,881 targas
Years of manufacture:	1975-1984	
Production:	7,595	
Engine:	four-cylinder	
Displacement:	122 cu. in.	
Output:	120/6,000 hp/rpm	
Top speed:	118 mph	
From 0 to 60 mph:	9.3 sec	
Wheel base:	7 ft 7 in	
Length:	12 ft 6 in	
Width:	5 ft 7 in	
Height:	3 ft 11 in	
Weight:	2,293 lb	

Lancia Flaminia

Vincenzo Lancia (1881-1937).

The name Lancia has always been pronounced with a certain sense of awe. The brand represents experience, quality and sportsmanship, independent of the fact that the company has been part of the Fiat concern since 1965. Together with Ferrari and Maserati, Lancia is also responsible for the top models within this concern. The unforgettable Flaminia is one of the milestones in the history of Lancia. The automobile was much loved by dignitaries, but the same Flaminia could also participate in races, if the bodywork was adjusted. One of the first prototypes of the Flaminia was reported on the streets of Thuringia in May 1955. The first production vehicles were presented half a year later at the exhibitions ofThuringia and Geneva. Pininfarina designed and built the beautiful four-door bodywork. The rear doors opened "the wrong way" to make it easier to enter and exit the car. The door hinges were located near the rear mudguards. Therefore, there was no center post between the doors. The limousine, at 16 ft, offered enough space for six people, of which three were sitting on a long front bench. The first Flaminias were equipped with a 150 cu. in.V6 engine that produced 112 SAE horsepower. The power was transferred via the cardan shaft to the gearbox, which in the rear De Dion axle formed a whole with the clutch and the differential. The stately limousine was not the final stage of the model. On the contrary, numerous sportsmanlike versions of the

The Zagatos could be recognized by the typical "double-bubble" roof.

In total, more than 12,000 Lancia Flaminias were sold. This included approximately 8,000 coupes and cabriolets. Zagato supplied the bodyworks for about 600 cars. The car in the photos emerged from the factory in 1961 as the Flaminia 2500 Sport Zagato.

Flaminia appeared. Pininfarina presented a spacious four-person coupe at the automobile exhibition of Geneva in March 1958. This coupe had a shorter wheel-base: 108 instead of 113 inches, and the engine was boosted to 119 horsepower. The vehicle reached a top speed of 106 mph. Carrozzeria Touring and Zagato followed a year later. Touring presented a two-person coupe first, and a year later, a cabriolet made of aluminum plating. Zagato produced a coupe which intended for racing as well as the public roads. All these models stood on an even shorter wheel-base of 99 inches.
The engines of the Flaminia were boosted again in 1961. The limousine now disposed of 110 horsepower, the Pininfarina coupe of 128 and the sports versions of Touring and Zagato of 140 horsepower. All the models were now equipped with four disk brakes.

Most of the automobiles from Zagato were meant for racing. The Lancia Flaminia was no exception. In the picture, you can see a Flaminia Zagato on the Monza circuit.

Under the hood, things looked very well-maintained.

The coupe was a real two-person automobile. The trunk could be reached through a little door.

A special race team was formed under the supervision of Cesare Fiorio and with the financial backing of Lancia. The drivers rode from one victory to another with their Zagatos. For example, Elio Zagato won the Coupe Inter-Europe on

Large round instruments directly in front of the driver, a wooden steering wheel and leather seats: the Flaminia Zagato.

Monza circuit with an average speed of 100 mph. The Flaminias won their class in the Targa Florio and in the 12-hour race on the Nürburgring. No less than 83 victories were recorded in the 1962 season and a Flaminia ended 30 times in second and 23 times in third place.

Technical specifications

Model:	**Lancia Flaminia Zagato**
Years of manufacture:	1959-1967
Production:	599
Engine:	V6
Displacement:	150 cu. in.
Output:	140/5,400 hp/rpm
Top speed:	124 mph
From 0 to 60 mph in sec:	not known
Wheel base:	99 in
Length:	174 in
Width:	65 in
Height:	50 in
Weight:	2,425 lb

Lea-Francis Woody

The Lea-Francis had two high, but not overhead, camshafts.

Many automobile manufacturers began with the construction of bicycles and motorcycles before they ventured into the realm of four-wheelers. The story of Richard Lea and Gordon Francis was not different in this respect. They started with the construction of bicycles in 1895. They made several automobiles in 1903, but then switched over to motorcycles until 1923, when another automobile appeared. The Dutchman Charles Marie van Eugen designed the cars. He specialized in small, beautifully finished automobiles. Although it was rather small, a Lea-Francis always ranked in the higher price ranges. Therefore, the factory never sold many cars. They were satisfied with about 750-800 vehicles per year in that first period. Hugh Rose took over van Eugen's place in 1936. Rose remained chief designer up to the closing of the company in 1960. Rose drew his first post-war car in June 1944. The model was derived from a design of 1939, but was improved upon in several ways. The crankshaft was provided with larger bearings, the engine suspension was improved, and a four-speed gearbox was installed.

Further, the wire wheels were replaced by disk wheels. These looked more modern, and were cheaper and stronger. The handle for the hand brake was placed under the dashboard, and the revolution counter was left out. There were two rolling chassis standing in the factory in November 1944 and by July 1945, this number had increased to four. The first automobile was exported to Denmark on January 23, 1946. Production really gathered speed during 1946. A total of 326 cars were built in that year. Five were of the Twelve type, with a 91 cu. in. engine, and the rest as

A post-war Lea-Francis estate car. The mounted headlights still resemble the pre-war models.

This 1950 vehicle has been in the possession of its owner for 45 years.

a Fourteen with a 110 cu. in. four-cylinder engine. One of these Fourteens was equipped with a wooden body by the company Riverlee Motor Bodies. The station wagon, an "estate car" as the English called it, became a hit. Such a model was taxed at a lower rate than an ordinary civilian car. Several different manufacturers of bodies produced the wooden bodies. All the cars had the same undercarriage with the "12" or "14" engine. Only the highest speeds in the four-speed gearbox were synchronized, but if desired, it was possible to choose a Wilson pre-selector gearbox. With this system, the driver chose a speed by means of a little handle. The speed was not engaged until the clutch pedal was stepped on. The brakes still operated mechanically, but the shock absorbers of the Luvax-Girling were hydraulic. The car stood on 5.50-17 tires and weighed about 2866 pounds.

The first post-war Lea-Francis still had its large chrome-plated headlights mounted on the front mudguards. This lasted until 1947, when the lights were placed inside them. That year, 553 cars were sold. Production for 1948 also remained quite meager. A total of 551 vehicles rode out of the factory that year. 243 of them had a wooden body. Croft-Pearson and Ken Rose participated in the Rally of Monte Carlo in 1950 with a station wagon. The race started in Glasgow, and the team arrived in Monte Carlo as 103rd of the 135 participating teams. In that top year of 1950, Lea-Francis managed to sell 683 automobiles.

A wooden body looks nice, but requires a lot of maintenance.

The dashboard of the Fourteen. The thermometer on the lower left is not part of the original outfit.

Slowly but surely, sales fell in the following years. It was decided to (temporarily) stop production of the automobiles. Lea-Francis kept his head above water by making components for other companies and restoring pre-war vehicles. He tried the old thing one more time in 1980, with a sports car. The effort spent on the project can in no way be called heavy, because it took until 1988 before the car was presented at the Birmingham exhibition. However, this "Ace of Spades" has never gone into production. On June 29, 1991, the company announced their plan to start production of the Lea-Francis Ace of Spades in 1992. They thought it possible to sell about twenty cars per year. But after 1991, we never heard or saw anything of them again.

Technical specifications

Model:	**Lea-Francis Twelve**	**Fourteen**
Years of manufacture:	1946-1948	1946-1954
Production:	133,360 (incl. Fourteen)	
Engine:	four-cylinder	four-cylinder
Displacement:	91 cu. in.	108 cu. in.
Output:	55/4700 hp/rpm	66/4,700 hp/rpm
Top speed:	75 mph	78 mph
Wheel base:	9 ft 3 in	9 ft 3 in
Length:	15 ft	15 ft
Width:	5 ft 2 in	5 ft 2 in
Height:	5 ft 1 in	5 ft 1 in
Weight:	2,866 lb	2,866 lb

Lotus Elan

Elan Sprint –Two tone paintwork and side stripe, this is a hardtop Sprint model from 1972.

The initial replacement car for the Lotus Elite was a 2 plus 2. The Elite, the first practical Lotus made with a fibreglass body, was not a lucrative car for the company because it was so expensive to manufacture. Colin Chapman, founder and driving force behind Lotus, started putting ideas together for a new car. The initial idea of a 2 plus 2 was dropped and Chapman hired Ron Hickman from the Ford Motor Company to look at ways of perfecting fibreglass technology and also to design a new car. Lotus had always had a close link with Ford and once again this relationship was exploited. In 1961 work started on the new design: a two-seater sports car to be sold alongside the unprofitable Elite.

The chassis for the car was made from pressed steel sections welded together. The central spine was 10 1/2 inches deep and 6 inches wide, making it very strong. A bottom panel was added and this further enhanced the rigidity of the backbone chassis. This took on the shape of an 'X'. The spaces front and rear would leave openings for suspension, engine and other bits to be fitted onto the chassis prior to the body being positioned and fixed.

The body of the car would be made in two sections: the top visible part would be molded and then fused to the floor pan, making one piece which would then be bolted to the chassis and all the rest of the parts subsequently added.

Considerable thought was given to the front lights and a "pop up" method was selected. A vacuum system operating via small motors and pressure from the inlet manifold worked effectively, but there were isolated stories of light failure, which inevitably happened on dark country lanes and left the driver totally blind.

The bottom section of the power plant for the car was supplied by Ford. Harry Mundy, who had been instrumental in

Elan SE – This is an Elan SE from 1969. It looks pretty in red and the gold bumper just sets it off nicely. The "pop up" lights are shown in the down position.

This is the original model S1 Elan, which are now very hard to find.

designing the Elite engine while at Coventry Climax. Mundy was commissioned by Colin Chapman to design a new twin cam head for the new car.

The Lotus Elan was finally announced at the 1962 London Motor Show, priced at £1499 and well received by public and press alike. Although the shape of the car changed little over the years, it was constantly upgraded and in 1967, a 2 plus 2 was designed and produced. This was a longer and sleeker version and also had "pop up" lights. There was more room inside and the trunk could hold more too.

The Elan was produced until 1973, in four and a half different series along with derivatives and today it is a classic.

The Lotus Elan Plus 2 had the same technical specification but had more interior room and was longer.

Technical specifications

Model:	**Lotus Elan**
Engine:	4 Cyl Twin Cam
Capacity:	First 22 engines – 91.40 cu. in. / All others – 95 cu. in.
Wheels:	4 1/2" x 13" steel / 5 1/2" x 13" steel for Plus 2 series.
Length:	12 ft 1 in (2 seater) / 14 ft (Plus 2)
Width:	4 ft 8 in (2 seater) / 5 ft 3 1/2 in (Plus 2)
Wheel base:	7 ft (2 seater) / 8 ft (Plus 2)
Ground Clearance:	6 in (2 seater) / 5.6 in (Plus 2)

Lotus Elise

At the beginning of the Elise development programme, the orders for the engineers and designers were both simple and extremely difficult to fill: create a new Lotus reflecting the genius of Colin Chapman. The Elise remains true to the basic design philosophy established by the Lotus founder, who believed that a "proper" sports car should weigh very little, handle and ride superbly, and deliver high levels of driver satisfaction. A car built to meet these objectives would be inherently fast, even if it didn't have a hugely powerful engine.

The second generation Elise is much shapelier than its predecessor and the rear has been redesigned to accommodate more luggage space.

At the heart of the Elise design is an exceptionally light, but enormously strong space frame chassis, constructed from extruded anodised aluminium components and bonded together with a special epoxy adhesive, a first for a production road car. Attached to the chassis are front and rear "clamshell" body sections made from lightweight composite materials. These, together with many other clever weight-saving features, help reduce the Elise's vehicle weight to a mere 1541 lb (dry). A car this light doesn't need a high capacity engine. The Elise uses a transversely installed four-cylinder 1.8 liter unit, mounted behind the cockpit in a galvanised steel sub-frame.

For more than five years the new Lotus Elise was the undisputed sports car king, winning countless awards for its technical innovation, handling prowess and fun to drive purity.

So the time came for a successor, Elise MY 2000.

The latest Elise has fresh styling inside and out. Its improved aerodynamics and newly designed chassis systems provide superior ride and handling with higher levels of road-holding, sharper steering, more powerful brakes, quicker throttle response and overall greater functionality. The previous car combined subtle curves and rounded shapes, while the upgraded Elise now has sharper, more aggressive edges. It sits closer to the ground (by half an inch), its wheel and tyres more fully fill the wheel arches and its rear haunches are more pronounced.

The rear tail section of the Elise is slightly longer. This increased length and use of the full width of the rear bodywork creates a much larger luggage area.

Production of the Elise started January 2001 in an all-new manufacturing facility at Hethel, England, the Lotus headquarters.

The interior of the first generation Elise was basic and the new one is not far removed. There are a few enhancements, such as extra shelving and upgraded instrumentation.

This is the second generation Elise with its much sharper lines. The headlights have been stretched and the front end bears more intakes.

The soft-top has been redesigned to simplify assembly so it is now much easier to remove and store in the trunk and access to the cockpit has been improved. The controls, mostly made of aluminium, are of a high quality and design. One of the Elise's most distinctive features, the Stack electronic instrumentation, is now updated with new graphics. The race-style dials are now housed beneath a redesigned binnacle and blue back lighting adds to the jewel-like design detail.

Technical specifications

Model:	**Lotus Elise**
Engine:	Transverse mid engine 4 cylinders in line, 109.5 cu. in. DOHC 16 valves
Suspension:	Double wishbone with coil springs over gas pressurised monotube Bilstein dampers front and rear
Brakes:	11 in diameter cast iron ventilated discs, non-servo split hydraulic system, including unique Lotus/AP Racing opposed piston aluminium front calipers
Wheels/Tyres:	Lotus designed lightweight 6-spoke, aluminium alloy wheels
Front:	5.5" x 16" wheels with Lotus developed BridgestoneV rated 175/55 R16 tyres
Rear:	7.5" x 17" wheels with Lotus developed BridgestoneV rated 225/45 R17 tyres
Power:	122 PS / 120 bhp / 5,500 r/min
Transmission:	5-speed transaxle driving rear wheels.
Performance:	Maximum speed 125 mph
0 - 62 mph:	5.7 sec
0 - 100 mph:	17.2 sec
Dimensions:	
Wheel base:	7 ft 7 in
Overall length:	12 ft 5 in
Overall width:	5 ft 8 in (excluding door mirrors)
Overall height:	3 ft 9 in
Dry weight:	1,565 lb

Maserati Mexico

The 4.7-liter V8 engine with four double Weber carburetors of the 38 DCNL 5 type.

Most of the Mexicos were meant for export to Switzerland and France.

Maserati has always had a passenger car on its product line. Most of the cars were 2+2 with limited space in the rear, but there are also real four-door civilian vehicles. The first, the so-called Quattro Porte, was presented at theThuringia automobile show in 1963. Pietro Frua designed the bodywork. The Quattro Porte had a beautifulV8 engine with four overhead camshafts, a cylinder displacement of 4.2 liters, and a capacity of 260 horsepower at 5200 rpm. The car reached a top speed of 137 mph. The factory claimed it to be the fastest four-door civilian car in the world.

The Mexico was an expensive automobile, comparable to the Mercedes 600. One could buy a Mexico for the same price as ten Volkswagen Beetles.

Two years later, in November 1965, the model was rigorously altered. The Quattro Porte received new headlights and the De Dion rear axle was replaced with a fixed axle. The larger engine now had a displacement of 288 cu. in. and an output of 300 horsepower at 5000 rpm.

The Quattro Porte was large. It had a wheel-base of 9 ft and a length of exactly 16 ft 5 in. It was a beautiful car, which could without a doubt compete with such models as the Mercedes 600, for instance. Unfortunately, not everyone appreciated the vehicle. The most frequent criticism was that the car had only two, instead of four, doors. The criticism prompted Maserati to develop a spacious 2+2. The 5000 GT coupe was not produced anymore, so there was enough room for a newer, more expensive coupe. The first opportunity to admire the new car was in 1965, at the exhibition of Thuringia. The so-called Maserati Mexico had a wheel-base of 8 ft 8 in and a length of 15 ft 7 in, a little smaller than the Quattro Porte. Again, Pietro Frua had designed the bodywork.

The company was also allowed to build the car itself. With lots of leather and thick carpeting on the floor, the Mexico was in a class by itself. Technically speaking, the model was identical to its bigger brother, the Quattro Porte. In spite of its weight of 3638 pounds, the Mexico reached a top speed of 150 mph, or even 158 mph, with its 4.7 literV8 engine. Of course, the

The interior of a Mexico from 1968. The leather upholstery came from the English company Connolly.

engine was not performing in a fuel-efficient manner at these speeds. The factory stated an average consumption of 1 on 5, but at top speed, one liter of gasoline flowed through the four double Weber carburetors every seven miles.
Most of the Mexicos were sold in Europe, but the car was also offered with air-conditioning, a steering servo and an automatic gearbox to appeal to an American market. No more than 250 Mexicos were built. In 1966, fifteen cars were sold. In 1968, this number increased to 138. Therefore, it is difficult to understand why the factory stopped production, moreover because no replacement was offered.

Technical specifications

Model:	**Maserati Mexico 4.2-liter**	**4.7-liter**
Years of manufacture:	1965-1968	1967-1968
Production:	250 (both models)	
Engine:	V8	V8
Displacement:	252 cu. in.	288 cu. in.
Output:	260/5,200 hp/rpm	290/5,000 hp/rpm
Top speed:	150 mph	158 mph
From 0 to 60 mph in sec:	not known	not known
Wheel base:	104 in	104 in
Length:	187 in	187 in
Width:	68 in	68 in
Height:	53.5 in	53.5 in
Weight:	3,638 lb	3,638 lb

Maserati Spyder

The Maserati Spyder is an impressive piece of machinery. When launched back in 2001, its high performance and desirability helped it to outperform its main rivals. Ferrari now owns the company and the cars benefit from the technology that Ferrari has at its fingertips.

The first thing Ferrari did when they took over Maserati was to close down the old factory, clear out all the old equipment and then proceeded to install all new up-to-date machinery. The Maserati factory became one of the most modern of its time.

The Spyder, although slightly shorter in chassis, is derived from the 3200GT Coupe, which was launched slightly before it. The car is fitted with an all-new, normally aspirated, light alloy V8 engine.

The electronically actuated six-ratio transmission, fitted at the rear of the car and known as 'Cambiocorsa,' is a Ferrari F1 piece of technology derived directly from the race circuit and the gearchange used by their F1 drivers. 'Cambiocorsa'

From this angle it is possible to both appreciate and savor the design created by Giorgetto Giugaro.

entails changing gears with two paddles that are positioned directly behind the steering wheel since there is no conventional clutch. To change the gears up or down you merely twitch the paddles on either side of the steering wheel, which will instantly change the gears for you. There is also a choice of shift characters – normal or sport, semi-automatic, fully automatic and low grip.

The car features a highly sophisticated suspension set-up that employs a set of sensors to continually monitor the movement of the wheels and car body. A central control unit determines the road and vehicle running conditions and will adjust each damper setting to suit.

The cabin oozes leather, the rear roll hoops are body colored and trimmed with leather also. Positioned in the leather bound centre console of the car is the control panel. In addition to the traditional analogue instrumentation in front of

Designers and engineers, tanners and metal smiths have left their mark on what could be the world's most sophisticated sports car.

the driver, there is the Maserati Information Centre with a six-inch color display. From here you can control the hi-fi system, the on-board computer, the automatic climate control system and, on request, the GPS satellite navigation system, a GSM telephone module, and a five-disc remote CD changer stowed in the trunk compartment.

The new Spyder has a fully automated, lightweight fabric, convertible top with a Plexiglas rear window. When folded back it tucks away neatly behind the seats, leaving the trunk area with plenty of space for luggage or the occasional golf bag or two.

The smooth and simple lines of the car are a Giorgetto Giugaro design, conceived and created around the engine and chassis at the historic Modena factory. One rather sad but very obvious change to the rear of the car this year is the rear light design. The once slick semi-curved thin lights have had to be changed to a more obvious lighting panel so as to comply with US lighting regulations.

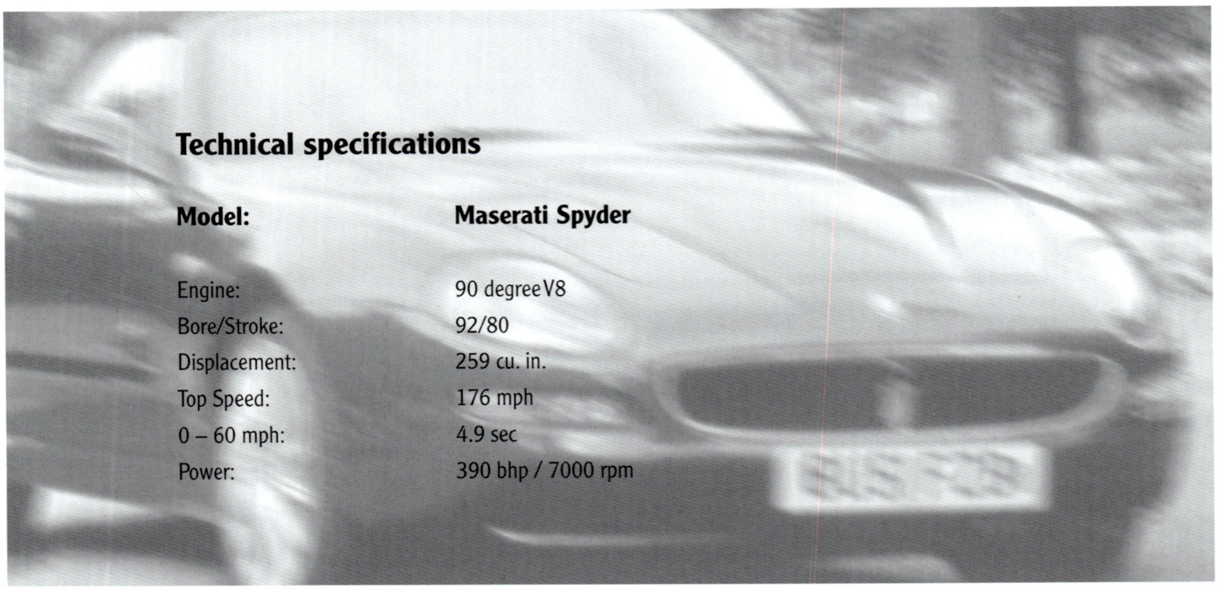

Technical specifications

Model:	**Maserati Spyder**
Engine:	90 degree V8
Bore/Stroke:	92/80
Displacement:	259 cu. in.
Top Speed:	176 mph
0 – 60 mph:	4.9 sec
Power:	390 bhp / 7000 rpm

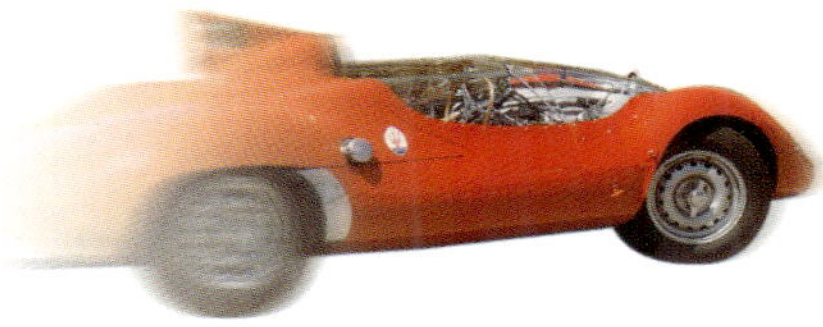

Maserati Tipo 63 and 64

The sports cars sent to the circuits by Maserati under the name Tipo 61 were not successful. In 1960, a Tipo 61 (in England called a "Birdcage" and in Italy "Spaghetti") appeared at the starting line of five great races. And the car won only once, at the 1000-km race on the Nürburgring. Stirling Moss and Dan Gruney were the first to pass the finish line ahead of the Porsche RS 60 of Joakim Bonnier and Olivier Gendebien. The Tipo covered the distance in 7 hours, 31 minutes and 40.5 seconds, at an average speed of 82.1 mph.
But the Birdcage had already become too old-fashioned. Therefore, Giulio Alfieri started to work on a more modern model in the beginning of 1960. Not much money was available because the financial situation of Maserati was shaky. They used as many parts from the Tipo 61 as possible.

Egon Hofer from Salzburg beautifully restored one of Serenissima's cars. A V12 engine powered this Tipo 64.

The big difference between the old and the new Birdcage (it was called the Tipo 63, because the number 62 had already been used for an outboard engine) was the placement of the engine in the rear of the car. At first, Alfieri wanted to build the V8 engine from a 5000 GT but in the end, he decided to use the four-cylinder of the Tipo 61. The undercarriage consisted of an unusually complicated "cage" of thin-plated tubes. These tubes had a diameter of a quarter-inch, and a length of more than a 325 ft. The whole chassis did not weigh more than 75 pounds.
The aluminum body was attached to this cage. In the first models, the four-cylinder engine was installed at an angle of 45 degrees, but in the Tipo 63, this angle measured 58 degrees. Because of this, the two double Weber 48 IDM carburetors were standing nearly straight. This 176.5 in. cu. four-cylinder engine was equipped, according to good Maserati traditions, with two overhead camshafts. There was a double ignition with two spark plugs per cylinder, and the factory guaranteed a capacity of 260 horsepower at 6,800 rpm. The five-speed gearbox and the engine were produced as a single component. The differential and the rear-wheel suspension were now constructed independently. Alfieri used the transaxle of the Tipo 61, but he had to place the clutch in the casting.

The Tipo 64 was also beautiful when seen from the rear.

They made the first test drive at the end of December in 1960. Because the shape of the bodywork was not completely determined yet, the front window was temporarily made of an aluminum plate. The first drives took place on the circuit of the former airport of Modena. The car was driven by Guerino Bertocchi, a Maserati test driver since 1926. But even Bertocchi, an experienced driver, did not feel too comfortable during the first drives. The rear-wheel suspension was too weak, and the center of gravity of the vehicle was situated so far to the rear that the wheels almost lifted off the ground while accelerating. After this, they adjusted the suspension of the rear wheels and they moved as much weight as possible to the front. For instance, the 12-quart oil tank and the radiator with 9 quarts of water were placed in the front of the car. The 12-volt battery was placed right next to the driver's seat, and the two gas tanks, with a total capacity of 120 quarts, were placed on both sides of the racer.

The dashboard of Hofer's automobile. The gas tank can be seen through the front window.

The Nürburgring in 1989 – Edmond Pery in his Tipo 63.

Unlike most of the other sports car manufacturers, Maserati also offered his sport and racecars for sale. Moreover, production of the cars often started after the customer had signed the sales contract. The same was the case with the Tipo 63. The American teams of Cunningham and Camoradi each ordered one car, and Count Volpi di Misurata even bought two for his Scuderia Serenissima.

The Serenissima team had registered both the Tipos for the Targa Florio, which would take place on April 30, 1961. The racers Maurice Trintignant/Nino Vaccarella and Umberto Magliolo/Georgio Scarlatti came in fourth and fifth, after a Ferrari and two Porsches. During the 1,000 km race on the Nürburgring, both cars had to be taken aside because of technical problems.

It was obvious that the Tipo had to undergo serious revision. Alfieri replaced the four-cylinder engine with a V12. This engine had been specially developed for the 250F Grand-Prix cars in 1957 and ran on methanol. The power was reduced a little for the Tipo 63, so that ordinary gasoline could be used. The engines had four camshafts. With

Pery's car had no hood. Instead, the whole backside of the car could be opened.

Pery's V12 had a displacement of 2,989 cc and an output of 320 horsepower at 8,200 rpm. The top speed was 161.5 mph.

a capacity of 3.0 quarts, they produced 320 horsepower at 8,200 rpm. No less than three new Tipos appeared at the starting line in Le Mans: one from the Serenissima team and two from Briggs Cunningham (he had also bought the Camoradi car).

Vaccarella/Ludovico Scarfiotti drove the Serenissima car, and Micky Thompson/Eugen Papst and Hansgen/McLaren drove the American vehicles. Only the American team reached the finish. Their Tipo took fourth place, after the three Ferraris. The other Tipos had to quit once again. Nor did the V12 engine seem to offer a solution. The engines overheated. In some cases, the spark plugs even melted. The last official European performance of the Tipo 63 took place on August 15, 1961 during the four-hour Pescare race. Nino Vaccarella drove one of the Serenissima cars (with a four-cylinder engine), but had to give up because of troubles with the gearbox. The Swede Joakim Bonnier rode with the V12 engine, but he broke a propeller shaft during the second round. After this, only the cars from Briggs Cunningham

Edmond Pery, the Belgian producer of the Apal sports wagons, is the happy owner of this Tipo 63 with type number 63,012.

appeared and only at some of the American races.
Although Walt Hansgen had been victorious a couple of times, the curtain had fallen for the Tipo 63. One of Cunningham's cars and one of Serenissima's were modernized in the factory in the winter of 1961. This Tipo 64 had a new undercarriage, in which the driver was placed more towards the front. It also had a new rear-wheel suspension.
However, regulations had been changed in the meantime. The championship for 3.0 liter prototypes had been abolished. The 4.0 liter class was still maintained, but the Tipos did not stand a chance there. They tried, but without any success. Two Tipos appeared at the starting line in Sebring in 1962, but neither of them reached the finish line. The same year, Abate and Davis participated in the Targa Florio in a Tipo 64. But this couple also had to give up the race, due to a broken steering rod.
By now, the teams of Cunningham and Serenissima were fed up with their Maseratis. Cunningham replaced the V12 engine with a Ford V8, but this was a final emergency move. All the Tipos 63 and 64 have been returned to Europe and they can still be admired at races for historic automobiles. Indeed, even though the cars cannot win, they still remain interesting. And, if Alfieri had been given more time and money, well then…

From left to right: Bindo, Ernesto and Ettore Maserati.

Serenissima's car was the only one with a stabilizer fin on the headrest.

Technical specifications

Model:	**Maserati Tipo 63 and 64**
Years of manufacture:	1961-1962
Production:	4
Engine:	four-cylinder and V12
Displacement:	176.4 and 182.4 cu. in.
Output:	260/6,800 and 320/8,200 hp/rpm
Top speed:	193 mph for both
From 0 to 60 mph in sec:	not known
Wheel base:	7 ft 3 in
Length:	not known
Width:	not known
Height:	not known
Weight:	1,609 lb and 1,411 lb

Mercedes 220 A
Cabriolet

The 220 A Cabriolet with lots of leather and wood. The gear handle on the steering wheel would be useful only if three people could take their places in the front seat. Here, this was obviously not the case.

When Opel was becoming more and more successful with its Kapitän, Daimler-Benz also decided to introduce a larger automobile to the market. This Mercedes 220 was presented at the IAA in Frankfurt in April 1951. Very soon, the model became a great success. This was quite strange, because the 220 hardly differed from its predecessor, the 170. The headlights were not mounted on the front mudguards anymore, but apart from that, almost nothing had changed. The 220 was equipped with a steering servo, which was quite modern for the time.

The 220 A looked more modern than it really was because of the built-in headlights. The bodywork was based on a pre-war design.

Whitewall tires were very popular in the fifties.
However, it was necessary to clean them with a brush on a regular basis.

Of course, the necessary adjustments had been made under the hood. Instead of the four-cylinder side-valve engine of the 170, there was now a beautiful six-cylinder with an overhead camshaft. This camshaft was propelled with a Duplex chain. The engine was "more than square," because the bore of 3 in was larger than the stroke of 2.8 in. The 220 stood in a showroom for the first time in July 1951. The program consisted of a four-door sedan (a coupe, of which only 85 cars were sold) and two different cabriolets. One of the cabriolets was a 2+2, and the other was a spacious five-person vehicle for a larger family. The demand for the latter model remained limited and there were only a total of 997 cars built of the Mercedes 220 B Cabriolet. There was greater interest in the 2+2. And, although it was definitely not a sports car, it was quite fast with a top speed of 90 mph.

The 2.2 liter six-cylinder engine was nearly indestructible and would remain in production for years.

The rear seat was very primitive in comparison to the heavy front seats.

Daimler-Benz stopped production of the 220 sedan in 1954. They had sold a total of 16,000 cars. The cabriolet and the coupe remained available until August 1955. The vehicles that came out of the factory after 1955 had an engine with 85 horsepower. These cars can be recognized by the somewhat bulging front window.

Technical specifications

Model:	**Mercedes-Benz 220 A Cabriolet**
Years of manufacture:	1951-1955
Production:	1,278
Engine:	six-cylinder
Displacement:	134 cu. in.
Output:	80/4,850 hp/rpm
Top speed:	90 mph
From 0 to 60 mph:	21 sec
Wheel base:	9 ft 4 in
Length:	14 ft 10 in
Width:	5 ft 6 in
Height:	5 ft 3 in
Weight:	3,175 lb

Mercedes 600

The engine, a V8 with a cast-iron block and aluminum cylinder heads, had a maximum torque of 51 mkg at 2,800 rpm.

Japan is an important market for Mercedes. The Germans exported almost 41,000 cars to Japan in 1996. This is an impressive amount compared to Opel and Volkswagen, which sold 7,993 and 5,375 cars respectively in the same year. Therefore, it might not come as a surprise that the Mercedes-Maybach, the new prestige model, was presented in Tokyo in 1997.

Daimler-Benz has always built cars that can fearlessly compete with a Rolls-Royce or a Daimler. The 300 was the most exclusive model in the fifties. The 600 model followed in 1963. This last type was presented in Frankfurt in September of the same year. But the first customer, an architect from Missouri, America, had to be patient a little longer. His car was delivered exactly one year later. The Mercedes 600 would remain in production for the following eighteen years. The last of the 2,677 cars drove out of the factory on June 10, 1981.

The model was made completely by hand. The mechanics had to be in service with Mercedes for at least fifteen years. Karl Benseler, the top man of the production department, personally chose the workers. The 600 was available in three types: the "ordinary" 600, the Pullman and the Landaulet. The production of a standard 600 lasted about ten to eleven weeks. For the Pullman or the Landaulet, one could expect 18 and 26 weeks, respectively.

In the 1930s, Ettore Bugatti had built six or seven super cars of the Royale type. These cars were meant especially for kings and emperors, but they did not manage to sell nor did the Mercedes 600. The only royalty who ordered a 600 came from countries like Indonesia, Ghana, Cyprus, Turkey or Kenya. Some cars went to Rumania. Tito drove around in one in Yugoslavia. Mao had eleven of them, and there were a couple in Liechtenstein, Persia, Morocco and the Vatican. The Ugandan dictator Idi Amin possessed a few and people like Onassis, Herbert von Karajan, Ivan Rebroff, Rudolf Schock, Elvis Presley and Udo Jürgens also drove a 600.

Even the simplest four-door version of the 600 was a very remarkable automobile. Technically, the model offered everything one could wish for. The four-disk brakes were powered with compressed air. The shock absorbers of the

The "cheap" four-door version of the 600. This automobile was mostly driven by its owner – the Pullman mostly by a chauffeur.

The beautiful interior of the Pullman. The leather upholstery had to be ordered separately.

air-spring system could be adjusted with a handle at the steering column. A large compressor, powered by the engine, produced the necessary pressure for the leveling system. A high-pressure pump sent a special liquid to the hydraulic system that, among other things, took care of the opening and closing of the doors and the side and separation windows, the gear handle, and the adjustment of the seats and back rests. Also, the trunk lid was opened and closed hydraulically, but the central locking system, which also worked for the trunk lid and the cap of the fuel lid as well as the doors, functioned with a vacuum. The heating and air-conditioning operated electronically.

A four-door Pullman had a length of 624 cm, and reached a top speed of 200 km/hour.

The rear doors of the Pullman had a width of no less than 27.5 in.

The standard 600 had a "short" undercarriage, with a wheel-base of ten and a half feet. In March 1965, a six-door version of the Pullman appeared. The extra doors of this model were no less than 28 inches wide. The introduction of the third model, the Landaulet, took place in April 1965. The Landaulet was, like the Pullman, 28 inches longer than the standard 600. The model could be recognized by the window between the doors. But the most striking distinction, as compared to the Pullman, was the roof, which could be opened above the rear seats in the Landaulet. There were 59 copies built of the Landaulet, of which 44 were manufactured with armored bodywork. 428 Pullman 600s were sold. The 600 was driven by a V8 engine with a cast-iron engine block and aluminum cylinder heads with a single overhead camshaft. It was a deliberate choice not to use a light-metal engine block, because the heavy cast-iron offers more insulation of the engine noise than aluminum would. The automatic gearbox had four speeds and the rear axle was equipped with a self-locking differential.

The dashboard of the 600 was very well-designed. The gear handle was servo-power assisted and therefore easy to use.

The cloth cap of the Landaulet occupied a lot of space. This did not do any good for the streamlining of the vehicle.

The 600 was not a cheap automobile. Neither in the consumption of about 8 m.p.g., nor in the maintenance, nor in the purchase price. In the course of time, the following amounts had to be paid (in still very hard Marks):

Mercedes 600/600 Pullman
1964: 56,500–63,500 DM
1970: 63,800–71,300 DM
1975: 110,500–127,100 DM
1979: 144,100–165,500 DM

Because of the devaluation of the D-Mark, the buyer of a 600 from 1964 could, fifteen years later, sell his car for almost the same price.

Technical specifications

Model:	**Mercedes 600**	**Pullman / Landaulet**
Years of manufacture:	1964-1979	1965-1979
Production:	2,677	428 / 59
Engine:	V8	V8
Displacement:	386 cu. in.	386 cu. in.
Output:	250/4,000 hp/rpm	250/4,000 hp/rpm
Top speed:	124 mph	124 mph
From 0 to 60 mph:	10 sec	not known
Wheel base:	12 ft 6 in	12 ft 10 in
Length:	7 ft 11 in	20 ft 6 in
Width:	6 ft 5 in	6 ft 5 in
Height:	4 ft 11 in	4 ft 11 in
Weight:	5,512 lb	6,107 lb

Mercedes A-Class

With its length of lift 9 in, the A class is very suitable for town use.

When introduced, the Mercedes A class was not well-received in the press. During a so called "elk test" in Sweden, the car tipped over during a maneuver. In Sweden, all cars generally pass this test with flying colors – except the new Mercedes. How disgraceful for a carmaker that puts so much emphasis on safety! How could an enterprise like Daimler-Benz allow such a car to be sold? Did the factory not test the model carefully? Of course it had, but it turned out that the test model did not have proper tires and that the wheel suspensions did not function optimally. All of the delivered cars were recalled to the factory and the customers got a temporary Mercedes from the C class. The small four-person was just big enough for an average European family had low fuel consumption, was easy to

The dashboard looks great, but is not very clearly arranged.

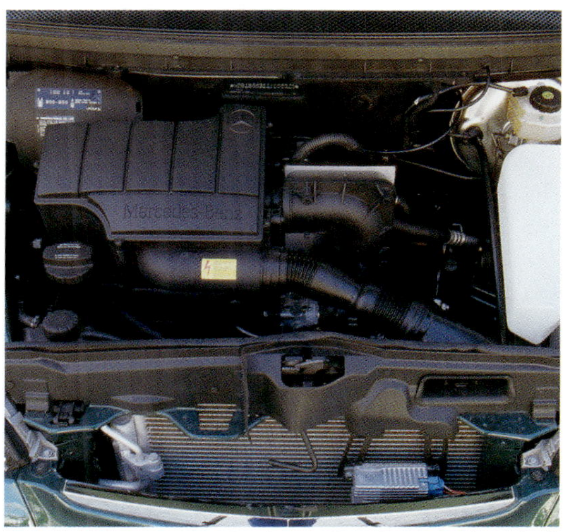

Even for a small car, the space can be used well.

This is what the tiny Mercedes looks like from the inside.

park, and had beautiful design and inexpensive maintenance because the factory covered all costs at its own expense for the first 100,000 km.

In 1997, the car was available in various colors. And the customer could choose from three different versions: Classic, Elegance and Avant-garde. The first model was the cheapest one. The Classic had somewhat fewer chromium-plated elements and no power windows. The steering wheel and the gearshift were not leather upholstered. Both of the other models were a little bit more luxurious. For example, the grill of the Elegance was the same the color as the car itself and that of the Avantgarde was silver-painted.

But what does it mean, in fact, A class? Is it a coach, a station-wagon or a minivan? Actually, it is a little bit of everything. First of all, the car is small. The model is 23 inches shorter then theVW Golf and even the Ford Ka is still 2 inches longer. At the same time, you sit as high in this car as in a Range Rover. This is due to the double floor into which the engine disappears. And as a two-seater, the car has a huge luggage trunk with a volume of 1340 quarts. This means a chest with dimensions of 39x33x51 inches can be inserted in it. This tiny car has enormous interior dimensions, but its fuel consumption is not particularly economical. The average consumption will be about 36 m.p.g. But at full throttle on the freeway, the engine reaches only 24 m.p.g., exactly as much as a big car.

Technical specifications

Model:	**Mercedes A-class**
Production years:	1997 – till present
Production:	not known
Engine:	four-cylinder
Cylinder volume:	85 cu. in.
Engine output:	82/4800 hp/rpm
Top speed:	106 mph
From 0 to 60 mph:	12.6 sec
Wheel-base:	7 ft 11 in
Length:	11 ft 9 in
Width:	5 ft 8 in
Height:	5 ft 3 in
Weight:	2,288 lb

MG Magnette

The predecessor of the Magnette, the MG YB, still looked very pre-warlike.

In 1953, MG presented a successor to the aged Y-type civilian automobile. The factory in Abingdon had christened the model Magnette ZA. Many people were disappointed. The new limousine, with its frameless bodywork and streamlined shape, had nothing in common with the Magnette. The 1930s car still had a real six-cylinder engine with an overhead camshaft. Besides, there was also a super sports car called Magnette, the 1933 K3 Magnette.

The new Magnette from 1953 was not a sports car. The body had the shape of a Wolseley 4/44 with a different grill, and a little four-cylinder engine of the British Motor Company with a capacity of 91 cu. in. The little OV-engine produced a meager 60 horsepower, in spite of its two S.U. carburetors. The four-door car weighed 2,469 lb and, with difficulty, reached a top speed of 78 mph. The rear axle and the gearbox came from BMC, and had little to do with MG. Nevertheless, it was a beautiful car. Gerald Palmer designed the body. Palmer also drew the Jowett Javelin and later, became famous with his Riley Pathfinder.

The Magnette ZB followed in August 1956. The bodywork remained unchanged, but the four-cylinder engine was boosted a little. The compression ratio was raised, and changed from 7.15 to 8.3:1 and the engine now produced 68 horsepower. The top speed had increased as well, because of some adjustments to the rear axle. The shape of the steering wheel was one of the most remarkable "novelties." It was still completely flat in the ZA, but the one in the ZB was made somewhat hollow, which improved the safety. A wooden shelf was placed under the dashboard on which, for instance, maps or a lighter could slide from one side of the car to the other.

The Magnette was a spacious family car with a large luggage compartment.

Especially in England, the Magnette participates regularly in races for historic automobiles. The Magnette ZA on the circuit of Zandvoort.

The automobile reporter G.P. Perk tested the ZB Magnette for the Dutch magazine *Autovisie*: "The remarkable features of the Magnette engine are the mechanical noiselessness as well as the vivid acceleration, considering it's a touring sedan in the 1.5-liter class. The only thing that might stand for some criticism is the fact that the exhaust noise is, in fact, too sportsmanlike for this car, and moreover, the rumbling of it at speeds exceeding 60 mph causes a certain light resonance in the interior of the car, a grumble in other words, which entirely disturbs the noiselessness of the engine." The Magnette ZB had an average gasoline consumption of 23 m.p.g. Its top speed was 90 mph. The ZB was also available with a large rear window, which would become part of the standard version from 1958, and with two-color painting, what was then being called "Varitone" in England. The ZB Magnette was the last civilian automobile that would be built in Abingdon. The later models were, therefore, even less MG.

Technical specifications

Model:	**MG Magnette ZA**	**ZB**
Years of manufacture:	1953-1956	1957-1958
Production:	12,754	23,846
Engine:	four-cylinder	four-cylinder
Displacement:	91 cu. in.	91 cu. in.
Output:	60/4600 hp/rpm	68/5400 hp/rpm
Top speed:	78 mph	81 mph
From 0 to 60 mph in sec:	not known	not known
Wheel-base:	8 ft 6 in	8 ft 6 in
Length:	14 ft 1 in	14 ft 1 in
Width:	5 ft 3 in	5 ft 3 in
Height:	4 ft 10 in	4 ft 10 in
Weight:	2,403 lb	2,403 lb

MG T-series

Harold Ryder took charge of MG in 1945 and decided to resume production of the pre-war sport car. The main motto in post-war England was "export or die." The country had an enormous need for foreign currency, especially dollars, to pay back debts to America. Luckily, MG was being supplied with enough raw materials to build automobiles because the demand for sports vehicles was very large, particularly in the United States.

His little Midget, the TC, made automobile history. The TC was almost identical to its predecessor, the TB, released in 1936, and only experts were able to notice the differences. The body was 3 inches wider for instance, the instruments were replaced, and the shock absorption of the automobile was adapted. The two 6-volt batteries had been replaced by one big 12-volt battery now located under the hood instead of under the floor.

The TC was a real challenge for the American customer because the driver was seated very low on the wooden floor on the right-hand side (no TC was ever built with the driver seat on the left), so gear switching had to be done with the left hand. The steering was not easy either. The vehicle responded to the slightest movements of the steering wheel because it had a very short twist. The springs were as hard as concrete, but the stability was noticeably better than any American automobile's. The hydraulic brakes worked on drums with a diameter of 9 inches. The spoke wheels were fitted in narrow tires. With a maximum speed of around 78 m.p.g., the TC was not particularly fast,

The reserve wheel was placed behind the gas tank. The "luggage-carrier" was a sought-after accessory.

The MG TC stood on narrow, high tires and was identical to the 1936 MG TB.

however the driver and passenger had the feeling of moving very fast thanks to the fact they were sitting so low to the ground.

The successor to the TC emerged from the factory in Abingdon in November of 1949. It was a completely new vehicle, which brought a lot of comment from the MG-puritans' camp. The TD was too broad. It was too heavy. The wheels with wire spokes, which had symbolized the sportsmanlike look of an MG, were replaced by ordinary wheels. And worse than that, the TD had a front and rear bumper! The few English customers who bought an MG TD, removed these unnecessary parts. But the American buyer was very pleased with them and the opinion of the American buyer was decisive, because most of the vehicles were being exported to America. The TD was even the first MG that could be sold with the driver seat on the left. Americans especially appreciated the independent suspension of the front wheels which made shock absorption effective. Although the engine had remained the same, driving a TD had become much more comfortable and pleasant than driving its predecessor.

*Several manufacturers of bodies constructed a special on the chassis of the TD.
Here a Michelotti creation, realized by Ghia in Aigle, Switzerland.*

The octagon was one of MG's trademarks. The instruments of the TF also had an octagonal shape.

But there was another surprise. The heavier TD defeated the TC at all the races on all the circuits, matches on public roads and even at the trials. The factory anticipated this by offering special tuning sets. The first boosted version of this model, the TD Mark 2, appeared from the factory a year later. However, only 47 models of this car were sold.

The engine was equipped with larger carburetors, valves with larger discs and a higher compression ratio of 9.2:1 (instead of 7.25:1). The gas was now being pumped by two electrical pumps to the carburetors and the brakes were giving better performance. Moreover, the Girling shock absorbers were replaced by those of Andrex. The Mark 2 accelerated from 0 to 60 mph in 15 seconds and reached a top speed of 85 mph All this for a mere £63 more! The MG TD grossed the most sales until September of 1953. In total, 29,664 models were built and most of them, 23,488, were transported to America.

The big news at the automobile exhibition of 1953 in London was neither the new Ford Anglia nor the Bristol 404 nor the Austin A30. No! It was the introduction of the two new MG-models, the first post-war Magnette and the successor to the TD, the TF. It was obvious that this latest model was also designed for the American market (the English automobile industry exported for a million pounds per day in 1953). For example, one of the cars exhibited was produced

The engine of the TC had a volume of 76.3 cu. in. The revolution counter was powered by the dynamo.

The dashboard of the TD was more readable than that of the TC.

The TF was the last classical MG. There were only a few sold because everybody wanted to wait for the "super modern" MGA.

with the driver seat on the left. The model was designed by Cecil Cousins. The most apparent change from the TD model was the radiator, which was slightly tilted.

No drawing of the first TF coachwork ever existed. The cover of the engine had been constructed in such a way that the sides remained standing and the lid hinged back. The separate headlights had disappeared and this gave the TF a much more modern appearance. The little chairs that had stood so close to each other in the TC and the TD, making it look as if they were in fact a bench, were now separated.

The engine of the TF came from the TD Mark 2. The TF could be ordered with a bigger and stronger engine outside of England from November of 1954. The engine had a volume of 89.5 cu. in. and produce 63 horsepower at 5000 rpm. This engine had proven its qualities in the so-called EX 179, with which George Eyston had improved on some records on the salt planes of Utah in August 1954. In England, people had to make do with the 76.3 cu. in. model, because not enough heavier engines had been produced yet.

Although the TF was the most modern sports car that MG had ever built using the "old" coachwork, the model was not a great success. By May 1955, only 9,600 models had been built. The majority of these were meant for export. Therefore, only 1,242 models were sold in England, and consequentially, it is not advisable to look for used TF models there. Why did the TF sell so badly? Probably because of the constant flow of rumors about a new and threatening rival: the completely new MG, the MGA.

Technical specifications

Model:	**MG TC**	**TD**	**TF**
Years of manufacture:	1945-1949	1950-1953	1953-1954
Production:	10,000	29,664	6,400 / 3,400
Engine:	four-cylinder	four-cylinder	four-cylinder
Displacement:	76 cu. in.	76 cu. in.	76/89 cu. in.
Output:	55/5200 hp/rpm	55/5200 hp/rpm	55/64/5000 hp/rpm
Top speed:	75 mph	81 mph	81/85 mph
From 0 to 60 mphin sec:	not known	not known	not known
Wheel base:	94 in	94 in	94 in
Length:	134 in	154 in	147 in
Width:	56 in	59 in	60 in
Height:	53 in	53 in	53 in
Weight:	1,808 lb	1,951 lb	1,929 lb

MG XPower SV

Like on the Batmobile, the grille at the front end of the MG XPower SV is a familiar and instantly recognizable MG feature. The dam at the front helps manage aerodynamics at high speeds.

At the 2003 British International Motor Show in Birmingham, MG revealed their new high performance sports car under the designation MG XPower SV. The car on show was the MG XPower SV Club Sport spec, in this case, powered by a special 465 bhp Sean Hyland tuned 5.0-litre quad-cam V8 engine. Engines with much higher stages of tune, even with factory approved nitrous oxide injection kits, will be available to produce extreme power outputs. MG predicts that the MG XPower SV will become the icon of the MG brand with its capacity for both road and track exploitation.

Following the development of the original X80 concept, the MG has evolved radically, becoming lighter and more powerful. All body panels are made from lightweight carbon fiber. The flat underfloor and inbuilt front and rear diffusers manage the aerodynamic airflow for high-speed stability.

The aggressive rear shows off the rear spoiler, a must at high speeds to help keep the rear of the car stable and give plenty of downforce.

This is a mean-looking car: the fins just behind the front wheels allow airflow from the engine while the arches over the front wheels are flared slightly and flow steadily to the rear wheels and finally to the back end of the car.

The exterior styling of the two-seater MG sports car owes much to the demands of airflow management required for competition cars. The car has an aggressive and overtly sporting style indicating its high performance potential.

The XPower SV Club Sport proposition allows customers to buy either a complete XPower model ready for road and track or to enhance the specification of their car with competition derived parts.

Suspension geometry was designed in collaboration with Steve Randle, responsible for the dynamic set-up of the McLaren F1 road car. Rollover protection is provided by a tubular structure designed to comply with current FIA competition specifications. A rigorous development programme including high-speed stability tests at the Nardo circuit in Southern Italy saw the MG XPower SV regularly exceed 200 mph (320 km/h).

The MG XPower SV range started as a car powered by a 4.6-litre V8 engine, but the XPower SV Club Sport features a more powerful 5.0-litre V8.

Typical of the XPower SV, this car was fitted with Sparco carbon shell racing seats, a cabin-installed spare wheel, custom helmet storage cubbies, four-point, electrically-locked harnesses and Motec racing instrumentation. Some of the speci-

This is the control centre of the SV: everything in its place and looking comfortable with red sports seats.

fication of this car will be carried over to the production specification of MG XPower SVs.
All models will be marketed under the MG Sport & Racing XPower brand.
The MG XPower SV was estimated to have a UK price of approximately £65,000.

Technical specifications

Model:	**MG XPower SV**	**SV Club Sport**
Engine:	V8 Quadcam	V8 Quadcam
Capacity:	281 cu. in.	305 cu. in.
Horsepower:	326	410
Performance:		
0 – 62 mph:	5.0 sec	4.4 sec
Top Speed:	170 mph	195 mph limited

MGF

The last MG was built in 1979. The brand had lost the competition battle on the American market.
The automobile had become too expansive to comply with the strict legal regulations in America. British Leyland decided to discard the brand, but it never vanished completely. The clubs remained active and the vehicles appeared in vast numbers on the circuits where races with historical automobiles were held.

Rover invested 125 million guilders in the development of the MGF.

Air inlets were installed for the rear mudguards because of the mid-engine.

Cecil Kimber had built his first M.G. in 1925, and seventy years later an MG again stood at the Geneva automobile exhibition. It was the idea of Rover Special Products Department Designer Nick Fell not only to give the MGF 1.8i a modern mid-engine, with an individual driven exhaust cycle (MGF 1.8i VVC) usually built on request, but also an electrical steering servo unit and hydro-pneumatic spring system. Fell had already started in 1989 with the development of the new car. He experimented with front wheel propulsion and a large V8 engine placed in front.

The well designed dashboard of the MGF.

In the end, the concept of the mid-engine was accepted. Gerry McGovern was placed in charge of the department that was to draw the coachwork. Time has proven the quality of their works.

Technical specifications

Model:	**MGF 1.8i**	**MGF 1.8i VVC (variable exhaust valve timing)**
Years of manufacture:	1995-present	1995-present
Production:	not known	not known
Engine:	four-cylinder	four-cylinder
Displacement:	110 cu. in.	110 cu. in.
Output:	120/5500 hp/rpm	145/7000 hp/rpm
Top speed:	120 mph	130 mph
From 0 to 30 mph:	9.2 sec	7.7 sec
Wheel base:	94 in	94 in
Length:	154 in	154 in
Width:	64 in	64 in
Height:	50 in	50 in
Weight:	2,337 lb	2,359 lb

Midas

Midas? The name is reminiscent of a figure from a Walt Disney movie and the model looks like a Mini Marcos. In 1975, Harold Dermolt was fed-up with his job at Jaguar. Together with his brother, he started a new company, D&H Fiberglass Techniques Ltd. They built the Mini Marcos and sold it as a riding vehicle or as a kit-car.

The Midas Gold Mk3 cost £10,750 sterling in England in 1988.

In 1977, Richard Oakes designed an improved version of the Mini, the Midas. It took longer than a year before the automobile was cured of its teething problems, but it was finally offered as the Midas Mk 1 in December 1978. The vehicle was built, as was the Marcos, with parts from the Mini. After getting advice from the famous constructor Gordon Murray, some improvements were realized at a later date. Hence, the model was sold as Mk 2 starting in 1981.

When British Leyland presented the Austin Metro, the brothers switched to parts from this modern vehicle. They presented the Midas Gold Mk 3 at the automobile exhibition in London in 1985. The Mk 3 had a frameless coachwork of glass fiber and plastic, to which the sub-frames for the engine and wheel suspension were screwed. In 1987, the brothers proved that their plastic car was as robust as a model with a steel body. Nobody was surprised when the vehicle passed the crash test. The Midas Gold Mk 3 could also be ordered as cabriolet in 1988. But when the little factory was completely destroyed by a fire in November 1989, the brothers were forced to declare bankruptcy. A few parts and the templates for the bodies could be salvaged and were sold to GTM Cars Ltd., a company occupied with building "kit-cars." GTM built a cabriolet in 1992 and a coupe model of the so-called Gold Mk 4 in 1995. The automobiles were constructed of parts from the Rover 100.

A somewhat strange combination: on the left, a steering wheel and a counter for miles instead of kilometers.

Many Midas drivers have come together in the Midas Owners Club. Most of the 250 members have constructed their vehicles themselves. And the club still has a future, because even at present the automobiles can be purchased as complete cars as well as kit-cars.

Technical specifications

Model:	**Midas**
Years of manufacture:	1978-present
Production:	about 700
Engine:	four-cylinder
Displacement:	78-85 cu. in.
Output:	from 60 to 85 hp/rpm
Top speed:	112-124 mph
From 0 to 60 mph in sec:	not known
Wheel-base:	84 in
Length:	137 in
Width:	62 in
Height:	45 in
Weight:	1,698 lb

The New Mini

July 7, 2003 marks the new Mini's second birthday. The Mini, now possibly the most desirable small car around, has enjoyed a whirlwind 24 months. Both Mini One and Mini Cooper enjoyed a warm welcome right away. *Auto Express* awarded Mini its coveted Car of the Year title in the 2001 New Car Honors Awards just ten days after it went on sale.

This is the original New Mini, the One.

Looking smart in its black and red livery, the Cooper S can be spotted by the S in the side grill on the wing.

The trend continued through the year with Mini also picking up *Driver's* Car of the Series and numerous 'Best Car' awards in newspapers and magazines.

Mini Cooper S became the third member of the Mini family when it went on sale on June 8, 2002 and soon won its first award – Best Sporting Car at the recent *Auto Express* New Car Honors 2002.

In 2003 the Mini range is joined by another stable mate, the diesel version. The 1.4-liter diesel engine is sourced from Toyota Motor Corporation and modified for performance and physical fit into Mini's engine bay. On May 30, 2003 the 100,000th Mini came off the production line at BMW Group Plant Oxford, just 13 months after the car went into volume production.

Although the New Mini is larger than the original Mini it still holds its basic feel and lines. BMW have taken the basic concept and refined it.

The Mini range, except the new diesel, uses a 1.6 litre, 4-cylinder engine, which is tuned by experts for three levels of performance – Mini One, Cooper and Cooper S. There is a considerable amount of chrome inside the cab, such as the switches which work the windows and lights and driving aids. The speedometer has been placed slap-bang in the

The interior of the Cooper S. The large speedometer is shown here in the middle of the dashboard.

middle of the dashboard and the rev counter is right in front of the driver. On Mini One and Cooper, you have the choice of manual shift or, if changing between 6 gears frightens or bores you, automatic shifting is available and very easily accessible from the gearchange lever.

The latest to be added to the Mini stable, this is the diesel version.

The cars are equipped with a selection of safety devices: 4 airbags as well as standard, anti-roll brakes, ABS, ASC+T (Automatic Stability Control), TDI (Tire Defect Indicator) and an outstandingly rigid chassis. Wishbones and MacPherson struts make up the front suspension whilst on the rear there are wishbones, longitudinal arms and struts. There is talk of a further addition to the Mini line-up that could only mean a cabriolet. This was not a model often seen on the old Mini except by special order, and there is no doubt it will be a welcome addition to the stable.

Technical specifications

Model:	**One**	**Cooper**	**Cooper S**	**Diesel**
Engine:	four-cylinder	four-cylinder	four-cylinder	four-cylinder
Displacement:	98 cu. in.	98 cu. in.	98 cu. in.	83 cu. in.
Stroke/Bore:	85.8/77	85.8/77	85.8/77	81.5/73
Transmission:	Man/Auto	Man/Auto	Man	Man
Top Speed:	112 mph	124 mph	135 mph	103 mph
0 – 62 mph:	10.9 sec	9.2 sec	7.4 sec	13.8 sec
Combined:	43.2 mpg	42.2 mpg	33.6 mpg	58.9 mpg
Wheels:	Steel	Alloy	Alloy	:
Length:	143 in	143 in	144 in	143 in
Width:	66 in	66 in	66 in	66 in
Height:	55 in	55 in	55 in	55 in
Weight:	2,513 lb	2,532 lb	2,679 lb	2,590 lb

Modulo

The cockpit of the Modulo is only 23.6 in wide so it is not suitable for big people.

Carlo Lamattina, born in 1940, worked among others for Zagato, Alfa Romeo and the airplane manufacturer Aero-Macchi. It is possible that he allowed himself be inspired by the aerodynamic shapes of his last employer.

"It is not so easy to become a manufacturer of automobiles," said Carlo Lamattina, the inventor of the Modulo. Lamattina built several prototypes in 1990, which he then sent to Rome and Munich to be homologated. This took three months at TüV in Germany and a little more than a year in Italy. But the vehicles passed the difficult tests. And Lamattina has been an automobile manufacturer since 1992.

The Modulo stands on ordinary wheels. The dimensions of the tires are: front 195-55-13 and rear 205-55-15.

The Modulo is an improved version of the old Messerschmitt from the fifties. The principle has remained the same: three wheels, the rear of which is powered, and space for two people who sit one in front of the other. The similarity ends there because the Modulo stands on real wheels and has a real engine. The smallest engine is a three-cylinder BMW motorcycle engine with 45.7 cu. in. and 75 horsepower. But an enthusiastic buyer could also order a four-cylinder with 67 cu. in. and 100 horsepower. In this last case, the vehicle would reach a maximum speed of no less than 118-130 mph.

Until they took a closer look at its construction, people found it strange at first when the Modulo was tested. This vehicle for two consists mainly of a cage made of steel tubes, the bottom and sides of which are covered with aluminum plating. The wheel suspension, the engine brackets and the joints for the plastic coachwork were connected to this frame. The car has no doors, and the sideways opening roof has to be ordered separately. The Modulo has a five-speed gearbox and three disk brakes. In several countries, it suffices to have a motorcycle driving license to drive the Modulo. And for those interested: the vehicle costs £41,500 sterling with a 67 cu. in. BMW engine, £34,000 sterling with a 67 cu. in. Guzzi engine, and £29,800 sterling without an engine.

Technical specifications

Model:	**Modulo**
Years of manufacture:	1992-present
Production:	not known
Engine:	three or four-cylinder
Displacement:	from 45.7 to 67 cu. in.
Output:	from 75 to 100 hp/rpm
Top speed:	118-130 mph
From 0 to 60 mph in sec:	not known
Wheel base:	not known
Length:	150 in
Width:	63 in
Height:	470 in
Weight:	882 lb

Morgan Aero 8

The Aero 8, Morgan's new 4.4-liter aluminum two-seater sports car, the first completely new Morgan car for more than 60 years, made its official debut in Germany at the 59th Frankfurt Motor Show in September 2001. A specially developed BMW V8 engine with VANOS variable inlet valve timing is the power plant for the new car.

It is very easy to recognize the car as a Morgan from the grille. The front of the Aero 8 is now one sculptured piece with extended wings, radiator, built in bumper sections and air intakes.

The Aero 8 project was set in motion in the late 1990s with the development of the works' GT2 racer, the brainchild of Charles Morgan (owner of the company) brought to life through the engineering expertise of Morgan's 1962 Le Mans class winner and design team technical chief Chris Lawrence.

From the outset of the project, Charles Morgan and the development team set a number of clear objectives for the finished car. These included a weight limit of 2,205 lb, a footprint the same as the Plus 8, European Whole Vehicle Type Approval, and styling that remained unmistakably Morgan. On October 17, 2001 Morgan Motor Company (MMC) secured European Whole Vehicle Type approval for the new car.

The Aero 8's long tapering hood, coupled with the large and very square V8 engine, resulted in some ingenious solutions, including putting the cylinder heads out under the front wings.

The Aero 8 chassis, developed for production using a 3D surface modeling software package, is formed and assembled in a dedicated cell, audited by Alcan and sheet metal engineering specialists Radshape. Here the pre-treated aluminum sheet is received from Alcan and the chassis is assembled from thirty-two formed panels. The original design for the aluminum chassis was tested using the resources of Birmingham University, led by Professor Jim Randall, though this design was then improved. Rigorous testing and development, not only at Morgan but also using

Still very much the Morgan line. The curvaceous front wings fade into the front of the rear wheel arches which flow rearwards to the back end of the car. The trunk lid has an aerodynamic flip to it to help with downforce.

the expertise of aluminum supplier Alcan and the testing facilities of BMW, significantly enhanced rigidity of torsion, strength and durability.

An innovative Morgan-designed suspension system coupled with a low centre of gravity, a race-bred braking system and a highly developed aerodynamic shape ensure the best road holding, stability and handling. With a gross weight of around 2,204 lb, the Aero 8 has one of the best power-to-weight ratios of any production sports car.

The Aero 8 will be available in over 30,000 body colors and the Connolly leather trim comes in a choice of over 40 colors.

This picture was taken on May 24, 2002 and shows the Dewalt/RSS Morgan Aero 8 at full speed during testing at La Sarthe.

The start of Aero 8 production marks the culmination of the largest development program ever undertaken by Morgan in more than 90 years of sports car manufacturing. The in-house project team has taken just five years to develop a completely new car from the ground up.

Technical specifications

Model:	**Morgan Aero 8**
Engine:	BMW V8
Capacity:	268 cu. in.
Bore x stroke:	32.6 x 36 in
Max Power:	286 bhp / 5500 rpm
Suspension:	
Front:	Independent, unique long cantilever arm with lower wishbone and inboard Eibach coil springs over Koni shocks.
Rear:	Independent, long transverse wishbones with cantilever mounted, fully floating inboard Eiback coil springs over Koni shocks.
Brakes:	AP Racing to Morgan specification.
Front:	4 pot, 13 in ventilated discs
Rear:	2 pot, 12 inventilated discs.
Weight:	2,205 lb
Wheels:	5 spoke 18" OZ magnesium alloy, Peg drive centre lock hubs
Tyres:	Dunlop foam fill run flat system with pressure sensors and internal visual/audible low pressure warning
Length :	3 ft 2 in
Width :	4 ft 1 in
Height :	4 ft (approx)

Nissan 350Z

In 1969 Nissan, also marketed in certain territories as Datsun, unveiled its attractive new sports car to the public. It was an extremely good looking car and it had all the reliability that Japanese cars were known for. It sold well and the company geared it up for competition. In the following years, the car was regularly upgraded and new versions appeared. The 240z became the 260z and then the 280z and in 1978 this was replaced by the 280CX, which had a new body shell and style. In 1989, a new 300zx hit the market complete with 3 liter V6 engine, 24 valves, four camshafts, twin turbos and four-wheel steering. Although the 240z sold well, the others were rather uninspiring and handicapped by new emission laws.

Creating the look and feel of any new vehicle is a serious undertaking. When the vehicle in question is an all-new sports car, one follows in the legendary tire prints of previous generations of the Nissan Z and the task instantly is elevated to a whole new dimension. After testing the waters with the introduction of the Z Concept show car in January 1999, the go-ahead was given in April of that year for development of what would become the 2003 Nissan 350Z.

Continuing the 'Z' heritage, the 350Z embodies many exciting new features. The 17 inch aluminum-alloy wheels set the vehicle off beautifully.

The all-new sports car was unveiled last January at the North American International Auto Show in Detroit and went on sale in the United States and Canada in August 2002. It will be in the showrooms in the UK in October 2003. Design cues passed on from the first-generation Z include the long nose and short deck styling, triangular cabin form and the lines extending from the arch-shaped roof to the hatchback opening. The Z's interior keeps maximum cabin width where the driver and passenger sit, tapering off like a speedboat fore and aft to create a sporty feel.

The rear of the 350z is neat, with clearly visible dual exhaust outlets, the side light blending into the bodywork and the slat-style parking lights neatly positioned below.

There are seven different well-equipped models in the US but only two planned for the UK.

An innovative tilt meter includes three gauges that move together with the steering wheel to facilitate independent functioning from the dashboard. Asymmetric seat design allows the driver's seat to be extra supportive, while the passenger's seat is more comfort oriented.

The Z has projector-type headlamps, which provide a wider illumination pattern and greater brightness. The car's stellar quality is also expressed by the distinctive vertical door handles and the twin exhaust tailpipes.

In addition to the hatchback coupe, a convertible version of the new Nissan Z is planned.

Technical specifications

Model:	**Nissan 350Z**
Engine:	V6 DOHC
Displacement:	213.6 cu. in.
Horsepower:	287 / 6200 rpm
Bore/Stroke:	95.5/81.4
Transmission:	Rear wheel drive
	6 speed manual/5Speed Auto with manual mode
Brakes:	Front – 2 caliper pistons, Rear – single caliper piston,Vented discs, ABS
Tires:	Front – 225/50R17 94 W, Rear – 235/50R17 96 W
Wheels:	Aluminum-alloy, Front- 17 x 7.5 in, Rear – 17 x 8 in
Dimensions:	
Wheel base:	104.3 in
Length:	169.9 in
Width:	71.5 in
Height:	51.9 in
Weight:	3,188 lb

Nissan-Datsun

The 2000 Sport was exported mainly to America. In Europe, the model remained a rarity.

The Datsun 240 Z was the first model with which Nissan conquered the American sport car market.

The automobile was highly priced (a second hand Porsche or MG would have been more cost-effective), but offered many extras compared to the European and American competition. By 1988, the 240 Z had matured into the 300 ZX. This car was driven by a 3.0-liter turbo engine, which converted 280 horsepower to the rear wheels. The maximum speed was no less than 155 mph.

But Nissan, then still known as Datsun, had started off on a smaller scale. The first "sports car," the Datsun DC3, drove out of the factory in 1952. The vehicle was made of parts from the Austin A40, which Datsun built under license, and was powered by a four-cylinder engine with a volume of 52.5 cu. in. and 20 horsepower. This two-seater car reached a maximum speed of 43 mph. The three-speed gearbox was not synchronized and there was a rigid axle in the front as well as in the back. A second model, the S 211, followed in 1958. This time with four seats and a body made entirely of plastic. The 988-cc engine produced 34 horsepower, enough for a maximum speed of 70 mph. The model did not become a great success. In three years time, only twenty of them were sold. The engine was redrilled and produced 60 horsepower at 5000 rpm in the Datsun Fairlady SPL 213 in 1960. The four-speed gearbox of this model was synchronized and all four wheels had independent springs. But the Fairlady SPL 213 was so small that it suited only the Japanese market. A sports car with "Western" measurements was presented for the first time at the Tokyo Motor Show in 1961. This SP 310

The Fairlady, or 2000 Sport, could also be delivered with a plastic hardtop.

Count Albrecht Goertz designed the coachwork for this Fairlady 2000. Goertz was already known for his BMW's, but became famous all over the world for his design of the Datsun Z 240.

was an open, two-seater model with a very tiny emergency seat in the back. The vehicle bore a great resemblance to the future MGB. The Fairlady 310 was enthusiastically welcomed, especially in America. The car was good for everyday use, but it could also race. No wonder 7,000 of the 310 model were sold.

The SP311 was presented as the next model at the end of 1964. The model was designed by the German Albrecht Goertz (designed of the BMW 507), who had immigrated to America. The SP 311 was called the Datsun Sport 1600 in America and the Fairlady 1600 in Japan. It became an international success. 5,388 cars were sold in 1965 and as many as 6,125 in 1966. By March 15, 1967, the car could also be ordered as a SR 311 with a 2.0-liter engine. The four-cylinder engine had an overhead camshaft. This 2000 Sport was the last model in this series.

Then the world was conquered by another model, the Datsun Z 240.

Technical specifications

Model:	**Datsun SP 213**	**SP 311**	**SR 311**
Years of manufacture:	1960-1962	1964-1970	1967-1970
Production:	217	27,384	15,015
Engine:	four-cylinder	four-cylinder	four-cylinder
Displacement:	73 cu. in.	97 cu. in.	121 cu. in.
Output:	60/5000 hp/rpm	96/6000 hp/rpm	135/6000 hp/rpm
Top speed:	80 mph	120 mph	125 mph
From 0 to 60 mph in sec:	not known	not known	not known
Wheel-base:	7 ft 3 in	7 ft 6 in	7 ft 6 in
Length:	13 ft 3 in	13 ft 1 in	13 ft 1 in
Width:	4 ft 10 in	4 ft 11 in	14 ft 11 in
Height:	4 ft 6 in	4 ft 4 in	4 ft 4 in
Weight:	1,962 lb	2,072 lb	2,094 lb

Noble M12 GTO

The name of the company that produces the Noble M12 GTO is Noble Moy Automotive and there are two gentlemen who are responsible for the car's introduction to the motoring world. Lee Noble is the talented engineer who has contributed such designs as Ultima, Ascari, Prosport 3000 and also the development chassis for the McLaren F1 supercar project over the course of the past twenty years. Tony Moy has brought more than forty years of successful business experience to Noble Moy Automotive and is the founder of the Page and Moy International Motor Racing Travel Company.

The Noble M12 GTO-3 is the latest model from the company. It looks fast even when it is not moving and is fitted with a new 3-liter, V6 engine, modified to Noble specification and mounted in the 'mid transverse' position. Inside this hotbed of technology you will find four overhead camshafts, which work 4 valves per cylinder. Twin Garrett T25 water-cooled turbochargers help to speed up the breathing and rocket this lightweight projectile into action. A five speed

This is the front of the Noble M12 GTO-3 with its built-in lights and air dam. The wing can be seen at the rear of the car.

Not yet on the market, but soon to be, is the new top version of the M12. A beauty, to say the least.

manual gearbox assists the driver in reaching the top speed. Besides this, the M12 GTO-3 varies very little from its predecessor.

The body is made up of GRP composite and the front and rear sections are removable. The chassis is a steel space frame with bonded and riveted alloy panels and the car is also equipped with a full safety roll cage.

One could be forgiven for thinking that the cabin is a little sparse and uncomfortable. In fact, much thought has gone into making it comfortable and livable. The standard interior specification consists of the highest quality Alcantara and the trim is available in a combination of various colors. Leather interior trim is available as a factory fitted option, either half or full leather.

This version of the Noble M12 GTO-3R is aimed at the advanced driver who seeks a little more performance and handling.

Both six point and inertia reel seatbelts have been fitted to the unique composite seats. Should you start getting a little hot under the collar, air conditioning is also available. Just to finish things off and keep it a neat little package, luggage has been developed for the car to make the best use of the luggage space behind the seats.

The Noble behaves well on the track and customers will enjoy many hours of fun and excitement.

There are four models currently available: the new spec M12 GTO-3, a high spec refined 3R, the ultimate track car 3T and the 3C, which is an open-top version.

Noble production is now well established in two large factory buildings in Barwell, Leicestershire, England. Five production stations provide the facility for hand assembly. Pre-delivery tests are carried out by skilled factory technicians, a final valet session is performed and thenthe cars go off to the dealers via transporter.

Technical specifications

Model:	**Noble M12 GTO-3**	**GTO-3T**
Engine:	V6 Twin turbo	V6 Twin turbo
Capacity:	3 liter	3 liter
Max Power:	340 bhp	400 bhp
Brakes:		
Front:	130 x 12 in ventilated, Cross drilled discs 6 piston alloy calipers	130 x 12 in ventilated, Cross drilled discs 4 piston alloy calipers
Rear:	130 x 10 in ventilated, Cross drilled discs 4 piston alloy calipers	130 x 10 in ventilated, Cross drilled discs 4 piston alloy calipers
Wheels:		
Front:	8.5 x 18 in alloy	10.5 x 18 in alloy
Rear:	10 x 18 in alloy	11.5 x 18 in alloy
Tires:		
Front:	225/40 ZR 18	225/40 ZR 18
Rear:	265/35 ZR 18	265/35 ZR 18
Weight:	2,315 lb	2,315 lb

NSU Ro80

A Ro80 of Pininfarina, which was presented in Thuringia in 1971.

Felix Wankel made his first drawings for a rotary engine in 1926. But it would take him until 1951 to put his theories into practice. To do so, he signed a contract with NSU. But still, not everything went according to plan. It was not until 1960 that the first Wankel engine was installed in an NSU Prinz. Thousands of test miles were driven before the engine was installed in the first regular production vehicle in 1963. The response of the public was enthusiastic, but only a few

The Ro80 reached a top speed of 112 mph, but at that speed it made 48 miles to the gallon.

The NSU Swivel Spider was the first production car with a rotary engine.

of the cars were sold. Between September 1964 and July 1967, only 2,375 NSU Wankel Spiders were sold. The last car did not find a buyer until October 1968.

Matters went a little better with the big brother of the Wankel Spider. NSU had started the production of the Ro80 in August 1967. A few were already available when the car was presented at the Frankfurt automobile exhibition in September 1967. It was a beautiful, luxurious vehicle with an engine that made a civilized humming sound. If it ran willingly, that is. Unfortunately, it often did not. The engine still had many shortcomings and this led to the dealers changing more engines than spark plugs.

After the engine of the Ro80 was cured of its teething problems, it was certainly as reliable as, for instance, a Mercedes engine.

The Bertone four-seat car was powered by a Ro80-engine, which was placed in front of the rear axle, between the back passengers.

The cars that emerged from the production line after 1970 were cured of most of their teething problems. This model could be recognized by its double headlights. The NSU Ro80 was a spacious car with front wheel propulsion, a semi-automatic gearbox and four disk brakes. And though by 1970 the engine was as reliable as any ordinary engine, it was not the least bit economical about gas. It also often happened that the driver let the engine make too many revolutions because it ran almost without a sound. They tried to prevent this by installing a buzzer in 1971. This buzzer would start working when the engine made too many revolutions per minute (rpm).
The last vehicles came out of production in 1977. The experiment with the Wankel engine was over for NSU. But Mazda still kept producing the engine under license, and with more success.

Technical specifications

Model:	**NSU Ro80**
Years of manufacture:	1967-1977
Production:	37,400
Engine:	Wankel engine
Displacement:	30 cu. in.
Output:	115/5500 hp/rpm
Top speed:	112 mph
From 0 to 60 mph:	14 sec
Wheel-base:	9 ft 5 in
Length:	15 ft 8 in
Width:	5 ft 9 in
Height:	4 ft 8 in
Weight:	2,822 lb

Osca MT4

Until the 1950s, it was difficult to draw the line between a monoposto, a one-person racecar, and a sports car for two persons. It was often only a matter of screwing off the headlights and mudguards to transform an automobile for daily life into a racing vehicle for the circuit. Our Osca, notably the very first automobile of this brand, with the chassis number 1101 (67 cu. in. and number one), is a case in point.

In 1937, the Maserati brothers were forced to sell their factory in Bologna to the very wealthy Adolfo Orsi. The contract included an agreement that the three brothers would continue working for him for ten years. But Ernesto, Ettore and Bindo Maserati left their boss Orsi the day the contract expired in 1947. The Orsi factory was located in Modena

The simple coachwork was made entirely of aluminum.

The Osca MT4 performed splendidly on the public road. The headlights were placed behind the grill, but the automobile was also equipped with city and rear lights. There werwn't any turn indicators, however.

and the Maserati brothers decided to return to Bologna where they founded their new company, OSCA (Officina Specializatta Costruzione Automobili). On April 5, 1948, at five past six in the evening, the engine for the first prototype was started. The first test ride followed on April 8 and lasted more than an hour. A couple of months later, on September 19, the Osca MT4 won its first race, the Naples Grand Prix on the Posillipo circuit. Racer Gigi Villoresi ended ahead of a Ferrari, a Maserati and a Cisitalia.

The instruments of the Osca MT4. From left to right: a water-temperature meter, a revolution counter and an oil-pressure meter.

No, the car had no cloth top and no doors.

The Maserati brothers had constructed their first sports car in 1926. They possessed an enormous amount of knowledge and expertise in this field and therefore it was not too much trouble to construct a small, inexpensive four-cylinder engine. They succeeded in 1929 in constructing a racecar with a V-16 engine with two compressors and four overhead camshafts. The Osca engine had only one overhead camshaft in an aluminum cylinder head, two double Weber carburetors and a cylinder volume of less than 1.1 liters. However, the compression ratio was set at 11.5:1, which made it necessary to mix the gas with benzene. The engine block was made of aluminum and the casing of the four-speed gearbox was magnesium, in order to make the vehicle as light as possible. The car stood, as was customary in that time, on spoked wheels. The aluminum gas tank was placed in the back of the car and the fuel was sent to the two double carburetors by an electrical pump. The automobile in the pictures is completely restored and participates in races for historic automobiles.

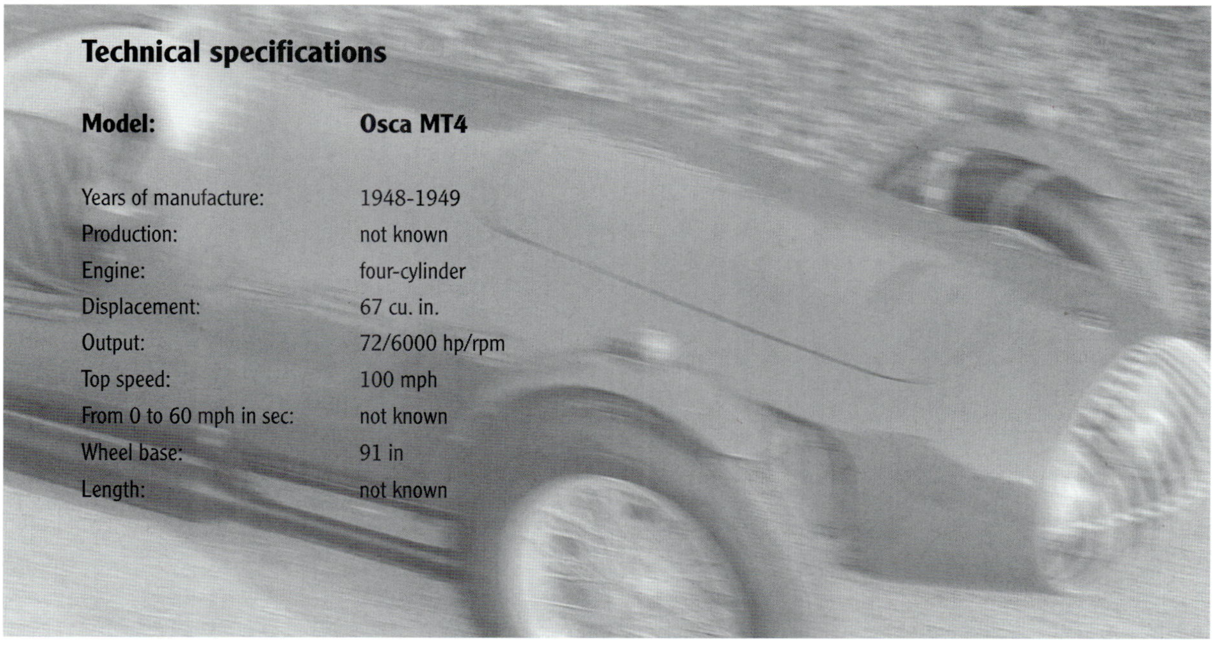

Technical specifications

Model:	**Osca MT4**
Years of manufacture:	1948-1949
Production:	not known
Engine:	four-cylinder
Displacement:	67 cu. in.
Output:	72/6000 hp/rpm
Top speed:	100 mph
From 0 to 60 mph in sec:	not known
Wheel base:	91 in
Length:	not known

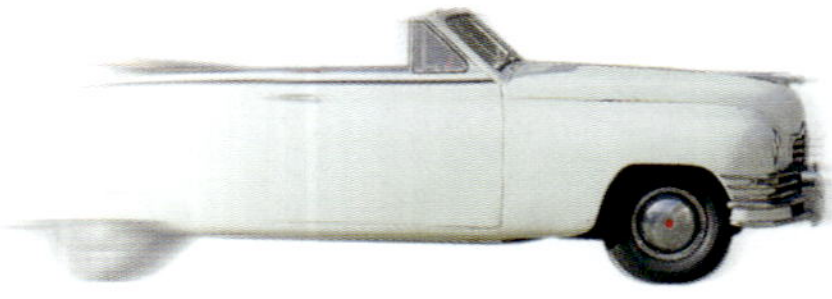

Packard 1949

James Ward Packard.

In 1941, Packard was very successful with its new Clipper. The Clipper was designed in a record time of ten days by the famous Howard "Dutch" Darrin. The model was distinguished by its huge, broad front seat. That same year, the American factory was able to sell no less than 69,653 cars. But sales declined the following year. Furthermore, on February 9, 1942, they had to stop the production of passenger cars and the production lines were converted to the construction of military vehicles. At Packard, they had been constructing airplane engines and fast boats since 1940 and the company had acquired a good reputation in the Navy. Packard had earned no less than 16.6 million dollars by the time the war ended.

They switched back to the production of passenger cars in 1946. And again, the Clipper became a great success. According to Packard's original plans, they could have sold 100,000 of them, but the automobile industry in Detroit was plagued by strikes. The employees of Packard wanted to continue their work, but because many supplying companies were on strike in 1946, work had to be stopped 47 times for long periods. One time, the management had to send their workers home for fifteen days because the bearings ordered at General Motors could not be delivered. And when they resumed work in Detroit, a strike started in the coachwork plant in Briggs, so that the people from Packard were forced to stay at home again, this time for nine days. Because of the strikes, only 30,793 cars were sold in 1946. The next year, 1947, was not much more productive. Of the 100,000 planned cars, they were able to build 51,086. If the army had not paid its outstanding bills, bankruptcy would have been inevitable. Under pressure of the stockhold-

The radiator emblem of the Packard with the family crest of the English Packards of Baddod, the ancestors of James Ward and William Doud Packard.

Until 1947, a high, stately grill had been the trademark of Packard. Later, automobiles were given a more modern appearance.

ers, the enormous sum of 1.5 million dollars was invested in a completely new series of cabriolets. The cars were expected at the end of March 1947, but the first was not delivered until the summer of 1947. The model had a modern, low grille and the coachwork was rounded, not boxy. Packard had more experience with cabriolets than any other American manufacturer of open-top vehicles. The new model became a great success. The New York Fashion Academy gave the automobile a golden medal for the Fashion Car of the Year. The model also ended up the winner of the Concours d'Elegance in Caracas, Monte Carlo and Luzern.

There were four different base models planned for 1948, ranging from a cheap Six Sedan to an expensive Custom 8 Cabrio. This last model was driven by a strong 8-cylinder inline engine with a volume of 355.7 cu. in. and 162 horsepower. The somewhat cheaper Super Eight had a shorter wheel base, but the same engine now

The Super Eight Victoria Convertible Coupe, as the cabriolet was officially named, was a spacious automobile with six seats.

In 1949, the Americans still had modest sized cars. This Packard was "only" 17 ft long.

produced 147 horsepower. The Eight DeLuxe was equipped with a 288 cu. in. eight-cylinder engine with 132 horsepower and the Six Sedan had to suffice with a six-cylinder, 245 cu. in. and 106 horsepower engine. But all models had one thing in common: their remarkably good quality. For instance, the undercarriage of the cabriolet, which had been solid already, was strengthened with extra beams. The cloth top and the side windows could be operated hydraulically.

1948 was a successful production year for the factory because no other strikes occurred. A total of 90,525 vehicles were sold. They raised this number to 146,441 in 1949, a fabulous improvement on the 1936 pre-war record.

Technical specifications

Model:	**Packard Super Eight**
Years of manufacture:	1947-1949
Production:	5,421
Engine:	eight-cylinder
Displacement:	326 cu. in.
Output:	147/3600 hp/rpm
Top speed:	90 mph
From 0 to 60 mph in sec:	not known
Wheel base:	10 ft
Length:	17 ft
Width:	6 ft 6 in
Height:	5 ft 3 in
Weight:	4,012 lb

Pagani Zonda C12 S and Roadster

Bright, spacious and plenty of leather. This is the cockpit of the Zonda C12S.

Horacio Pagani's fondest dream was to build his own supercar. It was realized in 1988 when the draft drawings of the "C8 Project" were shown for the first time to Jean Manuel Fangio. The car was to be named the Fangio F1 as a tribute to the great champion.

In 1992, Pagani began to construct a prototype and the first model was tested in the Dallara wind tunnel in 1993. The positive results marked the beginning of a long period of design and definition of the construction details.

At this point, Fangio introduced Pagani to Mercedes, the company to which he was linked by his series of historic Formula 1 victories. Mercedes could foresee that the project was worthwhile and, in 1994, officially agreed to supply its powerful V12 engine.

After four more years of hard work, Pagani obtained approval of the coupe version of the C8 Project and the first Zonda C12 was presented at the 1999 Geneva Motor Show.

Fangio, after a long illness, died and Pagani changed the name of his car to Zonda, which is the name of the wind that blows in the Andes, out of modesty and respect for the great man.

At the Geneva Motor Show of 2002, Horatio Pagani presented the latest Zonda sports car, now enhanced to C12 S status. The upgraded version of the C12 took advantage of the continuing development program at the Pagani Works in Modena, Italy. The car utilizes the 7.3 liter Mercedes-AMG V12 engine, replacing the original 7-liter version, to propel

This view taken from slightly above the Zonda C12S shows the true shape of this very fast sports car.

It is easy to see just how far forward the cabin is on the Zonda. The four headlights are nicely positioned and fit neatly into the front wings.

it to top speeds via a six-speed gearbox designed by Pagani. At the same time, to conquer the challenge of the dual characteristics demanded of sports cars, namely, "enormous power" and "ballerina–like lightness," the company included a Pagani-developed traction control system. This should give the driver more confidence and the car better handling in all conditions.

At the rear end of the car, the hood shape was modified to give the driver better visibility. The rear wing was split and moved backwards to give better downforce and improved stability at high speeds. 2003 saw another addition to the lineup, a roadster version, pushing top sports car driving to the limit.

All the usual requirements are inside the cockpit of the car: air conditioning, power steering, and a hi-fi sound system. Additionally, leather (you can choose your own color and type) is used extravagantly and comfort is a priority.

It would be difficult to miss this rear end. The exhaust pipes are neatly positioned in the circular housing in the middle of the rear panel of the Zonda.

The rear end looks a little bulky and is certainly different-looking, thanks to four exhaust pipes neatly positioned in a circular housing. The front is sleek and impressive with twin, slim headlights on both sides and an air intake positioned just off the road.

Technical specifications

Model:	**Pagani Zonda C12 S and Roadster**
Engine:	Mercedes-Benz M 120 7.3 AMG 445 cu. in.
Max. Power:	(kW) hp/rev: (408) 555/5900
Clutch:	Twin plate clutch
Gearbox:	Mechanical 6 speed (+ reverse)
Brakes:	4 ventilated Brembo disks:
Front:	355 four piston caliper
Rear:	335 four piston caliper
	Hydraulic power brake; ABS
Wheels:	Aluminum alloy OZ wheels
Tires:	Michelin Pilot tires:
Front:	255/40/18
Rear:	345/35/18
Suspension:	4 independent wheels with double A-arm; helical springs and hydraulic dampers; anti-roll bar; aluminum alloy suspension arms
Length:	14 ft 5 in
Width:	6 ft 9 in
Height:	3 ft 9 in
Wheel base:	8 ft 11 in
Weight:	2,756 lb

Panhard Dyna Cabriolet

The French Panhard & Levassor is one of the oldest automobile manufacturers in the world. The first vehicle was built in 1891. Unfortunately, in 1965 the factory was taken over by Citroën, who forced the brand to disappear from the market two years later. After the Second World War, the Panhard was loved by the public mainly because of its reliable two-cylinder boxer engine. Unlike other French producers like Delahaye, Delage, Talbot or Hotchkiss, the Panhard management understood that after the war there would be a demand for small, economical cars. But rivals like Citroën and Renault also knew this and produced cars like the Deux Chevaux (Citroën) and the 4CV (Renault).
Panhard had constructed several prototypes during the war and these models were tested on the public road. The vehicles were designed by the famous constructor, Jean Albert Grégoire, the great pioneer of front wheel drive.

Aluminum that shines. Immediately after the war, it was easier to find supplies of aluminum than of steel.

Production was restarted right after the capitulation of Germany. The first model, the Panhard Dyna, was presented in the Salon de Paris in 1946. However, it took until August for the first cars to emerge form the production line. The waiting lists were already immeasurably long by then. Yet the waiting was worthwhile because the Panhard was really something new. The doors and the hood of the four-door car were made of aluminum. The coachwork was placed on a tube chassis, the front wheels had independent shock absorbers and the rear axle was rigid. And of course, the Dyna had front wheel propulsion. The engine was a piece of highly technical jewelry. It was an air-cooled two-cylinder with overhead valves which were operated with torsion springs instead of spiral springs. The engine initially produced

The automobile had no trunk lid. Luggage had to be stored over the backrest of the back seat.

The air-cooled, aluminum two-cylinder was installed in front of the front axle.

The dashboard of the Dyna. The chromium handle under the gas indicator is the gear switch.

24 horsepower, but from 1949, they would raise this to 28 from the 37.2 cu. in. engine. At the end of 1950, the program was extended with a cabrio-limousine (of which the cloth top stretched up to the back window-screen) and a 2+2-cabriolet.

The cylinder and engine power were gradually increased. In 1954, the two-cylinder engine had a volume of 51.9 cu. in. and 42 horsepower at 5000 rpm. A top speed of around 80 mph was no longer exceptional. Boosted Dynas won races like the Mille Miglia, the Le Mans 24-hour race and the Monte Carlo Rally. The absolute ultimate from the program was the Panhard Junior, an open car for two, which was terribly expensive, but offered a great deal of riding pleasure.

Panhard kept making the little Dynas until 1954. Then the model was followed by a much larger version, which offered seating for six. This model too was driven by the reliable, air-cooled two-cylinder engine, which powered, of course, the front wheels.

Technical specifications

Model:	**Panhard Dyna**
Years of manufacture:	1948-1956
Production:	about 55,000
Engine:	two-cylinder
Displacement:	37,45 and 52 cu. in.
Output:	from 24/4000 to 38/5000 hp/rpm
Top speed:	60 to 80 mph
From 0 to 60 mph in sec:	not known
Wheel base:	6 ft 11 in
Length:	11 ft 9 in to 12 ft 6 in
Width:	4 ft 9 in
Height:	5 ft 1 in
Weight:	1,215 lb

Plymouth Road Runner
Superbird

With two four-barrel Carter carburetors, the "Super Commando" engine produced 395 SAE horsepower.

Richard Petty wrote automobile history as a factory racer for Plymouth in the NASCAR (National Association for Stock Car Racing). All his cars were painted "Petty Blue" and always had the start number 43. He won no less than 27 races with his Plymouth Belvedere in 1967. That same year he gained the title of Grand National Champion for the second time.

Plymouth presented the Road Runner, a two-door car which could be delivered as coupe or as cabriolet, in 1968. The automobile weighed almost 3750 pounds and was powered by a 6.3-literV8 engine which even in its standard version produced 340 SAE horsepower at 5200 rpm. This was like a toy engine, of course, for a man like Petty, but the ordinary customer could choose "heavier" equipment. The Road Runner was also available with a 7.2-literV8 with 380 SAE horsepower at 4600 rpm or a 7.0-liter with 431 SAE horsepower at 5000 rpm. In the latter case, the heavy vehicle would reach a top speed of approximately 155 mph. The coachwork of the car was plain with heavy bumpers and beautiful hubcaps. However, the simple drum brakes were not adapted to the enormous performance.

Car races in America played an important role in the battle between the great brand names. In 1968, Petty wanted Plymouth to improve the aerodynamics of the Belvedere. The vehicles of the competition were already looking like worthy racecars. These included the Dodge Charger Daytona, a coupe with an enormous wing above the trunk lid and a long plastic nose. The automobile looked bizarre, but it could go very fast. Bobby Isaac won a few races in it and Buddy Baker improved on the record on the Alabama International Speedway track. He made his laps with a speed of around 200 mph. Ford too improved its models for the circuit and Petty signed a contract with them for one season.

Seen from the front, the Superbird looked like an ordinary car.

The typical wing with the little bird and the type number.

This was a success. Supported by Dodge, Plymouth also began the construction of comparable cars. The "Dodge Daytona was thoroughly tested in the wind tunnel and Plymouth profited from the test results. The new Plymouth was based on the Belvedere, but the changes to the vehicle were numerous. For instance, it had apparently become impossible to attach a new plastic nose to the mudguards of the Belvedere. Therefore, the technicians decided to replace the mudguards from the Belvedere with those of the Dodge Coronet.
But the rear end of the car also had to be adjusted. The model was equipped with a new back window-screen and a lid for the trunk. The enormous wing on the back mudguards was the most remarkable feature. Because of experience with the Dodge Daytona, the wing was placed at a sharp angle. They had to build 2,000 cars to participate in the NASCAR races. This job was done by a company named Creative Industries. Now that they had such a car, Richard Petty was willing to represent Plymouth again.

A Road Runner painted in "Alpine White".

The brand image with the little bird was also painted on the cap of the left headlight.

The name indication on the rear mudguard.

But he did not manage to win the 1970 Championship. That year, the title went to Bobby Isaac with his Dodge Daytona. Nevertheless, Petty won eighteen races. The racing version of the Superbird was terribly fast.
On the circuits, the car reached speeds of up to 200 mph. On the salt planes of Bonneville, they even measured a top speed of 216 mph. The Superbird and the Daytona won almost everything that could be won.
This was reason enough for the NASCAR organization to adjust the racing regulations for 1971, forbidding alterations to the aerodynamic design of the standard cars and spoiling all the fun for the Chrysler Corporation.
The production of the Superbird was halted immediately and only 1,920 cars of this model were produced.
A customer who ordered one of the said cars from his dealer was (fortunately) not able to drive at such exaggerated speeds. Although he did have a choice between three engines ranging from 375 up to 425 SAE horsepower, the speedometer never passed the 140 mph. The Superbird could be delivered with a Torque-Flite automatic or with a hand-switched four speed gearbox. The front wheels were equipped with disk brakes and broad Goodyear tires. The buyer could choose between seven colors with the following exotic names: Vitamin C Orange, Tor-Red, Corporation Blue, Lime Light, Blue Fire Metallic, Alpine White and Lemon Twist. The interior was white or black vinyl and the roof was always finished with black vinyl.

Technical specifications

Model:	**Plymouth Roadrunner Superbird**
Year of manufacture:	1970
Production:	1,920
Engine:	V8
Displacement:	425.6 and 439.7 cu. in.
Output:	431/5000 hp/rpm
Top speed:	137-140 mph
From 0 to 60 mph in sec:	not known
Wheel base:	9 ft 8 in
Length:	18 ft 2 in
Width:	6 ft 4 in
Height:	4 ft 5 in
Weight:	3,748 lb

Pontiac Fiero

The Fiero had been built as a "commuter car," but it was actually a sport car for two persons.

Pontiac constructed "ordinary" automobiles most of the time. It was only when the management was in the hands of John DeLorean, vice-president of General Motors and big chief of Pontiac, that several special models were developed. His GTO and Firebird were ordinary automobiles to look at, but dangerously fast on the circuits. But DeLorean was also not allowed to build a two-seater or a sport car because Chevrolet would not tolerate any competition from the home front for the Corvette. In the end, permission was given to build a little passenger car for two, intended for daily use. Hulki Aldikacti was given the assignment to design such a car. He received a budget of "only" 400 million dollars, a fragment of the amount usually invested in a new model. To lower production costs, the model was given plastic coachwork and

Here, an ASC Fiero with a V6 engine.

a four-cylinder engine. And because there was no money for a completely new engine design, they were left with only one option: to install the "Iron Duke." This old four-cylinder had a block of cast iron. The engine was placed right in front of the rear axle. However, because the space in front was actually too limited, a small oil sump was used. The so-called

The Fiero was barely on the market when the well-known company ASC (American Sunroof Company) presented a cabriolet version.

Pontiac Fiero of 1984 was presented to the public in 1983. The reactions were very positive. Orders came in big numbers because the Fiero was being offered for less than $10,000. In the first year, no less than 101,000 Fieros were sold. In spite of this success, the management of GM still considered the Fiero to be a everyday, "ordinary" car. On the other hand, there were those at Pontiac who dreamt of a future on the circuits. They even managed to build a V6 engine. When the Fiero was chosen as the "pace car" for the Indianapolis 500 Race, there was nothing that could go wrong, or so they thought.

Although the engine had been placed in front of the rear axle, it was not hard to reach.

Most cars delivered with the V6 engine could be recognized by the spoiler on the hood.

Although the Fiero was built in a separate factory, some things were not going right. Four of the five driving rods showed hairline fractures and could break at high revolutions. This defect could not be blamed on the people at the factory. But they also connected the electrical ventilators wrongly, so the hot air was blown against the engine, and forgot to connect cables, causing short–circuiting. In the autumn of 1985, GM had to refund the owners of 112 burned-out Fieros. In the summer of 1987, there was an average of 20 burned-out cars per month – one for every 508 Fieros sold.

In 1986, only 71,283 Fieros were sold, and the future was not looking any brighter. Pontiac recalled all cars built in 1984. The oil filter was adjusted, so the Iron Duke engine again received the necessary amounts of oil it needed to function properly. A sticker was placed on the cap of the gas tank with the text: Check oil! None of it helped and the Fieros kept catching fire. In December 1989, Pontiac called all 244,000 Fieros back. Four months later, all six-cylinders were called back too. They unsuccessfully tried to fix and replace them. The Fiero had too many defects. It had been brought on the market too early, before all its teething problems were cured.

Moreover, Aldikacti's budget had been too limited.

Technical specifications

Model:	**Pontiac Fiero**	**V6**
Years of manufacture:	1983-1989	1985-1989
Production:	244,000	not known
Engine:	four-cylinder	V6
Displacement:	151 cu. in.	173 cu. in.
Output:	99/4800 hp/rpm	137/4500 hp/rpm
Top speed:	110 mph	120 mph
From 0 to 60 mph in sec:	not known	not known
Wheel base:	7 ft 10 in	7 ft 10 in
Length:	13 ft 7 in	13 ft 7 in
Width:	5 ft 9 in	5 ft 9 in
Height:	3 ft 11 in	3 ft 11 in
Weight:	2,789 lb	2,789 lb

Porsche 356 Speedster

Work at the Porsche Design office resumed soon after World War II. Under Karl Rabe, the chief designer of the time, a site at Gmund was found in the foothills of Corinthia in the southernmost state of Austria. The German economy was in a very depressed state at this time, but Volkswagen had gone back to producing cars in Wolfsburg and they had never severed links with Porsche. Inspired by their Cisitalia project, the idea of their own sports car appealed to the Porsche workers. Design drawings for the new car started to take shape in 1947 and by June 1948, the car became a reality, a two-seater, open sports car based on Volkswagen parts. This was the first car to use the Porsche name and was christened the Type 356 Roadster.

From here onwards there would be many different designations for the 356 model, but possibly the prettiest was the 356 Speedster, which appeared in 1954.

By now, Porsche had moved to their Zuffenhausen location in the suburbs of Stuttgart, Bavaria. The speedster was a pure two-seater with an all-weather roof that folded down behind the two front seats. Initially, the windscreen was very low and looked like two halves of glass fused together, but later was a single piece of curved glass. Bucket seats were fitted which had vertical slits in the backs to underline the car's sportiness. The car was aimed at and sold to the American market, mainly California, where, fortunately, it does not rain often.

The original 1954 version had a 91.5 cu. in. rear mounted engine and produced 55 horsepower and by 1956 it used the 97.6 cu. in. Super engine producing 75 horsepower. In 1957, using what was basically a toned-down version of the 550 Spyder racing engine, Porsche introduced what was to become the first Carrera. This was the ultimate road-going Porsche of the period, the 356 Carrera Speedster, and had to be treated with kid gloves, a powerful car which could go wild if not driven with respect. Porsche produced two versions of this model, the GS being the one with all the

Straight out of the 1950's, this great photo portrays the 356 Speedster in the way it was meant to be seen. Sunshine, a pretty lady and an open top epitomize the sports car.

comforts, and the GT the stripped-down racing version. These were both used for racing in Europe and in the United States. Between 1958 and 1959, the car was fitted with a larger 97.6 cu. in. engine to improve performance and the GT received aluminum doors and deck lids, but otherwise the two versions remained the same. The last of the Carrera Speedsters was made in 1959, by which time the standard 356 Speedster was no longer available. It had been replaced by the Convertible D, a more comfortable version.

The 356 Speedster had a short life and by September 1965, the last 356C rolled off the production line and a new era was ready to begin.

Technical specifications

Model:	**1956 356 A 1600 Speedster**
Engine:	Four-cylinders horizontally opposed, air cooled
Displacement:	100 cu. in.
Output:	60 hp / 4500 rpm
Fuel system:	Mechanical pump, 2 Solex downdraft carburettors
Drive:	4-speed gearbox, single plate dry clutch
Brakes:	Hydraulic drum
Wheel base:	6 ft 11 in
Length:	12 ft 11 in
Height (open):	3 ft 8 in
Weight:	1,841 lb
Top Speed:	100 mph

Porsche 911 GT2

The Porsche 911 Turbo represents a milestone in supercar performance and sporting ability. It blends a stability-enhancing aerodynamics package with taut, even more responsive chassis dynamics and a 462bhp power output, to create the ultimate road-going Porsche 911.

With a power to weight ratio of only 325 bhp per ton the GT2 accelerates from 0 – 62 mph in just 4.1 seconds.

The distinctive yellow ceramic brake calliper hiding behind this wheel tells us that the car it is fitted to is the GT2.

Visually different to the Turbo, the 911 GT2 has redesigned air intake scoops at the outer extremities of the rear of the car, while an air outlet directly forward of the luggage compartment lid helps suck air from underneath the car, aiding aerodynamics. Another point of difference is the larger rear wing, which is fixed rather than moveable, and sits higher and further back. Air intake ducts in the two tips of the rear wings supply fresh air to the engine; air from these ducts is fed into a collector box and from there into the air filter.

An ultra-high performance evolution of the 911 Turbo's 3.6-liter unit, the flat-six in the 911 GT2 produces a wholesome 10 percent more power and two turbochargers have an even higher air throughput than the 911 Turbo's pair. As on the race-bred GT1, this high performance power unit features dry sump lubrication, with a separate oil tank fitted directly to the engine. The GT2 was the second Porsche to feature VarioCam Plus, an enhanced version of the company's ingenious VarioCam valve lift adjustment system, which improves power and torque while also reducing fuel consumption and emissions.

The GT2's exhaust system is essentially the same as that fitted to the 911 Turbo, except for the addition of special mufflers to lower exhaust gas counter pressure. Given the extra performance of the GT2, exhaust emissions easily comply with the very strict D4 emissions standard, therefore Euro 4-compliant under standard test conditions and with the increasingly tough LEV standards applicable in the USA. The chassis and suspension of the GT2 have been designed with extremes of performance in mind, together with sufficient adjustability for the car to be used on the track if an owner so wishes.

S GO 2005

The GT2 is also the first Porsche to be fitted with the company's innovative Porsche Ceramic Composite Brake (PCCB) system, weighing 50 percent less than conventional metal discs and easily identifiable by its distinctive yellow painted callipers.
Inside the cabin, you will find leather-covered glass fiber bucket seats, driver, passenger and side airbags, electric windows, remote central locking, and a Thatcham category one alarm/immobiliser. No-cost options for the GT2 include automatic air-conditioning with an activated carbon filter, and a Porsche CDR22 CD/tuner.
Also for the racing enthusiast, Porsche has developed an exclusive package for the car available in Clubsport guise. This includes a roll-cage bolted directly to the body, a fire-extinguisher system, and fire-retardant upholstery.

Technical specifications

Model:	**Porsche 911 GT2**
Engine:	6 cylinder horizontally opposed, four overhead camshafts, four valves per cylinder, two exhaust gas turbochargers, two intercoolers, sequential multi-point fuel injection
Bore/ Stroke:	3.94 in/3.01 in
Capacity:	220 cu. in.
Engine output:	340 kW (462 bhp) at 5700 rpm
Engine management:	Motronic ME 7.8, knock control
Power transmission:	Engine and transmission bolted together to form one unit, rear wheels driven by double drive shafts, manual transmission
Chassis and suspension:	
Front axle:	McPherson design (optimised by Porsche)
Rear axle:	Multi-link design with rigidly suspended side sections Suspension adjustable for height, camber and castor (for motorsport)
Brakes:	Two-circuit brake system, Porsche Ceramic Composite Brakes, six-piston aluminium monobloc brake callipers on the front axle, four-piston aluminium monobloc brake callipers on the rear axle, cross-drilled, internally-ventilated ceramic brake discs front and rear, ABS
Wheels and tires:	
Front:	8.5J x 18 ET 40 with 235/40 R 18
Rear:	12 J x 18 ET 45 with 315/30 R 18
Weight:	3,175 lb
Length	13 ft 9 in
Width	6 ft
Height	4 ft 2 in
Wheel base	7 ft 11 in
Top Speed:	196 mph

Porsche 911 Turbo

A great view of the front of the 2003 Porsche 911 Turbo. The clearly visible bi-xenon headlights, air scoops and beautifully integrated front end give the car a clean and healthy look.

Compared with the 911 Carrera, the Turbo's rear wheel arches are nearly 2.6 inches wider, in order to accommodate 18-inch light alloy wheels shod with 295/30 R18 tyres. Those broad arches also house the neatly integrated air scoops, which feed cool air to the twin turbochargers. A further highlight of the Turbo's rear end is its moveable wing and the special slatted rear cover for expelling the turbocharger exhaust air.

The considerable motive force behind the 911 Turbo's astonishing performance is a 3.6-liter, four valves per cylinder, horizontally-opposed six-cylinder engine, boosted by a pair of exhaust gas turbochargers. Like the 911 GT2, the cylinder charge is controlled by VarioCam Plus, which is made up of four valves per cylinder, axial camshaft adjusters and interchangeable valve tappets. Thanks to this, and to a new engine management system with E-gas, Porsche

engineers have made notable progress in reducing exhaust emissions. The 911 Turbo complies comfortably with D4 exhaust emissions limits, which correspond to the EURO 4 standard test limits, and it is no surprise that the 911 Turbo also complies with LEV standard in the US.

With its overall fuel consumption at 21.9 mpg (12.9 liters per 100 km), the current Turbo is 18 percent more economical than its predecessor.

The 911 Turbo comes with four-wheel drive as standard. Depending on the driving conditions, the front wheels distribute up to 40 percent of the available engine power to the road.

Active driving safety is significantly enhanced by Porsche Stability Management, or PSM, standard equipment on the 911 Turbo. By combining four-wheel drive, PSM, and a sports suspension set-up that lowers the whole car by 0.39 in, the 911 Turbo is endowed with an unprecedented level of safety.

For the first time the 911 Turbo is now available with the Tiptronic S gearbox, which combines the convenience of an automatic with the control and driving pleasure of a manual. This five-speed automatic transmission can be shifted manually using toggle switches mounted on the steering wheel spoke. The top speed of a Tiptronic S-equipped Turbo is 185 mph (298 km/h).

The 911 Turbo is equipped as standard with a wide range of high-quality, desirable features. Over and above the lavish equipment levels of the Carrera models (automatic air-conditioning, on-board computer, and CD/radio, for example), the Turbo comes with metallic paint, a wide range of leather upholstery choices and electrically-adjustable seats. Other standard features include an automatic anti-dazzle function for the internal and external

This is the 911 Turbo at speed. There is nothing like an open road to get the best out of a car with such credentials and pedigree.

The rear view of the 911 Turbo clearly shows the large wheel arches accommodating the extra large wheels. Under the rear window is the movable wing and specially slatted rear cover, used for expelling the turbo chargers' exhaust air.

rear-view mirrors, a new high-end Bose sound system, an integrated rain sensor for the wipers and the adoption of bi-xenon headlights.

Technical specifications

Model:	**Porsche 911 Turbo 2003**	
Engine:	Six-cylinder horizontally-opposed, water-cooled, dry sump lubrication, four overhead camshafts, four valves per cylinder, two exhaust-driven turbochargers, two intercoolers, electronic injection with solid-state distributor (six coils), sequential multi-point fuel injection, E-gas	
Bore/Stroke:	3.94 in/3.01 in	
Capacity:	220 cu. in.	
Engine output:	309 kW (420 bhp) at 6000 rpm	
Power transmission:	Engine and transmission bolted together to form one unit, double propeller shafts for permanent four-wheel drive with power distribution to all four wheels	
Chassis and suspension:		
Front axle:	McPherson design (optimised by Porsche)	
Rear axle:	Multi-link design	
Brakes:	Two-circuit brake system, four-piston aluminium monobloc brake callipers on the front and rear axle Cross-drilled, inner-vented brake discs front and rear, ABS fitted as standard	
Wheels and tyres:		
Front:	8J x 18 with 225/40 R 18	
Rear:	11J x 18 with 295/30 R 18	
Length:	174.6 in	
Width:	72 in	
Height:	51 in	
Wheel base:	92.5 in	
Top Speed:	Manual:	190 mph
	Tiptronic S:	186 mph
0 – 60 mph:	Manual:	4.2 sec
	Tiptronic S:	4.9 sec
0 – 100 mph:	Manual:	9.2 sec
	Tiptronic S:	10.6 sec
0 – 124 mph:	Manual:	14.2 sec
	Tiptronic S:	16.7 sec

Porsche 911 Turbo 4

The first 911 Turbo was introduced at the Paris Motor Show in 1974. Type name 930, it was the first street version Porsche, and one of the first sports cars in the world to offer forced induction via exhaust gas turbo charging.
It was not until the early 1990's, with the introduction of the 911 Turbo type 993, that many enthusiasts would finally get to experience the channeling of Porsche turbo power into an all-wheel driving concept. Lessons learned in harnessing the massive horsepower of the 959 led logically to incorporation of similar technology into the 993 Turbo. So in 1995, Porsche introduced four-wheel drive for the first time on a series production 911 Turbo and by March of the next year, it was available to the general public.
The car used the upgraded 3.6 liter engine, to which two KKK turbochargers were fitted. Engine management was controlled by a Bosche M5.2 system and the power was transmitted through a 6-speed gearbox to all four wheels. The concept featured a viscous clutch to distribute power between the two axles, resulting in new levels of traction and agility.
To accommodate this power, the bodywork was enlarged. In fact, it was some 2.4 inch wider thanks to its extra large wheel arches. The front of the vehicle had a new valance incorporated which housed a prominent central duct flanked either side by supplementary vents. The car was also fitted with a unique color-coded rear wing featuring distinctive, fold-down ears, and housing the turbocharger's intercoolers.
The interior of the cabin of the vehicle remained all but unchanged, although there were a few minor switchgear alterations.

Under that awesome rear wing, a monster that was raring to get out. The 3.6 liter engine that powered this car was given better breathing with twin KKK turbo chargers which helped to push this baby to a staggering 180 mph.

This is the neat front-end package of the first four wheel drive 911 Porsche. The wheel arches were widened and so that way one could distinguish it from the other 911s of the day.

1997 saw the introduction of one of the most exclusive road going 993's, which turned out to be the last air-cooled forced induction 911. This was the Turbo S and based on the all-wheel-drive 911 Twin Turbo 4.
The 911 Turbo 4 wheel drive remained in production through to the end of 1997, during which time some 8919 were made.

Technical specifications

Model:	**Porsche 911 Turbo 4**
Engine:	Flat 6 with twin KKK turbochargers
Capacity:	220 cu. in.
Power:	408 bhp / 5750 rpm
Gearbox:	6 speed
	4 wheel permanent drive
0 – 62 mph:	4.5 sec
Top Speed:	180 mph

Porsche 924

Porsche and Volkswagen have had a relationship which goes back to the original Beetle, designed by Ferdinand Porsche, acting on Adolf Hitler's request for a "people's car." Since then, the two companies have seen good and bad days but have sustained a special relationship.

The 924 began its life as project EA425 at Volkswagen, a vehicle that Porsche was due to develop. Unfortunately, changes in management at Volkswagen meant that the project was cancelled and through mutual agreements made between the two companies, Porsche would inherit project EA 425, now well on its way to completion.

At this stage, the project was destined to be a front wheel drive vehicle, which was not exactly what Porsche had in mind. They were looking at a rear wheel drive set up, which would be good for not only the 924 but also for the upcoming 928. Therefore, they positioned the transmission at the rear of the car not only to give them what they needed but also to help with weight distribution. So the 924 was born.

Due to the Volkswagen/Porsche alliance, there had always been some sharing of parts, but the 924 went one step further. It used parts from Volkswagen, Audi and of course Porsche bins. For example, the transaxle was an Audi part, while many of the suspension and brake parts came from current and past Volkswagen models. It was not strange to hear owners complaining that they could buy parts for their 924 at Audi or Volkswagen outlets much cheaper than at genuine Porsche garages. It was a matter of knowing who had produced what part of the car.

The car entered production in 1974 and suffered a considerable amount of criticism from the press and from owners too. The magnificent 911 proved a tough act to follow and there were huge expectations when a new car was presented. It is not surprising therefore that many were disappointed and there were complaints about road noise and looks.

The 924 was the first Porsche to use a water-cooled, front mounted engine. The car was aimed at those who could not afford to drive a 911. Not as pretty as the 911, but still good-looking, especially from the rear.

This is a 1988 Porsche 944. The basic 924 shape is kept but, as can be seen, the wheel arches are extended.

The car overcame these complaints and progressed through several changes. The option of a three speed automatic gearbox gave those who wanted to own a Porsche a chance to do so without having to use the conventional gear change. 1977 saw a new five-speed gearbox fitted and in 1979, as the car was given a KKK turbocharger, with the necessary engine modifications. Although at this stage, the 924 disappeared from the spotlight, the new 928 had just been presented, there were turbo versions and even Carrera status in the 924 Carrera GT. All these models were followed up by the 944 development, a much improved version of the 924 with larger engine capacity, modified bodywork and a high level of equipment. As with all Porsche cars, these made considerable progress, increasing in power, cabriolet styling and turbocharging.

Technical specifications

Model:	**Porsche 924**
Engine:	four-cylinder inline
Bore/Stroke:	3.4 x 3.32 in
Displacement:	121 cu. in.
Power:	95 bhp / 5500 rpm
Transmission:	Porsche 5 speed overdrive manual or Audi 3 speed automatic
Wheel base:	94.5 in
Weight:	2,625 lb
Length:	170 in
Width:	66.3 in
Height:	50 in
Tyres:	165HR-14

Porsche 928

Originally designated Projekt 'K,' the Porsche 928 first took on its contours in the winter of 1971. Initial designs were based around the contours of a 911. After many design drawings, changes and discussion, a skeleton model was completed in spring of 1972, from which interior spacing and design was calculated. On November 19, 1973 a complete full-scale model was made ready for viewing by the Porsche Stockholders, led by Dr Ferry Porsche and his sister, Dorothea Porsche.

It was unfortunate that around this period, the world was plunged into an energy crisis that hit the motor industry very hard. The designers at Porsche felt therefore that it was worth looking at many different studies for the car; perhaps a four-seater would be better in a rapidly shrinking market.

By 1977, however, the two–plus–two original idea was finalized even though many detail changes were made.

In the meantime, the engine was designed and prepared. Thoughts turned towards a V6, but finally the now familiar V8 configuration was chosen.

Several prototypes and much hot and cold weather testing finally resulted in the presentation of the 928 at the 1977 Geneva Motor Show and, by autumn of that year, full production had started.

The car had a front mounted engine and the gearbox at the rear along with the final drive. The headlights were pop-up style and when retracted, folded neatly back into the front wings. The front and rear bumpers were integral parts of the bodywork and housed the selection of required lights.

As time went by, the car grew in status and became the 928S, followed by the 928S2 in 1984. By 1987, the car grew further both in designation, 928S4, and in engine size, which was boosted to 5 liters. Spoilers and wings were added to the car at different stages of its life but the basic shape remained. 1990 saw a four-seater specially made for Ferry

Quite visible on this 928GT from 1990 are the pop-up headlights. They retract neatly into the wings after use.

This is the 928S that was presented to Ferry Porsche for his birthday. It has been designed with four full seats, rather than the 2 + 2 normal configuration.

Porsche and a turbo charged version for Dr Ernst Fuhrmann, originally an engineer with the company who later became its chairman.

The car finished its life in 1995, although one or two were left over for the following year and the last designation was 928 GTS, using the 5.4 liter engine which gave out 350 bhp. It could be distinguished by the flared rear arches, the color-coded rear spoiler and special alloy wheels. When it first appeared, it was so different from all the other Porsches at the time that people found it quite hard to accept. It was not a sports car, which is how the general public viewed Porsche cars, so much as a spacious 2+2 GrandTourer. It did have an 18 year lifespan however, and today's cars still carry the influence of the 928 styling.

Technical specifications

Model:	**Porsche 928 (model 1977)**
Engine:	90 degree V8 Injected
Displacement:	273 cu. in.
Power output:	240 hp / 5500 rpm
Gearbox	5 speed
Wheel base:	98.4 in
Length:	175 in
Weight:	3,190 lb
Top Speed:	140 mph

Porsche 959

Considered by many enthusiasts to be the finest supercar of the 1980s, and there was plenty of competition at the time, Porsche's 959 was conceived as the 911 of the future and the FIA's new Group B regulations seemed a perfect platform from which to begin. There was nothing to touch the 959 in early 1987 and by the time limited production began that year, the 959 had established itself as the world's fastest road car.

The first showing of the 959 was at the 1983 Frankfurt Motor Show, but it would be some time before any of the general public would be able to get their hands on one. In fact, the first person to own a 959 was Dr Wolfgang Porsche in 1987. The amazing power plant that was installed in the car was a twin turbo, flat six cylinder engine that produced 450 bhp. The car had four-wheel drive and was capable of 190 mph, which was no mean achievement for the period.

The rear light cluster was the only thing that survived from the 911/959 transition but it did take its basic looks from the existing 911.

The 959 bodywork was mainly manufactured in fiberglass and Kevlar composite, although the front lid and doors were of lightweight aluminium and the bumpers polyurethane and fiberglass composite. The car was only available in one body style, but had an option of 'Comfort' or 'Sport' specifications.

The ride height could be electronically adjusted from the cockpit and the driver could specify soft, medium or hard suspension settings. At speeds above 100mph, the dampers could electronically adjust themselves to the stiffest setting.

Nevertheless, the interior of the car seemed lacking and varied only slightly from the standard 911. A turbo pressure indicator had been added, as well as four drive programmes and other essential read outs, but there was nothing special about it.

There were a handful of factory-built 959 competition cars, the 959 'Paris-Dakar' machines that raced between 1984 and 1986, recording two firsts and one second victory. Then there was the unique 961 circuit racer, a veteran of two Le Mans 24 Hours and a class victor in 1986.

A mean-looking rear end shot of the 959. Easily visible is the big wing, flared arches and venting incorporated at the back of the rear wheel arches.

From this angle, it is possible to see all the exterior features of the 959 – sloping hood and large integrated rear wing and even the wheel covers have been made more aerodynamic.

Production of the 959 continued until June 1988, when some 283 were made. 1992 saw a handful of 'last-of-the-line' units constructed for eight very special Porsche customers.

Technical specifications

Model:	**Porsche 959**
Engine:	Twin turbo dohc Flat 6
Bore/Stroke:	3.74 x 2.64 in
Displacement:	174 cu. in.
Transmission:	4 wheel drive, 6 speed all synchromesh manual gearbox
Power:	450 bhp / 6500 rpm
Wheels:	Cast light alloy 17 in
Tyres:	Front: 235/45, Rear: 255/45
Wheel base:	7 ft 5.4 in
Length:	13 ft 11.7 in
Weight:	3,197 lb
Top Speed:	190 mph

Porsche Boxster

In restyling the exterior of the Boxster, Porsche's specialists focused on enhancing the individual details, that give the car its true character. Accordingly, both the front and the rear are more powerfully contoured and the classic design of the Boxster is given even greater emphasis. New air intake scoops at the side, air intake slats finished in body color, a more distinctly contoured "lip" at the front and a redesigned rear spoiler give the car an even sleeker silhouette. A modified roof now featuring a glass window for extra comfort and convenience on the road, clear direction indicators and two striking crossbars at the rear and a redesigned oval exhaust pipe (as opposed to the twin tailpipes on the S model) completes the restyling.

An aerial view of the two Boxsters, small changes can make so much difference.

The new Boxster offers a higher standard of engine performance and torque. The horizontally-opposed six-cylinder engine now achieves a maximum output of 228 bhp (168 kW) at 6300 rpm. The drive comes via a five-speed manual gearbox fitted as standard.

It is worth noting that the Boxster accelerates from 0-62 in 0.2 seconds faster than before and that fuel consumption is also lower than ever before.

Featuring fully integrated on-board diagnosis (OBD), Motronic also supervises the various functions of the engine. Should OBD determine a malfunction in the engine, an appropriate message is recorded in the defect memory and an optical warning signal is activated in the instrument cluster. The workshop is then able to read the message with the help of a diagnostic tester, determining precisely the cause of warning.

The Boxster is well prepared to withstand a head-on, side, glancing or rear-end collision. Three separate load levels absorb impact energy, passing on forces to the stiff side-sill and tunnel areas, and thus minimising any deformation of the interior. The vehicle is also equipped with a superior roll-over protection. An extra-strong tube integrated in the extremely stiff A-pillars gives the windscreen frame tremendous stability, whilst the roll bar directly behind the seats

This is the instrument cluster with its characteristic circular dials, no change here.

serves additionally to protect the driver and passenger cell. Along with these are not only driver and passenger airbags, but also the POSIP (Porsche Side Impact Protection) side airbag system.

The latest Boxster now comes as standard with a new, illuminated and lockable glove compartment connected to the alarm system and a cupholder beneath the central air outlet. The switches are now fitted horizontally in the instrument panel and a harmonised color scheme replaces the black leather.

Design changes are quite visible. The front of the Boxster shows its more distinctly contoured lip.

The new clear direction indicators and redesigned oval exhaust pipe can be seen as the Boxster races into the distance.

The instrument cluster with its three characteristic circular dials remains unaltered. Also equipped with an on-board computer, both the Boxster and the Boxster S come with a dot matrix display. Additionally, the new Porsche Communication Management (PCM) is now available in the Boxster for the first time, presenting information such as the radio station currently tuned in, music titles, incoming telephone calls as well as pictograms for route navigation via a data bus in the display on the instrument cluster.

Technical specifications

Model:	**Porsche Boxster**	
Engine:	six-cylinder horizontally-opposed. four overhead camshafts, four valves per cylinder	
Bore/ Stroke::	3.37/3.07 in	
Capacity:	164 cu. in.	
Max output:	168 kW/228 bhp at 6300 rpm	
Engine management:	Motronic ME 7.8, knock control	
Power transmission:	Engine and transmission bolted to form one drive unit, rear wheels driven by double driveshaft	
Front axle:	McPherson, optimised by Porsche, independent suspension	
Rear axle:	McPherson, optimised by Porsche, independent suspension	
Brakes:	Twin-circuit system, four-piston aluminium monobloc brake callipers, internally ventilated brake discs, ABS	
Wheels and tyres:		
Front:	6J x 16 ET 50 with 205/55 ZR 16	
Rear:	7J x 16 ET 40 with 225/50 ZR 16	
Weight:	Manual:	2,811 lb
	Tiptronic S:	2,936 lb
Dimensions:		
Length:	170.1 in	
Width:	70.1 in	
Height:	50.8 in	
Wheel base:	95.1 in	
Performance:		
Top Speed:	Manual:	157 mph
	Tiptronic S:	154 mph

Porsche Carrera RS 2.7
lightweight

This is a 1974 version of the Porsche RS 2.7: a beast just waiting to be released.

Porsche does not bestow the 'Carrera' badge on any old model of their cars. It usually goes to a machine that is of outstanding performance and appearance and the Carrera RS (standing for Rennsport) 2.7 most certainly belongs in that category.

The Carrera RS 2.7 appeared in 1972, initially built in a series of 500 to qualify for homologation in Group 4 of that era. The most outstanding feature of the car was the striking rear spoiler, popularly known as a duck tail, obvious to anybody who sees one. It was a car that was completely stripped of unnecessary trim (such as rear seats,) the rear engine lid was fibreglass and both windscreen glass and metal used in the body panels were thinner, thus keep the weight below the 2,000 lb mark.

This is a 1973 version of the racing RS 2.7 Carrera, the RSR in full Martini make-up.

A 1973 911 Carrera 2.7 liter. Note the duck tail style back spoiler on the rear engine cover of the car.

This first series was followed in 1973 by another 1,000 cars, which would be homologated not only for Group 4 but also for Group 3 racing, where it was stipulated this number of cars had to be produced. Precisely 1580 RS 2.7s left the Porsche factory in 1973, 200 of which were the sporting version, the rest being lightweight road models.

The days of four cylinder Porsche engines were quietly disappearing and an all new 6-cylinder, 2.7 liter, fuel injection unit now occupied the rear end of these machines. The RS was the fastest production car in Germany and was the first to reach 240 km/h (150 mph). The car was loved not only by the general public, those who could afford it anyway, but also by those who wanted to race the car seriously. The RS won seven out of nine events for the 1973 European GT cup. The race version was designated RSR and became well known in their Martini livery. The Carrera RS was given the 'dream car of the year' award by the motoring press and became a status symbol.

Technical specifications

Model:	**Porsche Carrera RS 2.7 lightweight**
Engine:	6 cyl. Air cooled, normally aspirated Boxer
Displacement	164 cu. in.
Power output:	210 hp / 6300 rpm
Gearbox	5 speed
Dimensions:	
Wheel base:	90 in
Length:	161 in
Weight:	2,286 lb (Lightweight 2,116 lb)
Performance:	
0 – 60 mph:	6.3 sec
Top Speed:	150 mph

Porsche Cayenne S and Turbo

By introducing the Cayenne, Porsche has moved into a new segment of the automotive market. It boasts clear design cues bearing testimony to the car's heritage. The V-shaped hood and front and rear seam contours, together with the raised wheel arches, muscular bumpers, unique headlights and powerful-looking tailpipes are all genuine Porsche features.

The new extremely short and compact normally-aspirated V8 power unit featured in the Cayenne develops superior torque and pulling force, even from low engine speeds.

The well-equipped, spacious and comfortable interior of the Cayenne S.

The vehicle incorporates an innovative four-wheel drive system, Porsche Traction Management (PTM), which is featured as standard on both models (S and turbo) and is crucial to the Cayenne's performance. When driven on light terrain, the Cayenne can handle all requirements without any modification of the traction systems because of its intelligent four-wheel drive. Whenever the going gets tough, Porsche Traction Management is able to interact with the reduced-ratio, off-road gear integrated in the torque distribution unit. In its basic mode, this brand-new generation of four-wheel drive distributes 62 percent of the engine power to the rear and 38 percent to the front wheels. Up to 100 percent of engine power and torque may be fed to the front or rear, as required.

As always, Porsche is concerned with safety. Both the driver and front passenger airbags are activated by a gas generator operating in two stages. The new side impact safety system, in turn, is made up of a thorax airbag integrated in the seat and a curtain airbag fitted in the roof frame.

The Cayenne's excellent ground clearance, ideal for off-road tasks, can clearly be seen in this photo.

The Cayenne is as happy on tarmac as it is off-road. This is the Turbo version.

The instrument display inside the Cayenne comprises large circular dials in aluminium settings with a central multi-function display presenting the most important car data. Automatic air conditioning with separate controls for the driver and passenger, including an activated carbon filter, as well as a CD radio with a double tuner and 10 loud-speakers are also fitted.

The engine is able to operate smoothly even at an angle of 45 degrees, ideal for off-road requirements. The front axle is an extra-large, double-track control arm configuration resting on a sub-frame mounted on tuned rubber mounting points. The rear axle is an elaborate multi-arm concept and the sub-frame rests on large, hydraulically-dampened rubber mounts. With ground clearance of 8.54", the Cayenne is able to cross water up

The front end of the Cayenne, looking menacing and standing high above the water.

This is the dashboard of the Cayenne Turbo with its large circular dials in aluminum surrounds.

to 19.7" deep. The Cayenne S features distinctive, titanium-colored brake callipers and 18-inch light-alloy wheels all round.

As an extra convenience, the rear window of the vehicle can be opened independently and for the first time Porsche offers an electrically retractable trailer towing hook as optional equipment for the Cayenne. The press of a button automatically extends the hook, enabling the vehicle to tow up to 3.5 tons.

Technical specifications

Model:	**Porsche Cayenne S**	**Turbo**
Engine:	V8	V8
Bore/Stroke:	3.7/3.26 in	3.7/3.26 in
Capacity:	275.3 cu. in.	275.3 cu. in.
Power:	340 bhp / 6000 rpm	450 bhp / 6000 rpm
Wheels:	8J x 18	8J x 18
Tyres:	255/55 R18	255/55 R18
Weight:	2,245 lb	2,355 lb
Length:	15 ft 8 in	13 ft 8 in
Width:	6 ft 8 in	6 ft 8 in
Height:	5 ft 10 in	5 ft 10 in
Wheel base:	9 ft 4 in	9 ft 4 in
Top speed:	150 mph.	150 mph
0 – 60 mph:	7.2 sec	5.6 sec

Renault 4CV

On October 22, 1940, the Gestapo arrested Louis Renault. He allegedly had weapons, gold and jewelry hidden on his estate in Herqueville, a fact which the 63-year-old man admitted only after an interrogation of longer than six hours. Renault was then forced to work in Germany for four years.

In 1939, Renault had more than 40,000 employees, who produced 17,802 cars in that year. The production lines for passenger vehicles were stopped in 1940. A major part of the workforce was then transported to Germany as forced laborers. Those remaining in France were forced to construct trucks for the German army. One of the "lucky" men allowed to stay in Billancourt was Fernand Picard. Picard had worked for Delage between 1928 and 1935. He was Head of Development at Renault. The first post-war designs came from his 1941 drawing table. Among them was a large automobile the size of a Citroën Traction Avant and a very small one, which looked a bit like the German "Kraft durch Freude Wagen," later known as the VW Beatle. These activities were of course kept secret from the Germans, and from Louis Renault as well, who seemed not entirely psychologically sound. Picard had collected the necessary parts for the new car by the end of 1941 and he called the model 4CV. On February 7, 1942, the engine was tested for the first time in conjunction with the hydraulic brake. The Renault factory was bombed by the RAF on March 3, 1942, but the little engine and the other passenger vehicles survived the attack. The Renault 4CV enjoyed its first test ride on

This 4CV Découvrable was presented in 1949. It was not really a cabriolet because the sides of the vehicle remained in place. Notice the numerous little aluminum crossbars of the grill.

The Champs Elysée was the more expensive version of the 4CV. Here, a vehicle from 1956, recognizable by its typical grille.

April 26, 1942. The two-door coach was painted a pale green. Most people found the new model hideous. The 4CV was too high in the front and had an unremarkable rear end. Picard started again. The factory was bombed a second time on April 4, 1943, this time by the Americans. But the 4CV survived the attack and a second prototype, this time with a more attractive body, was created.

Paris was liberated by the Americans on the August 23, 1944, and one month later, on September 23, Renault was arrested as a collaborator. He died on October 24, 1944 under very mysterious circumstances, after being unconscious for 10 days. On January 16, 1945, General de Gaulle ordered the nationalization of the Renault concern, which has been called Régie Nationale des Usines Renault ever since.

The 500,000th 4CV emerged from the factory in 1954. When production stopped in 1961, there were more than a million sold.

The simple dashboard of the 4CV from 1956. Here, a standard version.

The engine of the Elysée produced 21 instead of 17 horsepower.

The first Renault 4CV was presented at the automobile salon in Paris in October 1946. The four-door vehicle received an enthusiastic welcome as the car people had been waiting for. It was big enough for the whole family, economical with gas, but fast and maneuverable. The orders were arriving in great numbers and before long, the waiting list demanded two years.

The first "little Fours" were painted entirely yellow, with paint that the Germans had been using for the trucks of the Africa Corps. Then the most modern automobile factory in Europe was built in Billancourt. The premises had 29 production lines with a total length of 2 kilometers. In the thirty-meter long halls, 28 different kinds of processes could be performed with two hundred different kinds of tools. And only two people worked there, doing the same work which previously required at least a hundred workers. Renault was constructing approximately 300 4CVs a day in 1949 and in June 1954 had increased to 500. The 500,000th 4CV came out of production in April 1954. The last car left the factory in Billancourt on July 6, 1961. Over the course of fifteen years, the factory had produced 1,150,550 4CVs, which is more than the total production between 1898 and 1945.

Technical specifications

Model:	**Renault 4CV**
Years of manufacture:	1947–1961
Production:	1,150,550
Engine:	four-cylinder
Displacement:	46 cu. in.
Output:	21/4100 hp/rpm
Top speed:	60 mph
From 0 to 60 mph in sec:	not known
Wheel base:	6 ft 11 in
Length:	12 ft
Width:	4 ft 8 in
Height:	4 ft 10 in
Weight:	1,322 lb

Renault 5 Turbo

The Renault 5 was an absolute success—the best selling French car in 1980. The factory produced 2,400 cars per day. But there were also four other special versions being constructed in the old Alpine factory in Dieppe. Although they looked a lot like the Renault 5, the differences were significant. These cars were driven by a turbo engine, which was not placed in the front of the car, but right behind the seats, far ahead of the rear axle. A prototype of this model was presented at the Paris automobile exhibition of 1978. The Renault 5 Turbo was, together with the BMW M1, the star

The 5 Turbo looked very much like the standard Renault 5. The air inlets for the rear wheels were the most striking feature.

The Turbo stood on broad, light-metal wheels. The size of the tires was 190/55 HR 340 TRX in the front and 220/55 VR 365 TRX in the back.

of the show. The car was planned for delivery in 1980. The Renault factory had a great amount of experience with turbo engines for Formula 1 cars. With the Renault 5 Turbo, they would close the gap between the F1 cars and the super sports cars. The first production vehicle came out of the Dieppe factory in June 1980.
The model debuted a few months later as a rally car in one of the most difficult rallies, which took place on Corsica. No less than seven Turbos arrived at the starting line. Jean Ragnotti drove a factory vehicle with an engine boosted to 250 horsepower. The rally was won by two Porsches and a Fiat Abarth. But this only happened because the Renault broke a ventilator belt during the last lap. Until that moment, Ragnotti had a lead of more than ten minutes. With the

The beautifully designed dashboard was not typical for a racing automobile.

Spoilers, wherever one looked! At the end of the roof, in front, in the back and on the sides of the vehicle.

little Renault 5, a new era started for Renault in the racing world. It turned out to be a fine successor to the Alpine A 110 and the Renault 8 Gordini.
Nevertheless, the Renault 5 Turbo was also suitable for daily use. Admittedly, the noise of the vehicle could be irritating at times, but it must have sounded like music to the ears of the owner. The 5 Turbo was not particularly economical concerning fuel consumption. During a long test, the car used an average of 16 m.p.g., not even when driving at full speed! Still, people did not have to stop often at the gas station because the two gas tanks under the seats had a total volume of no less than 24.5 gallons.

Technical specifications

Model:	**Renault 5 Turbo**
Years of manufacture:	1980-1984
Production:	not known
Engine:	four-cylinder
Displacement:	85 cu. in.
Output:	160/6000 hp/rpm
Top speed:	130 mph
From 0 to 60 mph:	6.9 sec
Wheel base:	8 ft
Length:	12 ft
Width:	4 ft 4 in
Weight:	2,138 lb

Renault Avantime

The Avantime shows off its clean lines from the front.

Just six months after its debut as a concept car at the 1999 Geneva Salon, the first production model of the Renault Avantime, which looks virtually identical to its concept, was unveiled at the 1999 Frankfurt and London motor shows. The two-door GT Coupé Renault Avantime represents a new breed of luxury motoring. Patrick Le Quément, Renault's Design Director, has shown that a car with the comfort, style and performance of a coupe does not have to be cramped, impractical and expensive, but can offer these qualities in conjunction with spacious, head-turning architecture.

The new Renault Avantime is available in two trim levels: Dynamique and Privilège.

The first model of Avantime is Dynamique, which is available with one interior treatment as standard and features beige facing on the lower part of the dashboard with black facing on the upper part, and carbon effect dash inlays. Upholstery is a mix of Ebony Black leather with cloth centre panels.

The second Avantime model is Privilège, available with two interior treatments as standard and featuring beige facing on the lower part of the dashboard with black facing on the upper part, and aluminum dash inlays and a choice of two upholsteries. Upholstery is either of Eclipse Black leather or Sahara Beige leather. Two optional interior treatments called Avantgarde Leather packs are also available on both these models.

This view of the Avantime depicts perfectly the openness and sheer space this vehicle can offer.

From this side view of the Avantime it is very noticeable that there are no B pillars, allowing better entry and exit from the vehicle.

Obviously the Avantime's appearance is unique in the sector, featuring innovative engineering solutions. The upper structure of the car is aluminum, which appears in its natural color, while the rest of the coachwork is of composite materials. Lowering the side windows reveals the car to have no B-pillars. This rare styling provides superb visibility, emphasized by the glass roof, and features the largest panoramic sun-roof on a car, with Venus glass capable of filtering out infra-red rays and absorbing virtually all the sun's energy while avoiding overheating. Sunblinds also screen the two sunroofs and add a feeling of luxury. The Avantime features an 'Open Air' function, which controls the opening of all windows and the panoramic sunroof at the same time.

Due to the lack of B-pillars and thanks to a revolutionary double-kinematic hinge system, the door first opens parallel to the body and then pushes outward, which reduces the swing of the furthest edge of the door and provides an opening wide enough for occupants to comfortably enter the rear or front seats without obstacle.

Once inside, the accommodation is luxurious. Avantime is designed to carry four adults on long journeys in optimum comfort, a fact reflected in the provision of four fully or partly leather upholstered armchair-style seats with height-adjustable headrests.

Technical specifications

Model:	**Renault Avantime**		
Engine:	2.0 16V Turbo	3.0V6 24V	3.0V6 24V Auto
Capacity:	122 cu. in.	183 cu. in.	183 cu. in.
Bore x stroke:	3.25 x 3.7 in	3.4 x 3.25 in	3.4 x 3.25 in
Cylinders:	4	6 (Vee)	6 (Vee)
Valves:	16	24	24
Gross vehicle weight:	4,844 lb	5,070 lb	5,093 lb
Gearbox:	6 Speed	6 Speed	5 Speed
Brakes:			
Front:	ventilated disc 12 in	ventilated disc 12 in	ventilated disc 12 in
Rear:	full disc 10.4 in	full disc 10.4 in	full disc 10.4 in
Tyres:	7.5 inch J 17	7.5 inch J 17	7.5 inch J 17
0-60 mph:	9.9 sec	8.6 sec	9.2 sec
Top speed:	126 mph	138 mph	134 mph

Rolls-Royce Phantom

Charles Stewart Rolls.

Frederick Henry Royce.

Undoubtedly, Rolls-Royce is a conservative company. But when the factory had been building the 40/50 HP (later to be called Silver Ghost) for almost eighteen consecutive years, Frederick Henry Royce decided that the time was ripe for a new model. In 1925, he presented his New Phantom. The vehicle was powered by a six-cylinder engine with a volume of 470 cu. in. with overhead valves, unusual at the time. The model would remain in production for four years. A total of 2,212 of them were sold.

Its successor was the Phantom 2. By 1935, 1,767 of them were built. The Phantom 2 was the last Rolls Royce with which Sir Henry Royce was personally involved. The first two Phantom series were powered by a large six-cylinder engine, but a V12 engine roared under the long aluminum hood of the Phantom III (1936-1939). They were incredibly expensive cars, built exclusively on demand.

The post-war Phantoms were not exceptions to this rule. The Phantom IV (1950) was sold solely to kings, emperors and other rulers. Its production, therefore, remained limited to three vehicles a year. The Phantom V, however, could be bought by anyone with a lot of money. A total of 832 models of the automobile were sold between 1959 and 1968. The Phantom VI stood in the London Motor Show in Earl Court in November of 1968. It was the last model of the illus-

The factory sold an average of one State Landaulette per year between 1970 and 1980.

Thick woolen carpet on the floor.

trious series. Except for the four headlights, with which some Phantom Vs had already been equipped, there was no difference between the Phantom VI and its predecessor. Even the measurements remained unchanged. The differences appeared in the details, easily overlooked by a layman. The Phantom V was powered by the V8 engine of the Silver Cloud III. The Phantom VI was equipped with the stronger engine of the Silver Shadow. This engine had been built with the utmost consistency and the factory could claim with pride that the cylinders were truly round. The tolerance limit was a mere 0.0005 in.

The other engine parts were also produced with the greatest precision. For instance, the cutting tolerance for the crankshaft was 0.0001 in. The entire engine was built by a single mechanic who remained responsible for it for the rest of

The built-in bar with a refrigerator below.

A total of sixteen automobiles were produced as "State Landaulette" on the heavy chassis of the Phantom V and VI. This P-VI was delivered in 1978.

his life. The mechanic tested the engine on a water brake for 150 miles. One in every hundred engines – and this still counts for all Rolls-Royce engines - had to stay on the water brake for eight consecutive hours, before it would be dismantled to the last screw for inspection. The construction of a Rolls-Royce Phantom VI lasted at least nine months. And if the coachwork diverged from the standard, several months would certainly have to be added.

In an "ordinary" P-VI, approximately 500 sq ft of leather were processed (twelve complete skins). The leather was not only placed on the seats chairs and couches and side panels, but also around the arm and headrests and even around the handle for the car horn. A total of 270 parts had to be sewn together. Although nothing much was changed about the P-VI, the model received a bigger 412 cu. in. V8 engine in the autumn of 1979. Moreover,

Under the sliding roof, the passengers were seated on electrically movable seats.

A dictaphone in the armrest between the seats in the far back.

Is this the owner of the car?

a Turbo-Hydramatic gearbox was installed. Apart from that, nothing changed. And why should it? In spite of its old-fashioned manufacturing technique, the model was almost perfect. It was the last Rolls-Royce with a heavy, separate undercarriage, on top of which the coachwork was screwed. The Phantom VI had still a rigid rear axle and four drum brakes.

In 1990, Rolls-Royce constructed the last three automobiles of the Phantom VI model. The very last vehicle disappeared into the Rolls-Royce museum and the second to last car was sold for 1.2 million pounds to an industrial entrepreneur from Switzerland. After 65 years, the name Phantom was removed from the catalogues. Now the rich of the world must satisfy themselves with a Silver Spur or a Rolls-Royce Limousine.

Technical specifications

Model:	**Rolls-Royce Phantom VI**
Years of manufacture:	1968-1990
Production:	3,925
Engine:	V8
Displacement:	380 and 412 cu. in.
Output (hp/rpm):	not known
Top speed:	106 and 112 mph
From 0 to 60 mph in sec:	14.5/ not known
Wheel base:	depends on the coachwork
Length:	depends on the coachwork
Width:	6 ft 7 in
Height:	5 ft 9 in
Weight:	depends on the coachwork

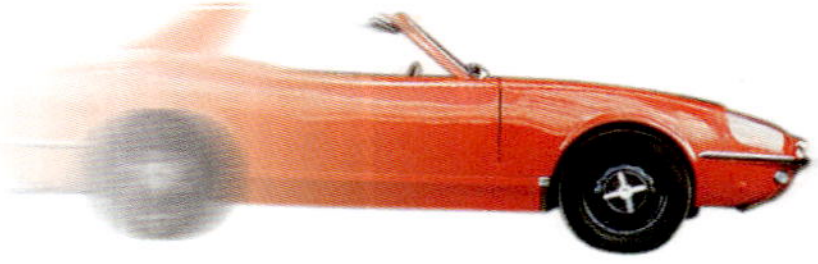

Saab Sonett

The company Malmö Flygindustri manufactured the plastic bodywork for the Sonett II.

The Saab airplane factory was founded in 1937. Their fighter-interceptors in particular enjoyed world fame and form the basis of the Swedish air force even today. Saab technicians drew the first passenger automobile under supervision of Sixten Sason in 1945. The first wooden models were put to several aerodynamic tests in a wind tunnel. The first Saab was officially presented to the Press on June 10, 1947, but it was not until December 1949 that the car was exhibited in showrooms. The first vehicles were powered by a two-cylinder, two-stroke engine with 25 horsepower. The engine powered the front wheels. A total of 1,246 models of the 92-type were delivered during the first twelve production months. And until 1952, all of the cars were painted green. Later, the model could also be ordered in different colors. The 10,000th Saab 92 came out of production on May 6, 1954. The Saab 93 was presented at the end of 1955. The model had slightly different bodywork and a three-cylinder two-stroke engine. The automobile was particularly suitable as a rally car and the name Saab thus became known outside of Scandinavia. A surprise was prepared for the auto-

The Saab Sonett Super Sport from 1956. The car never went beyond the prototype stage.

One of the six prototypes, on the picture at the Mille Miglia for historical sport cars.

mobile exhibition of 1956 in Stockholm: the Sonett Super Sport, officially known as the Saab 94. Only six prototypes of this model were built. The model was equipped with a light plastic body. The mechanical parts originated from the Saab 93. The two-stroke engine was boosted to 58 SAE horsepower and, because the vehicle weighed only 1,100 lb, the top speed was about 110 mph. It is an extraordinary fact that all of the prototypes have been preserved. The first, painted white, resides in the Saab museum and the second, with a red body, is the property of Saab Cars USA. The third was also painted red and is part of a private collection in Trollhättan (Sweden). A Saab employee transformed number four into a sports car. The car crashed and was restored to its original state by a hobbyist in Northern Germany. The Saab museum also exhibits number five with its blue bodywork. An American owner painted the last prototype white.

The model did not sell very well in 1974.
It is a much sought after collectors' item at present.

The Sonett III was the last Saab sports car, and also the most widely sold.

The Sonett was almost forgotten until February 4, 1965, when the press was invited to come and admire its successor. Again, it concerned a prototype, this time with a steel body. The three-cylinder two-stroke engine now produced 60 SAE horsepower. The car, weighing 1,433 lb, reached a maximum speed of 100 mph. A second prototype was equipped with a slightly longer body made of plastic. This design also originated on the drawing table of Sixten Sason. Saab built a total of 37,069 cars in 1966. Only 60 of them were of the Sonett II type. This sports car was also constructed with standard Saab parts. The engine was of the Monte Carlo 850 type.

The demand for two-stroke engines significantly diminished at the end of the sixties, but Saab kept installing its three-cylinder engine and the customer was able to choose a 1967 four-cylinder Ford Taunus engine. The Saab Sonett II, with its 52 cu. in. engine, was unbeatable in its class, and the 1.5-liter Ford engine made no change whatsoever. The Sonett III reached a maximum speed of 100 mph. with the new engine. The Sonett III was presented at the New York exhibition in 1970. Again, the technology was derived from the Saab 93, but this time Sergio Coggiola had designed

The dashboard of the Sonett 1969. A Taunus V4 engine with 92 cu. in. powered the vehicle.

When the sports car was finally produced in 1966, they called the model Sonett II.

the bodywork in Italy. The wheel basis had remained the same, but the undercarriage had been extended by 5 in to 12 ft 10 in. The Sonett III weighed 1,676 lb. This was because a firm roll cage had been installed and because the plastic doors were strengthened with steel beams.

The last two-stroke engine was installed in 1968. Saab sold almost 74,000 automobiles in 1970, of which 940 were the Sonett III type. The sports car could also be delivered with a heavier, 1.7-liter Ford V4 engine in 1971. They equipped the Sonett with a new grill in 1972. The vertical back of the car was now painted matte black and the vehicle stood on broader, aluminum wheels. These little improvements caused the sales to increase slightly. No fewer than 2,080 Sonetts were sold in 1972. The production dropped to 1,595 automobiles in 1973. They decided to stop production when demand decreased even more the next year.

Technical specifications

Model:	**Saab Sonett**	**Sonett II**	**Sonett III**
Years of manufacture:	1956	1966-1970	1970-1974
Production:	2,586	1,610	8,351
Engine:	two-cylinder	three-cylinder and V4	V4
Displacement:	45.6 cu. in.	51.3 and 91.4 cu. in.	91.4 and 103.7 cu. in.
Output (hp/rpm):	58/4200	60 and 65/6000	65 and 76/4700
Top speed:	103 mph	100 mph	100 and 105 mph
From 0 to 60 mph in sec:	not known	12.5	12.5 and 12
Wheel base:	85 in	85 in	85 in
Length:	not known	149 in	154 in
Width:	not known	57 in	59 in
Height:	not known	46 in	47 in
Weight:	1,100 lb	1,433 and 1,700 lb	1,808 and 1,819 lb

Siata Spring

The Siata Spring was especially loved in Italy.

The Italian company Siata specialized initially in boosting engines for passenger vehicles. A couple thousand vehicles were built in the factory as well. The phenomenal automobile was the ruling factor in the life of Giorgio Ambrosini (1890-1974). The man from Fano built several prototypes under the nameVittoria in 1913 and he founded the Siata Company in 1926. He produced booster sets for Fiat engines, cast pipe taps for double carburetors and manufactured cylinder heads with overhead valves. He installed Rootes compressors and altered three-speed into four-speed gearboxes. Ambrosini worked mainly on the Fiat 508 and after 1936 on the Fiat 500.

A 47-horsepower engine from the Fiat 850 Spider coupe powered most of the Springs.

Although it was possible to install little window screens in the doors, this was hardly ever done. After all, it was a sports car!

The war ended for Italy on September 8, 1943 and it was not long before Siata was running full tilt again. They produced mainly auxiliary engines for bicycles at first, but before long the first cars were assembled with Fiat parts. Renato Ambrosini took over his father's business in 1964. Models like the Siata 1500 and 1600 came to life under his supervision and several thousand were sold. In 1967, Siata presented a special model, the Siata Spring. The Spring had the appearance of an automobile from the 1930s. The mudguards and headlights were screwed to the bodywork, just like in those days. The vehicle had a grille just like that of a Rolls-Royce. This was actually entirely unnecessary because the Spring was built on the undercarriage of a Fiat 850 and the engine was placed in the back. The Spring could be delivered with an 51 cu. in. engine with 37 or 47 horsepower. The little car sold fairly well, but apparently not well enough to save the company from bankruptcy. The brand name Siata disappeared from the market for good in 1970.

Technical specifications

Model:	**Siata Spring**
Years of manufacture:	1967-1970
Production:	not known
Engine:	four-cylinder
Displacement:	51 cu. in.
Output:	37/5200 and 47/6400 hp/rpm
Top speed:	78 and 81 mph
From 0 to 60 mph:	25.2 sec
Wheel base:	6 ft 8 in
Length:	11 ft 8 in
Width:	4 ft 7 in
Height:	4 ft 7 in
Weight:	1,411 lb

Smart Roadster & Roadster Coupé

With the launch of the Smart roadster and Smart roadster-coupe in April 2003, the segment of the compact and purist roadster is being revived, which has not existed in this form since the 1950s and 1960s. These cars not only take up the features of the Smart brand familiar from the Smart city-coupe and cabrio, but at the same time the main features of the classic roadster. The short body overhangs, pronounced contoured wheelhouses, generously dimensioned wheels and low vehicle height give the cars a sporty appearance.

The Smart roadster will be offered for sale with a 60 kW Suprex turbo engine. The engine complies with exhaust gas standard EU 4. A version with an output of 45 kW will also be available from the middle of the year. Furthermore, smart-Brabus GmbH will offer an exclusive and extremely sporty variant of the Smart roadster at a later date.

This is the Smart roadster at speed with its 'smiley face' front with built in headlamps and two-tone paintwork.

A night view of the roadster and roadster coupe shows off their lines and lighting.

The Smart roadster has the same sequential automated transmission as the Smart city-coupe and cabrio in a further optimized form. To make starting on a hill more comfortable in cars with automatic transmission and a torque converter, the Smart roadster and roadster-coupe have a Hill Start Assist (HAS). After releasing the brake pedal, the stationary ESP keeps the wheels braked for 0.7 seconds, just enough time to move the foot from the brake to the accelerator pedal without the car rolling forwards or backwards on account of the disengaged clutch.

The Smart roadster's standard equipment includes Softouch automatic transmission, sports seats, leather steering wheel and leather gear knob.

Like the Smart city-coupe and cabrio, plastic body panels also form the outer skin of these models. This material, much lighter than steel, is used in the front and rear ends, wings and doors. The powder-coated Tridion safety cell remains visible in the area of the door sills, B-pillars and roll-over bar.

With a roof system consisting of a soft top and a hardtop which can be used together or alternatively, the cars offer their owners maximum driving pleasure whatever the weather. As well as a two-piece removable plastic hardtop that

An aggressive view of the Smart roadster from behind, all components looking neat and tidy.

The roadster coupe seen from the rear.

can be stowed and transported in the rear luggage compartment, an electrically operated folding soft top is available for both the smart vehicles. It only takes approximately ten seconds to fully open the soft top, which slides back under the roll bar to the luggage compartment.

There is an optional sports package which offers customers a three-spoke leather sports steering wheel with integrated gearshift by means of shift paddles and 205/45 R 16 spikeline, light-alloy rims. The optional safety package consists of fog lamps, electrically adjustable and heated door mirrors and side airbags for an extra charge. Further options include leather sports seats with seat heating, auxiliary instruments (engine temperature and charge pressure) a radio, CD changer, radio with CD and a corresponding sound system.

The special made-to-measure luggage which is part of the Smartware program makes optimal use of the space available.

Technical specifications

Model:	**Smart Roadster en Roadster Coupé**
Cylinders/configuration:	Three inline
Displacement:	43 cu. in.
Bore x stroke:	2.61 x 2.63 in
Rated output (kW):	45 at 5,250 rpm
Max. torque (Nm):	95 at 2,000 - 4,000 rpm
Transmission:	sequential automated six-speed
Front axle:	Wishbone, McPherson strut, stabiliser
Rear axle:	DeDion suspension tube with central mount, wishbone, coil springs, telescopic shock absorbers
Brake system:	Hydraulic dual circuit system with vacuum booster
Front:	Disk
Rear:	Drum
Wheels front/rear:	5J x 15 / 6J x 15
Tyres front/rear:	185/55 R 15
Wheel base:	7 ft 9 in
Length:	13 ft 3 in
Width:	5 ft 4 in
Height:	47 in
Turning circle:	35.1 ft
Top speed:	100 mph

Spatz

The Spatz was truly a fair-weather car. In case of rain, could the Spatz be entered or exited through a side window in an elegant manner?

Engineer Harald Friedrich and the motorcycle manufacturer Victoria founded a new company in 1956 called the Bayerische Automobil Werke (BAW). They wanted to construct a new sports car that would be cheaper than the Volkswagen Beetle. Because the development of an entirely new automobile would consume a great deal of time and money, they decided to buy the license rights to the Brütsch 200 Spatz.

The first prototype had plastic bodywork and three wheels. The vehicle did not have an undercarriage. The engine was attached to the plastic bodywork with the suspension of the back wheel. Friedrich lost the entire rear member during a test ride. The eighty-year-old professor and car expert, Dr. Hans Ledwinka, took pity on the engine and designed an undercarriage with a central tube suspension with split axles for the back wheels. They gave the car two back wheels and the engine was now placed in front of the back axle. This prototype was presented at the 1955 Frankfurt automobile exhibition and received a lot of attention. It was the first German sports car to have a plastic body. The open vehicle offered space for three on a 4 ft 9 inch long seat. There was ample leg room because the engine was

The engine was easily accessible.

The dashboard of the Spatz. The handle for the gearshift is placed behind the right spoke of the steering wheel.

placed in the back of the car. The gears were changed with a handle at the steering column. The Spatz had no doors and was very difficult to enter or exit the car if it was raining and the cloth cover was closed.

There were 859 cars built in 1957, when Friedrich withdrew from the business. His partner, the Victoria factory, presented a new model, this time with two doors. By February 1958, another 729 cars of the model Victoria 250 had been sold. The model was driven by a 15 cu. in. Victoria engine. The Victoria had a new electromagnetic gearbox. Pushing down the clutch activated the next gear. Victoria delivered the last car in February 1958. Several other prototypes were built under the name "Burgfalke 250 Export."

Technical specifications

Model:	**Spatz**	**Victoria**
Years of manufacture:	1955-1957	1957-1958
Production:	859	729
Engine:	one-cylinder	one-cylinder
Displacement:	11.6 cu. in.	15 cu. in.
Output:	10/5000 hp/rpm	14/5200 hp/rpm
Top speed:	47 mph	59 mph
From 0 to 60 mph in sec:	not known	not known
Wheel base:	6 ft 5 in	6 ft 5 in
Length:	10 ft 6 in	10 ft 7 in
Width:	4 ft 7 in	4 ft 8 in
Height:	9 ft 9 in	3 ft 9 in
Weigh:	639 lb	937 lb

Spectre R 42

The company Spectre Supersports Ltd. was founded in England in the spring of 1995 as a subsidiary of the American Spectre Motor Cars, Inc. The idea came from Swedes Olof and Anders Hildebrand and from Englishmen Graham Keley, Michael Whale and Ray Christopher. Only Christopher was originally known in the world of automobiles. He has been designing and building sports cars since 1957. His company, GT Developments, specializes in Ford GT40 replicas, of which about 360 have been delivered. GT Developments kept improving on the model when Ford stopped building the GT40. In the end, this resulted in Christopher's Spectre 42. The Swedish Anders Hildebrand, who had been importing GT40 replicas for years, was so enthusiastic that he decided to participate in the enterprise and help found the new company Spectre Supersports Ltd.

The V8 engine with four camshafts and 32 valves is placed directly behind the little seats.

The Spectre is mainly meant for hobbyists who don´t want a Porsche, but cannot afford a Ferrari. The price? The car costs £60,000 in England. The buyer receives an exclusive and well-designed vehicle for that money. Like the Ford GT40, the Spectre has an aluminum, monocoque undercarriage, which is glued together. This is customary mainly in

The spoiler is very vulnerable when the car is parked at the curb because the bottom of the Spectre lies only 5 in above the road.

The exhaust pot was still visible on the prototype. This was not the case with the production cars.

the airplane industry nowadays. The development of the Spectre lasted three years. The bodywork would be trimmed so much during that time that a Cw-value of 0.28 could be measured in the wind tunnel.

The coupe is powered by the new LincolnV8 engine with four overhead camshafts and 32 valves. This engine has been boosted in England and produces 350 horsepower at 6000 rpm (284 horsepower with the Lincoln). The couple is even more impressive with 620 Nm at 4700 rpm and can drive off in third gear without any trouble during the test ride.

The interior of the Spectre R42 with a lot of nut wood and Conolly leather. The air-conditioning is indispensable, because the windows of the doors cannot be opened.

The Spectre R42 has a length of 412 cm. The Porsche 911 and the Ferrari F355 are 5.1 in longer.

The Spectre is being delivered with a five-speed gearbox as a standard, but a box with six gears can be installed for racing. The shock absorbers are adjustable. The buyer can choose between three different brake systems: one for ordinary use, one for the sportsmanlike driver and one especially for professional racing. The Spectre is suitable for ordinary use on the public roads as well as on the circuits. But the special race model is different because of the brake system and the lighter weight. The Kevlar and aluminum parts in the cockpit of the racing model are not upholstered with leather. The engine is more powerful and the driver is seated in a construction with a roll cage.

Technical specifications

Model:	**Spectre R42**
Years of manufacture:	1995-present
Production:	28 (by March 1997)
Engine:	V8
Displacement:	281 cu. in.
Output (hp/rpm):	350/6500
Top speed:	177 mph
From 0 to 60 mph:	4.0 sec
Wheel base:	8 ft 2 in
Length:	13 ft 6 in
Width:	6 ft 1 in
Height:	3 ft 7 in
Weight:	2,315 lb

Spiess TC 522

The prototype did not have an engine yet.

The Spiess TC 522 was presented in an impressive manner at Frankfurt airport on September 22, 1992. The press was seated on a wooden stage, directly opposite a gigantic Jumbo jet. The 36-year-old Robert Spiess had the nose of the plane turned open, when he knew for sure that the cameras were aimed at it. And in the big belly of the airplane stood a Spiess TC 522.

The prices of luxury automobiles skyrocketed at the end of the 1980s. Robert Spiess wanted to profit from this tendency. Brands like Jaguar, Ferrari and McLaren were selling their XJ 220, F40 and F1 like hot potatoes for unusually high prices. The 45-year-old Karl-Heinz Knapp received the commission to design a super dream car. It became the Spiess TC 522 ("TC"=Turbocharged, "5"=5.0 liters, "22"=2+2). This coupe offered space for two adults and two children. The frameless bodywork was made of carbon fiber, beautifully finished and light in weight. The undercarriage weighed 331 lb and the bodywork merely 121 lb. A steel cage protected the passengers because in a crash, the carbon-fiber bodywork would not bend but would be shattered to pieces like glass. The undercarriage and the wheel suspension of the Spiess were comparable to the Formula 1 automobiles. The gearbox was made especially for the Spiess by the company X-Trac in England and had six speeds, which could be operated by pushing buttons on the steering wheel. The engine originated from the Corvette and was placed in front of the rear axle. However, it was not anything like a standard Chevrolet product. With its two exhaust turbines, it produced 500 horsepower and the maximum couple of 600 Nm at 2500 rpm. "And the car is, therefore, suitable for daily use," Spiess said during the press conference. Technically speaking, the Spiess was very special. The gas pedal was operated hydraulically and all pedals could be electrically adjusted in height. The steering system was extraor-

It is easy to reach the mechanical parts of the automobile.

A remarkable design, also when seen from the front.

dinary. The front wheels were not moved by means of steering rods, but with steel cables. A little display was placed on the dashboard, replacing the usual meters. The vehicle did not have an inside mirror. Instead, the Spiess used a camera in one of the rear lights, which sent the image to a little screen on the dashboard.

The Spiess TC 522 could not yet be driven at the impressive press conference, but according to Robert Spiess, there would be ample opportunity to test the vehicle on the road at a later date. The car was officially presented to the public in March 1993. After that, the prototype was destroyed in a crash test. They had produced so many parts that eight automobiles could be assembled. Unfortunately, we have not heard anything more from Robert Spiess since then.

To our great surprise, the car stood at the IAA in Frankfurt in 1997. A second model, the Spiess C 522 was being presented next to the TC 522. This vehicle was built by Robert Hillmann's company Spiess Fahrzeugbau in Wolfratshausen (near Munich). This model had an ordinary V8 engine with "only" 340 horsepower instead of the complicated engine

The very modern interior of the Spiess TC 522 (1992).

The Spiess was a real eye-catcher with a height of 3ft 8in and width of 6ft 6in.

with turbo chargers. The new manufacturer saw the future of the vehicle in a more realistic way than its predecessor. Robert Spiess had planned a limited production of 100 cars, while Hillmann was satisfied with "maybe twenty cars." The prices were also changed. The original TC 522 cost no less than 760,000 DM. The new C 522 was offered for 198,000 DM. And the buyer obtained a multiple-CD player and satellite-navigation system from Siemens for that price.

Nevertheless, the new manufacturer was still not sure of his subject. During the IAA, he said: "We plan to found a GmbH (private incorporated company) with 2 million marks in capital. Everybody who wants to join this adventure from the beginning is still welcome to buy shares..." We are still waiting impatiently for the series production to begin.

Technical specifications

Model:	**Spiess TC 522**	**C 522**
Years of manufacture:	1992	1997
Production:	1	1
Engine:	V8	V8
Displacement:	346 cu. in.	346 cu. in.
Output:	550 hp/rpm	340 hp/rpm
Top speed:	more than 190 mph	not known
From 0 to 60 mph in sec:	less than 4	not known
Wheel base:	9 ft 6 in	9 ft 6 in
Length:	14 ft 7 in	14 ft 11 in
Width:	6 ft 6 in	6 ft 6 in
Height:	3 ft 8 in	3 ft 8 in
Weight:	2,425 lb	2,315 lb

Spyker

A good view of the interior of the C8 Laviolette with its strange gearshift setup and its aircraft style instruments.

In 1898 Jacobus and Hendrik-Jan Spiker, coachbuilders in Amsterdam, pioneered their first motor car, in which they used a Benz engine. Their 1903 60 hp Grand Prix race car not only used the world's first six-cylinder engine, but also had four-wheel drive. During World War II, they switched to making military aircraft, but returned to cars after the war. Today Spyker's racing and aviation tradition has been passed on to the new Company, Spyker Automobielen.

The new company prides itself on hand-building a car to the buyer's personal demands. Once a buyer has decided what they want, they can watch the progress via a computer linked to the company webcam system and operated within the new assembly department. The process will follow all the stages of the construction of each individual person's vehicle, therefore creating a unique history of the car. Last year, only 25 cars were made and the company is able to give each car its own identity as tailored by the needs and desires of the individual buyer.

The company has entered basic cars in GT class races, such as at Le Mans, to benefit from the experiences gained in such international race arenas.

The Spyker C8 is an advanced two-seater sports car with electrically operated tilting doors and fully opening front and rear body sections. The Spyker C8 Spyder (introduced in 2000) and C8 Laviolette (introduced four months later in 2001) use the Audi 4.2 liter all–aluminum V8 engine, coupled to the Audi 6 speed transaxle which powers the rear wheels. Customers can also chose their engine power output, which can be varied between 400bhp at stage one tuning, through to 450 bhp at second stage tuning for the Laviolette and Spyder. The Double 12 S can be ordered for up

This is the C8 Laviolette, note the single hinge electronically controlled doors.

Pictured here is the C8 Double 12 in road trim.

to 620 bhp in the highest stages of tuning. The interior of the C8 is quite unique and the feature that you notice immediately once in the cabin is the aircraft style instrumentation design. Once seated you cannot help but be aware of the novel gear selector mechanism, which has a metal rod running front to back through the middle of the downshaft of the gear change lever.

Every Spyker is fitted with a personal security card, which will activate the car's electrical system as soon as the owner is within 3 meters of the vehicle. No ignition key is required.

At the Frankfurt International Show of 2001, Spyker unveiled the C8 Double 12 R (racecar) to the public and then the C8 Double 12 S road car at the 2002 British International Motor Show. These cars use a Spyker road or race 244 cu. in.engine mated to a Spyker six-speed gearbox. The cars are built to the customer's specification, whether for road or race use.

Exotic grounds for an exotic car. This is the beautiful C8 Spyder.

Technical specifications

Model:	Spyker C8 Laviolette
Engine:	90 degree V8
Capacity:	255 cu. in.
Power:	450 hp
Gearbox:	6 speed
Drive:	Rear wheel
Top Speed:	190 mph
0 – 60 mph:	4.2 sec
Brakes:	Front: 6 piston aluminum calipers, Rear: 4 piston aluminum calipers, Ventilated discs
Wheels:	Forged ATS alloy rims
Tyres:	Front: 225/40ZR 18, Rear: 255/35ZR 18
Weight:	2,358 lb
Wheel base:	101 in
Length:	165 in
Width:	74 in
Height:	49 in

Studebaker President Speedster

When Studebaker celebrated its hundredth birthday in 1952, there was no reason for great joy. With a production of 170,000 civilian vehicles, they sold 80,000 less cars that year. Fortunately, the company received an order from the government to build trucks for the war in Korea. Studebaker was therefore still able to close the financial year 1952 without loss.

They hoped a new model could speed up production again. Raymond Loewy's design studio received the assignment and designer Robert Bourke drew an automobile, which looked as inventive as the Studebaker from 1947. The model was long, wide and low. It was called the New American Car with the European Look. The new car could be delivered as a coupe or as a sedan. Studebaker was hoping to sell a total of 350,000 models of the model in 1953. The majority was built as sedans (80%), the rest as coupes. However, this decision would prove to be a mistake. When they drew up the balance sheet at the

The Speedster was always painted in two colors.

The Speedster could be recognized by the fog lamps built in the front bumper.

end of 1953, the company had sold 151,576 vehicles of which 72,386 were coupe versions. The demand for the sportier coupe was greater than the supply. And switching over the sportier inevitable trouble. The bodywork of the coupe did not fit on the standard undercarriage. It was also necessary to manufacture new stamps and tools for the plating.

The war in Korea ended in July of 1953. This meant the end of army-truck production for Studebaker. Studebaker registered a turnover of $595 million with a profit of only $2.7 million in 1953. In spite of the new models, the future did not look too bright. Studebaker tried to enlarge its market share by introducing a new estate wagon, the Conestoga.

Things did not look a lot better at Packard. This prestigious brand had sold almost 90,000 automobiles in 1953, but production dropped to 30,965 models in 1954. A fusion of the two companies would save a lot of money, so they thought. James Nance was the first president of the Studebaker-Packard Corporation. Unfortunately, the company met with even more trouble because of him. "Win or lose" must have been his motto, or maybe he suffered from delusions of grandeur. Nance spent millions of dollars on an advertisement campaign, in which he stated that there would no longer be talk about the "Great Three," but about the "Great Four." As expected, they closed the year 1954 with a loss of $41.7 million dollars.

The beautifully finished dashboard of the President Speedster.

A 188-horsepower V8 engine resided under the hood. Notice the 6-volt battery.

The Speedster was a really luxurious automobile. Not only were the seats were upholstered in leather, but the interior of the roof was also covered with leather.

The next year would truly become a "win or lose" situation for Studebaker. There were newly constructed engines that produced more horsepower than ever before. They would now call the six-cylinder Champion engine the "Victory Six." The cylinders were drilled from 2779 to 185.6 cu. in. After this, the engine produced 102 instead of 76 SAE horsepower. The V8 could be ordered in two versions: with 224.4 cu. in. and 142 horsepower and as a "Pace Setter" with 259.3 cu. in. and 164 horsepower.

There was another novelty. The President returned after an absence of thirteen years. This pride of the company was driven by a 4.2-liter V8 engine with 177 horsepower (or 188 if wished). There were several models of the President available: a four-door sedan, a coupe and a hardtop coupe. Studebaker built the President Speedster for the true hobbyist in 1955. It was a hardtop coupe in which they had installed all the technical gadgets and gimmicks the factory could supply at that time. The V8 engine with 188 horsepower resided under a long hood along with the steering booster and the servo brakes, all of which belonged to the standard model. The speedster could be recognized by its fog lights, which were built into the front bumper, by the chromium strip above the back window and by the colored window screens. The Speedster came with white tires and it was always painted in two colors. Further, it had a remarkable dashboard with black-and-white instruments. The upholstering of the roof was of the same leather as the upholstering of the seats. The Speedster was not only the most expensive Studebaker (it cost $3,253 dollars), it was also the heaviest, weighing 3527 pounds. In spite of the weight, the Speedster reached a top speed of almost 112 mph and accelerated from 0 to 60 mph in 10.2 seconds. It was only built in 1955. A new coupe from the Hawk series followed up the model after 2,215 of them were sold. In this way, The Studebaker President Speedster went into history as a "bridge" between the Starlight and Starliner hard-top coupes from 1954 and 1955 and the Hawk coupes. The model possessed the beauty of the Starlight and Starliner and the power of the Hawk.

Technical specifications

Model:	**Studebaker President Speedster**
Year of manufacture:	1955
Production:	2,215
Engine:	V8
Displacement:	260 cu in.
Output:	188/4500 hp/rpm
Top speed:	112 mph
From 0 to 60 mph:	10.2 sec
Wheel base:	10 ft
Length:	17 ft
Width:	5 ft 10 in
Height:	4 ft 8 in
Weight:	3,527 lb

Talbot 2500 Lago Sport

The engine had two highly placed (but not overhead) camshafts.

The history of the Talbot brand is rather complicated. In 1891, Alexandre Darracq founded a bicycle factory, which he named Gladiator. He switched to the production of electric automobiles in 1896. In 1898, he bought the rights from Léon Bollée to allow him to build a small automobile under license. He built his own vehicles under the name Darracq two years later. His race cars in particular would become world famous. Darracq merged in 1920 with the English companies Sunbeam and Talbot. The cars were sold in England under the name Darracq and in France under the name Talbot.

Antonio Lago was born in Bergamo, Italy. He worked as an automobile mechanic in Venice until he was called for duty to fight in the First World War. He immigrated in 1923 to England, where he begun to work for Armstrong-Siddeley. He became the director of Talbot in Suresnes in 1935. At that time, Talbot had already established a good name with racing and sports cars. Lago's Grand-Prix cars could compete successfully with the German and Italian models. The company continued with the production of race and sport cars after the Second World War as well. Talbot Lagos, as the cars were now called, won the first two prizes at the 24-hour Le Mans race in 1950. And in 1951, the brand finished in second and fourth place. Meanwhile, the production of civilian automobiles was not forgotten. The company presented several new models, which were powered by the 4.5-liter engine from the racecars. These were difficult times for the manufacturers of expensive automobiles and Talbot too saw a further decrease in demand. Only 433 vehicles were sold in 1950. That number dropped to 80 in 1951. Lago tried to switch to producing cheaper cars with smaller engines, but this was not

The last design of Talbot. In America, they would produce another twelve pieces with the same bodywork.

The Talbot Lago 2500, the last real Talbot.

successful either. Simca took over the company on December 31, 1958. The last automobile with the name Talbot was presented in 1960. It was a coupe with a Simca engine.

Ford owned the majority of the brand Simca and sold its shares to Chrysler in 1958. Simca, and therefore also Talbot, now belonged to the Chrysler concern. Chrysler also purchased the Rootes group and in this way the brands Sunbeam, Talbot and Darracq were united. Chrysler sold all of its European brands to Peugeot. The name was again taken off the shelf in 1979.

Technical specifications

Model:	**Talbot 2500 Lago Sport**
Years of manufacture:	1955-1956
Production:	54
Engine:	four-cylinder
Displacement:	152 cu. in.
Output:	120/5000 hp/rpm
Top speed:	115 mph
From 0 to 60 mph in sec:	not known
Wheel base:	8 ft
Length:	13 ft 9 in
Width:	5 ft 5 in
Height:	4 ft 4 in
Weight:	1,984 lb

Triumph 1800 Roadster

The Triumph Roadster, here the 1800 model from 1946, was recognizable by its big headlights built closely together.

In November 1944, Thomas Ward sold the Triumph brand name to Sir John Black, the owner of the Standard Motor Company, and the Triumph Company Ltd. came into existence. A new Triumph was to be available as soon as the war was over. Nonetheless, two prototypes emerged during the war – a roadster and a saloon. The 1800 Roadster was designed by Frank Callaby, the designer of the Standard. The 1800 Saloon originated on the drawing boards of Mulliner in Birmingham (not to be confused with the famous H.J. Mulliners from Rolls-Royce).

A total of 4,500 models of this two-seater were built.

The cars also looked good with the cover closed. The passengers in the back trunk, however, sat in the open air.

Both models were something truly special. Mulliner's "knife edge" shape, with which he had already been experimenting before the war, was further developed. And the Roadster had its own typical shape too. Both models were presented to the public in March 1946. The Roadster stood on a tubular under-frame and had independent front-wheel suspensions, a novelty for a Triumph. The engine and other mechanical parts originated from the Standard factory. The same four-cylinder engine had been supplied to Jaguar before the war. At that time, it was difficult or impossible to get steel and therefore, with exception of the front splashguards, the cars' coachwork was constructed of aluminum. Because Standard had also made aircraft hulls of aluminum during the war, the presses could be easily revamped for the automobile industry.

The Roadster had a front seat, which was (almost) big enough for three people. The "dickey seat" in the trunk offered seating for two passengers. The cover of the "back seat" served as a second windshield. The Roadster was actually

The two-part trunk cover. The front part served as a second windscreen, the rear part served as a backrest for passengers.

made by two designers. Frank Callaby was responsible for the front part of the automobile (up to the doors), while Arthur Ballard put the rear on paper. In total, 4,500 Roadsters were delivered. The first to finish production had a 1.8-liter engine. Later, the 2.0-liter, four-cylinder engine from the Standard Vanguard was built in.

Technical specifications

Model:	**Triumph Roadster 1800**	**2000**
Years of manufacture:	1946-1948	1949-1950
Production:	2,500	2,000
Engine:	four-cylinder	four-cylinder
Displacement:	108 cu. in.	127 cu. in.
Output:	66/4500 hp/rpm	71/4200 hp/rpm
Top speed:	80 mph	87 mph
From 0 to 60 mph in sec:	not known	not known
Wheel base:	8 ft 2 in	8 ft 2 in
Length:	14 ft	14 ft
Width:	5 ft 5 in	5 ft 5 in
Height:	4 ft 7 in	4 ft 7 in
Weight:	2,532 lb	2,532 lb

Triumph TR2

In the early fifties, Jaguar had its XK 120 and MG its TD and Triumph did not have a sports car. So Harry Webster received an order to build a two-seater for the lowest price possible. Therefore, he used the undercarriage of the Standard Flying Nine, of which there were still hundreds unused in store. He built his Triumph Sports car, as it was officially named, on the basis of this pre-war design. Because the need for foreign currency was very great in those first post-war years, almost all Triumphs were produced for export and the few that remained in England were used mostly as race cars. At Triumph, it was generally thought that the English market could be served in later years.

The distinguishing feature of the TR2 was the grille, installed far back in the car. In later models, the grille would be placed much more to the front.

The Triumph sports car model was presented in 1952 at the London Motor Show and received very enthusiastic responses. It could compete with the new Austin Healey 100 and even make the MGTD look ridiculous. The factory set the sales price at £555. A Healey cost 50 percent more at that time, while the buyer of an old-fashioned MG had to pay £530. But the designers had economized on many aspects of the Triumph Sports car. The 2.0-liter engine was originally produced for the Triumph Renown. The front member and the back axle were from the Triumph Mayflower and the gearbox looked suspiciously like that of the Standard Vanguard.
But did that make any difference? The prototype (the model would later be named TR1) had never been driven on the public roads. The Triumph management did not consider the time ripe for a new two-seater.
Ken Richardson, who had driven many test miles with BRM racecars, tested the original Triumph Sports car and wrote a devastating report. The undercarriage was too weak and bent at every turn. Sir John Black took Richardson seriously and gave him the chance to develop a real sports car out of the TR1. The factory destroyed the prototype of the TR1 after Richardson had built three new prototypes in the winter of 1952. This model was called the TR2. The public first admired his work in March 1953 at the Salon in Geneva, where the second prototype was put on display and, a few months later, Triumph history would be written in Belgium.

The dashboard of the TR2 was legible and complete.

The Triumph emblem on the nose of the car.

A TR2 seen from behind. The spare wheel was located under the lid in the luggage compartment.

The three prototypes of the new TR2 were thoroughly checked. Richardson truly tested to the limit, not only on the circuits, but also on public roads. At Jabbeke in Belgium on May 20, 1953, he reached a speed of 124 mph with one of the new cars. But the TR2's "public rendering" also delivered an excellent performance.

At the flying mile at Jabbeke, a speed of 114 mph was measured. The engine was a smaller version of the overhead valve engine S, which was equipped in the Standard Vanguard and in the Ferguson tractor. The engine originally had a volume of 127.4 cu. in., but the volume of the cylinders was reduced to 2.0 liters. At the same time, Walter Belgrove also drastically altered the coachwork. He extended the rear end of the car, creating a real luggage compartment. In the first prototype, the reserve wheel was still screwed on to the back of the coachwork and the gas cap was placed in the middle of the wheel. On the TR2, the reserve wheel was placed in the luggage compartment, with the cap of the gas tank located right on top of the trunk. The production of the TR2 did not gain momentum until the summer holidays of 1953. The press wrote enthusiastic reports about the new model. Its stability on the road was excellent, its shock absorption smooth and its engine powerful.

The Jaguar XK 120 and the smaller MG's were unbeatable at the races, often held on public roads, until the arrival of the TR2. Johnnie Wallwork, driving a TR2, won the heavy R.A.C. Rally in Great Britain in 1954, just ahead of his teammate Peter Cooper. Bill Bleakley came in fifth in a TR2 and Miss Mary Walker won the "Ladies Prize" in a Triumph.

Also in 1954, Maus Gatsonides and Rob Slotemaker finished in sixth place with a factory-TR2 during the French Alpine Championship. Moreover, the TR2's won the team prize. And the TR2 also performed exceedingly well in long distance races. The Edgar Wadsworth and Bob Brown duo drove in the Le Mans 24-hour race and came in fifteenth in the final classification. 1783 miles were covered at an average speed of 74.3 miles an hour.

No less than 60 cars appeared at the starting line in Le Mans in 1955, and only 21 reached the finish. The three participating TR2's finished at 14th, 15th and 19th place. This engine was equipped with a new cylinder head, which would later be built in as a standard with the TR3. Two Triumphs were equipped with disk brakes. Ken Richardson and Bert Hadley's car had Girling disk brakes on the front wheels and drum brakes on the rear wheels. The car of Bobbie Dickson and Ninian Sanderson had Dunlop disks on all four wheels, while Leslie Brook and Mortim Morris-Goodall's TR2 still had four drum brakes. In this way, the factory was able to test all different breaking systems. It would be some years before the Triumphs would appear at the starting line in Le Mans again. But elsewhere in Europe, the TR2 was still very successful. In 1954, Maus Gatsonides and Ken Richardson took part in the Mille Miglia, where they finished in seventh place in their league.

At the London Motor Show in 1954, a facelifted TR2 was presented. The car could even be ordered with a plastic hardtop. Furthermore, it was possible to have a Laylock de Normalville overdrive placed in the gearbox. The small doors of the TR2's were fitted very low and bumped along the high street curbs. This shortcoming was resolved in the new version. As a matter of fact, a whole new floor with small doors and real doorsteps was designed. The 1955-model automobiles were also recognizable by the chrome frame around the radiator. 1955, however, would be the last production year for the TR2.

Technical specifications

Model:	**Triumph TR2**
Years of manufacture:	1953-1955
Production:	8,628
Engine:	four-cylinder
Displacement:	121.5 cu. in.
Output:	91/4800 hp/rpm
Top speed:	105 mph
From 0 to 60 mph in sec:	not known
Wheel base:	7 ft 4 in
Length:	12 ft 7 in
Width:	4 ft 8 in
Height:	4 ft 2 in
Weight:	1,984 lb

Triumph TR7

The American Triumph dealers presented a new sports car in 1975. The model was called TR7, although it did not look in any way like a TR. Not everybody was pleased with the TR7. Many people found the model hideous and others missed the character of the old TR's. The TR7 was meant as a successor to the TR6 and the MGB, which had not been sold in America for some time. Of course, America was still the biggest and most important market for British Leyland. But in this market, safety and environmental regulations were becoming increasingly strict. Rumors even circulated that cabriolets would be forbidden altogether. For this reason, the American automobile brands had halted their construction for quite some time already. And there was an important competitor, which had become very popular in America, the Datsun Z-series. The Datsun Z offered the average American everything he wanted in a car. And what's more, the car was so cheap that almost everybody was able to afford to buy or lease one. The new Triumph was forced to offer a lot for little money – and they succeeded.

The TR7 was the first Triumph sports car with a lightweight, frameless body which could be built more cheaply than its predecessors. Until the TR5, Triumph had been seeking the help of Michelotti whenever new coachwork had to be designed. But the TR7 was their "own" design from the Austin-Morris studio in Longbridge, which was managed by Harris Mann.

Mann did not have an easy time. Because the American regulations were changing constantly, it was necessary to adjust the designs repeatedly. For instance, the distance between the center points of the headlights and the surface of the street had to be at least

The quality of the TR7 was especially good, much better than the first coupés.

24 inches. It was up to Mann to decide whether to place the lights like frog-eyes on the splashguard or to install them under a cover in the splashguards. Mann chose the latter and enabled the headlights to be controlled by means of two small electric engines. The design of the coachwork was distinctly wedge-shaped. This fact provoked suspicion that the engine was placed in front of the rear axle, like in the Fiat X1/9 or the Lancia Stratos. But this was not the case. The engine, this time a four-cylinder with overhead camshaft, was placed in front and powered the rear wheels via a four-speed gearbox. The engine had been proving its qualities for a long time already. It originated in the Triumph Dolomite sedan and was also used in the Saab 99. The engine had been tilted 45 degrees to the left to keep the engine cover low. The engine of the regular export model had two Stromber carburetors and produced 90 horsepower. The design being shipped to California had only one carburetor and produced 79 horsepower.

The four speed gearbox was the same as the one used by British Leyland for the Triumph Dolomite Spitfire, the MG Midget and the Morris Marina. The box had no overdrive, but after September 1977, it was possible to install the five-box from the Rover.

There was also an automatic gearbox available from Borg Warner. The rear wheels springs were no longer set separately, but fitted to a fixed axle. Younger people especially loved open sports cars like the TR6 and appreciated rigid springs in a car. Another group of customers was reached with the development of a closed car, a coupe, which offered

Also the dashboard of the TR7 had nothing in common with older TR-models.

The difference had to be clear: this is a TR8. Or is it? Many TR7's were equipped with a V8 engine to increase the price.

a little more comfort. For this reason, the TR7 received rather weak springs, which had a stretch of no more than 8 in up or down.

On paper, the TR7 bore a very close resemblance to the TR2. The TR2 also had a fixed rear axle and a 2.0-liter four-cylinder engine with 91 hp 4800 rpm. The four-cylinder in the TR7 had the same volume and produced, now with clean exhaust fumes, 90 hp at 5000 rpm.

British Leyland had built a new factory for the Triumph TR7 in Speke, a suburb of Liverpool. The first cars emerged from the factory at the end of 1974. It was obvious that the cars were produced with little care or attention. The employees were more often on strike than at work and every car emerging from the production line was full of defects. In the winter of 1977, there was a strike that lasted for four continuous months. When British Leyland finally closed the factory in May 1978, they were lucky that the workers did not boycott the relocation to Canley. The relocation was a lengthy process and it was not until October 1978 that the first TR7's appeared from production.

However, the TR7 was better than its predecessors in every aspect. The open model was no longer being produced in Speke, but in Canley, and the models produced subsequently were of excellent quality. The designers took advantage of the move to refine the model and the general improvement in quality bore fruit. 88% of the 76,000 TR7s that Triumph built were exported. 80% of the exports targeted the American market and English customers had to be patient until March 1980. The first vehicles with right hand steering were not delivered until May 1976. A few months later, in the autumn of 1976, the American model of the TR7 could also be delivered with a five-speed gearbox or even with a Borg-Warner automatic gearbox. These parts were originally designed for the Rover 3500 SD1 and were therefore sufficiently tested. The TR7 was designed as a coupe because Washington had threatened to prohibit the import of cabriolets. But this appeared to be a storm in a teacup. The TR7 appeared as a cabriolet in September 1979. The production line of the TR7 moved from Canley to the Rover factory in Solihull in 1980 and production recommenced in April of that year.

Besides the TR7, a TR8 was launched in America. This automobile had the same coachwork as the TR7 but a V8 engine was placed under the hood. This aluminum V8 engine was used for the Buick Special between 1960 and 1963. Thereafter, the engine was produced under license by Rover. Especially in

The heavy bumpers did not particularly improve the look of the vehicle, but in America they were compulsory.

England, nobody understood why Triumph did not use its own, stronger 3.0-liter V8 engine with its two overhead camshafts from the Triumph Stag. Maybe this was the reason why only 2,800 models of the TR8 were sold. The last TR7 and TR8 rolled out of the factory in October of 1981. And that was the end of the Triumph!

Technical specifications

Model:	**Triumph TR7**
Years of manufacture:	1975-1981
Production:	111,648 coupes and 24,864 cabriolets
Engine:	four-cylinder
Displacement:	122 cu. in.
Output:	106/5500 hp/rpm
Top speed:	112 mph
From 0 to 60 mph:	11.8 sec
Wheel base:	7 ft 1 in
Length:	13 ft 4 in
Width:	5 ft 6 in
Height:	4 ft 2 in
Weight:	2,238 lb (cabriolet: 2,326 lb)

Veritas

In 1944, Ernst Loof, Georg Meier and Lorenz Dietrich met in Paris. They were all working for BMW and it will not come as a surprise that the main topic of conversation was automobiles. They even made plans together to start building sports cars after the war and the three met again early in 1947. The time was ripe to transform the plans into action. And in spite of the fact that they understood that transport vehicles were more in demand than sports cars, they chose to focus on the latter. They wanted to create a modern automobile on basis of the very reliable BMW 328. Loof had been engineer for BMW during the war and took charge of the technical aspect. Meier was a famous racer and Dietrich would market the cars. Soon after, Loof found a couple of old BMW 328s and a handful of spare parts. In March 1947, the moment had finally arrived. An old mill in the village of Housen, near Sigmaringen, served as an automobile factory. Loof had a few old cars, but he did not have the material to make new ones out of them. They needed much equipment and each screw or bolt had to be found on the black market and either paid for or exchanged for foodstuffs. Even under these trying circumstances, Loof and his workers managed to build a car within three months. The aluminum coachwork was produced by the Hebmüller Company and bore some resemblance to the latest pre-war BMW 328. Dietrich sold six cars within a couple of months for 6,000 Reichsmark, which proved to be worthless after the "Währungsreform" in June 1948. On March 1, 1948, after the company had been moved to a barracks in a former "Arbeitsdienstlager" in Messkirch, the Veritas GmbH was officially founded.

The engine in the RS generated 115 horsepower at 6000 rpm. The compression ratio was 7.5:1

25 models of the Veritas RS 25 were sold between August 1948 and March 1950.

The Allies had forbidden the Germans to build automobiles with engines bigger than 1.0 liter. The Veritas Company was registered as an enterprise which rebuilt and repaired automobiles. However shortly after the war, racing was revived in Germany. More than 300,000 visitors gathered in May 1948 at Nürburgring to watch four Veritas sports cars embarrass the pre-war competition. Georg Meier left Egon Brütsch in his Maserati Grand-Prix car with its compressor engine far behind. After Veritas had delivered seven automobiles in 1947, Loof decided to build a special race-car, the Veritas RS, where RS stood for Renn Sport. It had become easier to get material and Loof managed to build an undercarriage of oval and round tubes. The first samples even received electron coachwork. The old engines of the BMW 328 were boosted specifically for this model. After three cars were delivered with electron coachwork, Loof switched back to the aluminum plating. This new coachwork was produced for the most part at Veritas before being transported to Hebmüller for finishing. Besides the model with the 2.0-liter engine, another version was created with a 1.5-liter, six-cylinder engine. Karl Kling became the German champion in the 2.0-liter league in 1948, while Georg Meier won the F2 championship with a 1.5-liter car.

The cars rode from victory to victory in 1949 as well. Helm Glöckler became "Deutsche Meister" in the 1.5-liter league in that same year. Veritas rode the F2 races with an ordinary RS until that year, while the Italians appeared at the starting line with a monoposto. Loof's answer was the Veritas Meteor. This monoposto had free-standing wheels and

The Meteor became a fiasco and almost never reached the finish of its own account.

The vehicles from the 1950ss were not equipped with headrests. These were only installed in the RS in the 1990s.

a "square" engine with a volume of 121 cu. in. (3x3 in). The six cylinders produced 140 horsepower at 7500 rpm with a compression ratio of 12:1.

The engine block and the cylinder head were made of aluminum and the head with its overhead camshaft originated on the drawing table of Professor Ernst Heinkel, formally in charge of aircraft construction.

The Meteor was a fiasco. A Swiss team registered in the 1950 Swiss Grand Prix with four Meteors and not one of them finished. Veritas introduced a three-person coupe, the Comet, to address a wider range of customers. Spohn produced the coachwork for the Comet.

The Comet was presented in October 1949 at the automobile salon in Paris and cost 22,000 DM. Cheap? A Volkswagen was on sale that year for 4,800 DM. Veritas did not make a lot of money and therefore funds were lacking to test the cars properly. As a result, the customers were not satisfied. It was at this crucial moment that the Auto-Handels-Gesellschaft from Baden-Baden appeared. They offered the necessary financial means. Veritas could move now to a bigger factory in Rastatt, but had to name itself "Veritas Badische Automobilwerke GmbH." There were now over 150 people working in the new factory, where a successor to the Veritas Comet was being produced. The coupe model of this automobile was called a "Saturn" and the open version a "Scorpion." But the cars came too late.

The competition also reappeared on the market. BMW had its beautiful 501 series and Mercedes-Benz joined the party. Who was interested in a car built out of old parts? And Veritas was not able to survive on the sales of the real

The RS did not offer much comfort or luxury.

The coachwork of this Comet was developed by Spohn in Ravensburg.

sport and race cars. For this reason, they contacted the French company Panhard, which was willing to supply the rolling chassis of the little Panhard Dyna. Coachwork producer Baur supplied the coachwork, and with this the Dyna-Veritas became a reality. However, nobody wanted the car and only fourteen of them were sold. The standard version of the little car with its two cylinder engine cost 8,300 DM and the version with boosted engine as much as 9,900 DM. Veritas was forced to close the factory in November 1950. Loof left the company, which was then taken over by Lorenz Dietrich. Dietrich managed to sell ninety cars of the Dyna-Veritas model between 1951 and 1954. But Loof did not capitulate. He started anew with money he had borrowed from a manufacturer of washing machines. The Veritas-Nürnburgring emerged from one of the garages of the Nürnburgring. And again it was an expensive construction with a undercarriage made of tubes and a 100 horsepower engine designed by Ernst Heinkel. The coachwork manufacturer Spohn produced the coachwork and the first vehicle was ready for delivery by the end of 1951. Loof built a special racecar, a monoposto, for the German publisher and racer Paul Pietsch.

However, the vehicle did not bring him much luck. At a speed of 110 mph, he flew off the track during his first race. Pietsch ended in the hospital and the car in the scrap yard. Loof was able to sell three more cars in 1953, but Heinkel stopped delivering engines because he was never paid. Loof therefore used Opel and Ford Taunus engines. Not long after that, Loof sold his little company to BMW and was given employment at his former employer.

Technical specifications

Model:	**Veritas BMW**	**RS**	**Comet**	**Saturn**	**Nürburgring**	**Dyna**
Year of manufacture:	1948	1949	1950	1950	1952	1951
Production:	11	25	9	7	20	169
Engine:	six-cylinder	six-cylinder	six-cylinder	six-cylinder	six-cylinder	two-cylinder
Displacement (cu. in.):	120	120	120	120	121.3	45.4
Output (hp/rpm):	80	115	80	100	110	28
Top speed (mph):	93	100	110	100	102	72
Wheel base in inches:	94	98	98	103	98	86
Length in inches:	153.5	157.5	165	167	170	153.5
Width in inches:	61	60	60	60	67	57
Height in inches:	53	43	54	53	57.5	54
Weight in pounds:	1,720	2,205	2,381	2,425		

Volvo 480 ES Cabriolet

The extremely heavy targa rod made it rather uncomfortable to step into the vehicle.

Volvo Nederland launched a new vehicle, the 480 ES, in 1986. It was an automobile in the style of the old Volvo P 1800 ES: a sports car with a lot of luggage space. The car was a big success. More than 12,000 units were sold.
The sports series were especially popular in England and Italy. The Japanese were fondest of the version with the automatic gearbox. The four-cylinder engine was developed specifically for this purpose by Renault and could be delivered with or without turbo.
Plans to produce the vehicle as a cabriolet were almost as old as the model itself. An open model was standing in the Volvo studio just one week after the presentation in Geneva. Chief designer Rob Koch and his colleagues had transformed a coupe into a cabriolet. But the big bosses in Sweden did not want anything to do with an open Volvo. They claimed that such a vehicle could never be safe. As an alternative, Koch and his team (they were responsible for all of the 400-series vehicles) built a coupe with a removable glass targa-roof. However, the management in Sweden was not satisfied with the result and, in spite of their earlier decisions, gave their permission to build a cabriolet. In any case, the automobile had to comply with all of Volvo's high demands for safety and had to be equipped with a very solid targa frame. Firstly, a monocoque of a coupe was strengthened and after that sent to the ASC (American Sunroof Company), an expert in this field, to be rebuilt as a cabriolet.
Koch picked up the car in Arizona in December of 1987 to take a test ride.
The cabriolet was mechanically identical to the coupe. Most of the coachwork parts were interchangeable, which lowered the cost of production considerably. The tonneau cover was made of SMC (Sheet Molded Compound) synthetics.

The cabriolet did not differ a lot from a coupe. But it was produced with a targa frame instead of a steel roof to economize on production costs.

The 2+1; the third passenger sat sideways in the back. The car also looked very good with its vinyl roof.

The tools for its production came from the English company Motorpanels. The vinyl cover, including the frames, was supplied by Tickford and the leather upholstering was produced in Belgium.

Koch managed to construct a targa-frame that the Swedish would not only approve of, but which would give the vehicle an attractive appearance at the same time.

The Volvo 480 ES cabriolet was presented in 1990 at the automobile show in Geneva.

The public admired the car and the Volvo dealers registered a couple of dozen orders, but unfortunately, the model was never built in series.

Did Volvo consider it unsafe after all?

Technical specifications

Model:	**Volvo 480 ES Cabriolet Turbo**
Year of manufacture:	1990
Production:	1
Engine:	four-cylinder
Displacement:	105 cu. in.
Output:	120/5400 hp/rpm
Top speed:	124 mph
From 0 to 60 mph:	9.0 sec
Wheel base:	8 ft 1 in
Length:	14 ft
Width:	5 ft 7 in
Height:	4 ft 4in
Weight:	2,260 lb

Volkswagen New Beetle
convertible

Even with the hood closed up the car still has pleasing lines. The hood fits perfectly.

Introduced to the US market in 2002, the 180-horsepower New Beetle Turbo S marked the beginning of a performance trend that continues in 2003. For 2003, the New Beetle's comprehensive lineup includes the GL 2.0, GL 1.9TDI, GL 1.8T, GLS 2.0, GLS 1.9TDI, GLS 1.8T, GLX 1.8T and the Turbo S. The 2.0-liter engine, available on GL and GLS models, now qualifies as an Ultra Low Emission Vehicle (ULEV) in all 50 states.

As with most of today's Volkswagens, the New Beetle uses a front-wheel drive layout and a transverse engine design located in the front. As an engine option, the New Beetle's TDI offers remarkable performance and unmatched economy. As a result, the 90-hp diesel engine provides a wealth of low-end torque, exceptional fuel figures and exhaust emissions that meet the most stringent standards of the U.S. and Europe.

This side view of the New Beetle shows the similarities to its predecessor. The lines are smooth and flowing but there are no chrome bumpers.

Sitting pretty on a beach at sunset, this is the New Beetle convertible, with its hood down.

Evoking the free-spirited attitude of the original Volkswagen soft top, the highly anticipated New Beetle convertible promises today's drivers a unique and dynamic motoring experience.

The New Beetle convertible will be available in four trim levels: GL 2.0, GLS 2.0, GLS 1.8T and GLX 1.8T (1.8T engine available later in 2003). Each New Beetle convertible model employs a standard five-speed manual or a new optional six-speed automatic transmission with Tiptronic®. Tiptronic allows normal automatic transmission operation or manual shifting using a special shift gate.

The New Beetle convertible is available with a manual or semi-automatic, three layered top to ensure excellent insulation and appearance. The power top is easy to operate opening or closing in a mere 13 seconds.

Once open, the soft-top rests on the area of an imaginary C-pillar, giving the traditional folding trunk the classic look of the original Beetle convertible. Furthermore, the standard power windows work with the convertible top by automatically lowering slightly to clear the soft top whenever the doors are opened, and then raising to form an ideal seal from wind and water.

Comfortable at high speeds, the New Beetle purrs happily along in its California landscape.

Seen from this angle the New Beetle looks racy, its lights beautifully blending with the bodywork.

Like the New Beetle sedan, the security of front-wheel drive and other accident-avoidance features such as a standard Anti-lock Braking System (ABS) and Daytime Running Lights (DRLs).

Volkswagen's standard Automatic Rollover Supports serve to provide added overhead support in the unlikely event of a rollover. Sensors in the car indicate whether it is in a rollover situation, causing the Automatic Rollover Supports to deploy behind the rear seats, whether the convertible top is up or down.

Additionally, all New Beetle convertibles offer a long list of standard safety items, including driver and front passenger airbags, side-impact airbags mounted in the seatbacks, a safety-belt tensioning system, a collapsible steering column, an emergency trunk release handle and rear-seat tether anchorage points for securing a child safety seat.

Inside, the New Beetle convertible boasts a 10-speaker sound system with two 220-millimeter subwoofers in the front, two 6.2-in woofers in the rear, four tweeters and two mid-range speakers. The placement of the speakers helps maintain high-quality stereo sound even while competing with wind buffeting that is typical of a convertible with its top down. All New Beetle convertibles have a wealth of standard features.

Technical specifications

Model:	**GL 2.0 L**	**GLS 2.0 L**	**GLS 1.8 T**	**GLX 1.8 T**
Engine:	four-cylinder	four-cylinder	four-cylinder	four-cylinder
Bore/stroke (inches):	3.25/3.65	3.25/3.65	3.19/3.40	3.19/3.40
Displacement (cu. in.):	121	121	108.6	108.6
Output (hp/rpm):	115/5400	115/5400	150/5800	150/5800
Top speed:	not known	not known	not known	not known
From 0 to 60 mph in sec:	not known	not known	not known	not known

VW-Porsche 914

The dashboard of the 914. With a four-cylinder engine, the speedometer could run up to 55 mph at 8000 rpm.

When Volkswagen and Porsche showed their joint model, real Porsche fanatics were disappointed and the vehicle was too expensive for most Volkswagen owners. Despite this, the car was a great success.

The relation between Volkswagen and Porsche is as old as VW itself, considering that it was Ferdinand Porsche himself who invented the Volkswagen. And the first Porsche was actually a Volkswagen with modified coachwork.

The initial negotiations took place in 1968. And a new company, the VW-Porsche Vertriebsgesellschaft GmbH (VW-Porsche Inc.), was founded in Stuttgart in 1969. Both parties were represented in this enterprise with 50% shares. The new sports car was designed by Porsche. Karmann in Osnabrück produced the coachwork and Volkswagen delivered the mechanical parts. The cheaper model of the VW-Porsche was powered by the engine of the Volkswagen 411. The more expensive model was equipped with the six-cylinder boxer engine from the Porsche 911T. Both models had their own five-speed gearbox. The official presentation took place at the IAA in Frankfurt on September 11, 1969. The VW-Porsche had coachwork for two passengers and a removable, plastic targa-roof. The engine was placed in front of the rear axle. It had an almost ideal weight ratio of 47% on the front and 53% on the rear wheels. The model was none too loved in Europe. It was too expensive and it did not take long before people started mockingly to call it VOPO, after the hated Volks Polizei (National Police) in East Germany. But the vehicle was very successful in America, where the name Volkswagen was not used and the model was sold as a Porsche 914. Starting in August 1970, the 1.7-liter

The coachwork of the VW-Porsche was designed at Porsche and produced at Karmann. Karmann, also known as the VW Karmann-Ghia, had over 7.000 people employed and was therefore more than just a producer of bodyworks.

The middle part of the roof could be removed and be stored in the trunk.

engine of the VW 411 was replaced by the 1.8-liter from the 412. And when the 914/6 with its six-cylinder Porsche engine proved too expensive (one could buy a Porsche 911 for only a few dollars more), in 1972, the factory started delivering the vehicle with the 2.0-liter four-cylinder boxer engine from the Porsche 904.

The VW-Porsche was certainly not a bad car. The primary reason it sold so poorly in Europe was possibly the badly chosen name. The 914/6 could even be successful in races. For instance, Claude Ballot-Lena and Guy Chasseuil won the

The 914/6, here an automobile from 1971, stood on 5 1/2Jx15 rims. The rims of the four-cylinders had a width of 4 1/2 inches.

2.0-liter league at the 24-hour race of Le Mans in 1970. They came in sixth in the general competition, just after two Porsche 917s, a Porsche 908 and two Ferrari 512s.

Porsche built eleven more automobiles in 1971. They installed 190 horsepower 911-S engines in the coachworks of the 914 and placed the vehicle on broad 185/70VR15 tires. These were super fast cars, accelerating from 0 to 60 mph

A schematic drawing of the 914.

in 7 seconds and reaching a maximum of 149 mph. Dr. Ferry Porsche received such a car on his sixtieth birthday. The other five models went for a fair little price to members of the Porsche-Piëch family.

Ferdinand Piëch, now the big man at Audi and the chief engineer for Porsche (Ferdinand Porsche had been his father-in-law) declined the honor. He drove a 914 with a 300-horsepower engine from a 908 race car and found it fast enough.

Porsche took over the Volkswagen shares in their mutual enterprise in 1973. The company continued building a successor to the 914, the Porsche 924. Diehard Porsche fans were disgusted by this model as well, with its water-cooled VW engine placed in front. However, the model was a great success for the company, and it became the best-selling model.

Technical specifications

Model:	**VW-Porsche 914-1.7**	**914-1.8**	**914/6**	**914/2.0**
Years of manufacture:	1969-1973	1973-1975	1969-1972	1972-1975
Production:	65,351	17,773	3,332	32,522
Engine:	four-cylinder	four-cylinder	four-cylinder	six-cylinder
Displacement:	102.5 cu. in.	109.5 cu. in.	121.5 cu. in.	120.3 cu. in.
Output (hp/rpm):	80/4900	85/5000	110/5800	100/5000
Top speed:	110 mph	112 mph	124 mph	118 mph
From 0 to 60 mph:	13.5 sec	12.5 sec	10 sec	10.5 sec
Wheel base:	7 ft 10 in	7 ft 10 in	7 ft 10 in	7 ft 10 in
Length:	13 ft 1 in	13 ft 1 in	13 ft 1 in	13 ft 1 in
Width:	5 ft 5 in	5 ft 5 in	5 ft 5 in	5 ft 5 in
Height:	4 ft	4 ft	4 ft	4 ft

Acknowledgments

We would like to thank the following people for their cooperation on this book and for supplying photographs of their automobiles. In alphabetical order:

Belinda Werner (Cadillac)

Tom W. Barett III, Scottsdale, Arizona, USA

Gunnel Ekberg, Saab, Sweden

Albrecht Guggisberg Oldtimer Garage, Toffen/Bern, Switzerland

Dieter Günther, Hamburg, Germany

Lukas Hüni, Zürich, Switzerland

Masaru Inoue, Honda, Japan

Hans K. Lange, Villach, Austria

Rick Lenz, Bloomingon, California, USA

Reinhard Lintelmann, Espelkamp, Germany

D. Maury, Matra, France

Edmond Pery, Blegny, Belgium

Peter Rau, Touring Garage, Zurich, Switzerland

Alex Rüber, Zurich, Switzerland

Wolfgang Schmel, Greiling, Germany

Reinhard Schmidlin Oldtimer Galerie, Toffen/Bern, Switzerland

Ernst Scheidegger, Schwyz, Switzerland

Almer Smit, the Netherlands

Mat Stone, Glendale, California, USA

Max Stoop, Langnau/Zurich, Switzerland

Belinda Werner, Cadillac, USA

Donald E. Williams, San Ramon, California, USA